C000243786

Perceptions of Islam in European Writings

Ahmad Gunny

THE ISLAMIC FOUNDATION

Published by
THE ISLAMIC FOUNDATION,
Markfield Conference Centre,
Ratby Lane, Markfield, Leicester LE67 9SY, UK
Tel: (01530) 244944, Fax: (01530) 244946
E-mail: i.foundation@islamic-foundation.org.uk
Web site: http://www.islamic-foundation.org.uk

Quran House, PO Box 30611, Nairobi, Kenya

PMB 3193, Kano, Nigeria

Copyright © The Islamic Foundation, 2004/1424 H

All rights reserved. No part of this publication may be reproduced, stored in a retrieval system, or transmitted in any form or by any means, electronic, mechanical, photocopying, recording or otherwise, without the prior permission of the copyright owner.

British Library Cataloguing-in-Publication Data
Gunny, Ahmad
Perceptions of Islam in European writings
1. Islam – Public opinion – History 2. Public opinion – Europe – History 3. Public opinion – France – History 4. Islam in Literature 5. Islamic countries – Foreign public opinion, European 6. Islamic countries – Foreign public opinion, French
I. Title
305.6'97

ISBN 0 86037 373 8
ISBN 0 86037 378 9 pbk

Typeset by: N.A. Qaddoura
Cover design: Nasir Cadir

Printed in Great Britain by
Antony Rowe Ltd, Chippenham, Wiltshire

Contents

Preface

This book is not to be viewed as defensive apologetics on behalf of Islam. Rather it is an attempt to put forward a scholarly, Muslim, point of view which can accommodate other views in a healthy debate on some aspects of Islam and the West. As my aim is to achieve consensus I use those Islamic sources which have won the esteem of the Muslim community throughout the centuries. Yet I remain firmly committed to the notion of fidelity to European thought.

In the later stages of preparation of the work the following colleagues at the Oxford Centre for Islamic Studies provided generous assistance: Muhammad Akram elucidated some of the Islamic sources for my benefit and Pat Harvey widened my perspective more than once. Yahya Michot organized a series of seminars on Islamic science at the Centre, which I found most stimulating. I am grateful to them and to James Piscatori who encouraged me at all times. The views expressed in the following pages are, however, entirely mine.

I wish to thank the Voltaire Foundation, Oxford, the editors of the *Journal of Islamic Studies* and the *International Journal of Islamic and Arabic Studies* (Bloomington) for permission to use material from my articles published by them.

I am most grateful to Dr. M. Manazir Ahsan, Director General of the Islamic Foundation, and his colleagues for accepting to publish a work which I hope will interest Muslims and non-Muslims alike. I believe it would compliment Tariq Ramadan's books *To be a European Muslim* and *Islam, the West and the Challenges of Modernity*, which have been published by the Islamic Foundation in 1999 and 2001.

The support of my family throughout is much appreciated.

Ahmad Gunny

Transliteration Table

Consonants. Arabic

initial: unexpressed medial and final:

ء	'	د	d	ض	ḍ	ك	k
ب	b	ذ	dh	ط	ṭ	ل	l
ت	t	ر	r	ظ	ẓ	م	m
ث	th	ز	z	ع	'	ن	n
ج	j	س	s	غ	gh	هـ	h
ح	ḥ	ش	sh	ف	f	و	w
خ	kh	ص	ṣ	ق	q	ي	y

Vowels, diphthongs, etc.

Short: ـَ a ـِ i ـُ u

long:

ـَا ā ـِي ī ـُو ū

diphthongs:

ـَوْ aw

ـَيْ ay

Introduction

Images of Islam in eighteenth-century writings (1996) actually surveyed a period stretching back to the second half of the previous century. The present study continues the enquiry and is primarily concerned with an intellectual history of Western, mainly French and English writers', responses to Islam from about 1787 to the 1890s. However, in order not to interrupt the flow of ideas, it also discusses works of an earlier period, as these form part of the tradition of writing on Islam, especially on the Qur'ān and the Prophet, in the West and are relevant to later debates. Although it may have played a less important role in Western thought between the 1650s and the 1790s than it does today Islam fully deserved the attention given it in *Images*. The emphasis there was on the religion itself, with its doctrinal and moral ramifications. In a sense, discussion of Islam at any time can hardly avoid reference to the teachings of the Qur'ān and the Prophet. In fact, in the present work, the Qur'ān and the Prophet are never far from the scene, acting as a common thread that joins the varied themes being treated such as travel, women, culture, politics, philosophy, theology and anthropology.

As we move on from the age of the Enlightenment, the focus of writers' interests shifts increasingly to what the French call *civilisation*, that is, society, education, culture, politics and economics. These interests now also develop into anthropological and ethnographical studies which appear to shed new light on the perception of Muslim communities by Europeans. However interesting may have been the previous period in European history when curiosity about Islam was just beginning to displace traditional hatred, its responses to Islam were incomplete. A similar analysis in the nineteenth century may probably convey the same impression of incompleteness. Why, then, set limits, chronological and geographical, to the investigation? The advantages of such a strategy seem to outweigh its disadvantages. It might be better to have partial reactions than to be faced with the sweeping generalisations that mar the achievement of those authors who have chosen to evaluate Islam over many centuries at a time.[1] If the span of the investigation is too long it encourages one to pass over major writers very quickly. The result may then be an exercise in rhetoric. I use this word with its old meaning of the art of persuasion. Cicero and Quintilian, for example, showed how orators and, later, writers became selective and suppressed all evidence that might enhance the case of their opponents and concentrated on promoting their own causes.[2] Extreme selection inevitably leads to distortion. But however brief the period covered, selection is still unavoidable. At least when the period is relatively short attention may be focused on major writers and all or nearly all aspects of the works of those selected can be examined at close quarters with a view to achieving a balanced evaluation. The argument must rest on a number of carefully chosen writers, texts and ideas. The objective of this work therefore is not to discover whether European writers were 'right' about Islam in one respect or 'wrong' about it in another. That would appear too clear-cut an approach as such polarization rarely happens. The objective is rather to show to what extent they were fair, balanced and accurate in their evaluation in light of the information available to them and also to add a new dimension to the Orientalism debate and to studies in eighteenth- and nineteenth-century Islam. There is, of course, some justification in not allowing oneself to be imprisoned within a strict chronological boundary of about a hundred years if this narrows the perspective.

Some might think that the general idea of assessing what European writers of the Enlightenment and the colonial eras had to say about Islam is not particularly original. But even in Shakespearian studies where so many books have been published over the centuries there is still scope to produce something new. With regard to European writings on Islam the possibilities seem as good, if not better. Why? The reason is that despite much talk of pluridisciplinary studies these days, few books, genuinely pluridisciplinary and demonstrating a deep knowledge of both the European and Islamic material, exist on the theme 'Islam and the West'. Writing truly pluridisciplinary works in this area represents a formidable challenge to any scholar. This challenge does not seem to have been fully met yet, although some stimulating books exist such as those of Norman Daniel, *Islam and the West*, 1960, Edward Said, *Orientalism*, 1978, Hichem Djait, *L'Europe et l'Islam,* 1978, Claudine Grossir, *L'Islam des Romantiques*, 1984, Albert Hourani, *Islam in European thought*, 1991, Bernard Lewis, *Islam and the West*, 1993, Mohammed Sharafuddin, *Islam and Romantic Orientalism*, 1994, Derek Hopwood, *Sexual encounters in the Middle East*, 1999 and Emily Haddad, *Orientalist poetics*, 2002.[3] *Orientalism: A Reader*, 2000, edited by A.L. Macfie and reviewed by me in *Journal of Islamic Studies*, September 2002, pp. 372-374, is a valuable selection of essays by various scholars on criticisms of Orientalism and the counter-criticisms to which they gave rise. The authors selected represent every shade of opinion in the debate.

Although the above-mentioned scholars have contributed or are contributing to our understanding of the intellectual relations between the West and the Islamic world, there is something missing in their works. Grossir, Sharafuddin and Haddad, who deal with the literature of the imagination mainly, show the impact of the Islamic Middle East on Romantic writers, Haddad even opening new perspectives on the aesthetic significance of Orientalism on nineteenth-century poetry. Djait is very perceptive about non-Romantic writers such as Voltaire and Renan. However, some factual errors concerning Islamic teaching are to be found in the studies of the group of three authors. Even in Djait there is little reference to or proper understanding of Islamic sources. These are essential if one wishes to project Muslim views. Being a Muslim is not sufficient by itself to convey such views. Hourani and Lewis have distinguished themselves in Arabic, Turkish and Islamic studies. While Hourani's above quoted work, like Lewis's, is an interesting collection of essays, it cannot match his remarkable volumes on Arabic thought and peoples. Moreover, Lewis's book is highly controversial. I cannot share his view that Jean Gagnier was being cautious if he described Muḥammad as 'God's mortal enemy' in his biography. Hopwood has sound views on the nineteenth-century political scene, but lays too much stress on the sexual element in the relations between French, British and Arabs, to the detriment of other aspects of these relations. Perhaps the most thought-provoking of these scholars remains Said. However, his selection of writers or aspects of their works is open to question. Why, for instance, is Boulainviller, the author of the most favourable European biography of the Prophet in centuries, excluded from his analysis? Why is his evaluation of Gobineau based solely on the latter's *Essai sur l'inégalité des races humaines*? One detects that he had a thesis to prove. Should the perspective that Said has sought to impose, namely of a West that permanently dominates Islam, not therefore be varied?

Strange as it may seem, studies projecting a scholarly, Muslim, point of view on the subject of Islam and the West are rare. Yet a Muslim perspective that avoids anachronism and assesses texts only according to information available for the period under consideration is essential to a dialogue between equals as is fidelity to European thought. Otherwise it will be a dialogue of the deaf between Islam and the West. It is not implied that a

Muslim view is the only one that can be accommodated. Muslim and non-Muslim views can surely co-exist. After all, non-Muslims are not being asked to abandon their own beliefs: what is simply required of them is that they should respect those of Muslims and not seek to sabotage their publication by Western publishers. How else would it be possible to have dialogue if the views of one of the partners were not heard? In this connection, Hamilton Gibb argued in *Modern Trends in Islam* (1947) that it was not for Protestant Christians to refuse to Muslims, either as a community or as individuals, the right to reinterpret the documents and symbols of their faith in accordance with their own convictions (p. xii). Jacques Berque, for his part, stated in his *Leçon inaugurale* (1956) at the Collège de France that the Western scholar must work in partnership with those who know their societies and cultures from within.[4] Who are these persons? It does not follow that an Arabic-speaking or Muslim-born person automatically fits the description. For instance, Tahar ben Jelloun, winner of the prestigious Prix Goncourt with his novel *La nuit sacrée* in 1987, makes his heroine Zahra take the form of a man and lead the *ṣalāt ul-janāza*, the funeral prayer, for her dead father. Muslim readers are not amused by the licentious comments accompanying the prayer and are bewildered when she and the congregation prostrate themselves on the floor of the mosque. There is no prostration during this particular prayer! The image of Islam in this part of *La nuit sacrée* lacks in authenticity and the novel gives the impression of being aimed at non-Muslim readers who know nothing of Islam. Even the eminent scholar of Arabic civilization, Albert Hourani, could be mistaken about the order of proceedings at Friday prayers in his exciting *A History of the Arab peoples* (1991). The implication is that in order to present a faithful picture of Islam one needs to demonstrate amongst other things a familiarity with, and a desire to be true to the spirit of, its teaching and long-established practices. Fidelity to European thought, on the other hand, requires one to demonstrate deep knowledge of it and, above all, the firm resolution to refrain from the use of rhetoric against it. These criteria are by no means easy to satisfy.

In the wake of Vatican Council II (1965) the Anglican Church produced its own statement on dialogue between Jews, Christians and Muslims in an Appendix to the Lambeth conference of 1988. It includes the following: 'The essential condition of any true dialogue is a willingness to listen to the partner ... For understanding is more than intellectual apprehension. It involves the imagination and results in a sensitivity to the fears and hopes of the other. Understanding others means allowing them to define themselves in their terms rather than ours.' The statement appears to validate the approach being taken here. It expresses fine sentiments with which few would disagree. In practice, however, the view that Muslims cannot be trusted to be objective about their religion and that the only objective analysis can come from non-Muslims continues to prevail and to inspire much of the writing on Islam.[5] On this reckoning, the same objective analysis in Christian and Jewish studies could only come from non-Christians and non-Jews!

In the broad framework to the argument the reader might wish to take note of significant historical landmarks bearing on some aspects of the relations between Europe and the Islamic world, as these landmarks should act as a foil to perceptions of Islam based on the imagination. It should become clear that works of the imagination do not have pride of place here in any case, although they are not entirely neglected. The historical events to be borne in mind include the invasion of Egypt by Napoleon in 1798. However, only those events likely to shed some light on the writings of the authors discussed later are assessed here. French imperialism had its paradox: Napoleon's adventure in Egypt also had a positive aspect in that the impressive army of scholars and scientists accompanying him subsequently produced a massive work of scholarship which is still used today.

This, naturally, is no plea for colonialism. For a reasoning that makes French imperialism a prerequisite for the existence of French scholarship would be very much like that of Pangloss in Voltaire's *Candide* – that is, to have chocolate one had to have syphilis before! Nevertheless, Egypt's French connection was strengthened under Muḥammad 'Alī (1805-49), vali of Egypt, who saw the benefit of having Egyptian military officers, doctors and engineers trained in France, if only to suit his own purposes. The connection developed throughout the century.

It is generally recognized that the Napoleonic wars were being fought outside as well as inside Europe. Napoleon's occupation of Egypt was brief, 1798-1801. However, it cannot simply be viewed as an episode in the war with Britain: it had long-lasting repercussions. It marked the beginning of Anglo-French domination of the Middle East for more than one hundred and fifty years and new relationships between the European powers and the region. The first military alliance between the Ottomans and Britain led to the expulsion of the French from Egypt in 1801. After their expulsion, the French tried to go to Syria, but they were compelled to move.[6] Like Persia soon afterwards, Egypt was exposed to Anglo-French rivalry. The Napoleonic wars showed the military superiority of European states, especially with regard to the organization of the army. Afterwards European armed power and influence over the Islamic world increased considerably as a result of growth in factory production and rapid changes in means of communication. Europe needed raw materials for its factories and food for its increasing population. From about 1820 much of Egypt's cultivable land was used for the production of cotton which was exported to the mills of Lancashire via Alexandria. Under Khedive Ismā'īl (1862-79), Egypt severed its administrative links with the Ottoman Empire, but only to become a cotton plantation serving the needs of the European market. Despite revenue accruing from the Suez Canal, built with French and Egyptian capital and opened in 1869, Egypt was unable to pay off its debts to European creditors. Egyptian nationalism struggling against European interests finally led to military intervention by Britain in 1882.

Relations between Persia and France developed when Fath ʿAlī Shāh Qajar (reigned 1779-1847) was refused assistance by Britain, under the treaty of 1801, to ward off Russia's attack on Azerbaijan.[7] Napoleon himself hastened the process of rapprochement with Persia by sending secret missions there, including one led by Amédée Jaubert (1779-1847), a pupil of the Orientalist Sylvestre de Sacy with a deep understanding of Oriental customs and a good command of Persian. A dual alliance between France and Persia culminated in the Finkenstein Treaty of 1807. Persia was to break off relations with Britain and to expel British East India Company agents from its soil. The Treaty revived Napoleon's old dream of conquering India: Persia was to be his passage to India. But it was never implemented as Napoleon abandoned Franco-Persian friendship for Franco-Russian entente. Napoleon's broken promises may explain why the Shah felt obliged to side with Britain in the end. But Mirza Shafi, his Prime Minister, remained faithful to France despite being offered large sums by Harford Jones Brydges, British consul in Baghdad. One may therefore understand, to a certain extent, Gobineau's sympathy for the Persians later in the century.

After its expulsion from Egypt, the French army was keen to establish French power overseas and was encouraged by a report on Algeria that suggested that the Arabs and Berbers would, in their dislike of the Ottoman authorities, welcome the French if they respected Islam, their women and property.[8] So it invaded Algeria in 1830, purporting to liberate it from Ottoman oppression, but it really started a brutal colonization of the interior under General Bugeaud. Local resistance under ʿAbd al-Qādir (1808-83) finally crumbled in 1847. By that time French rule had extended to the edge of the Sahara. By confiscation and other means the French acquired land: immigrants (French *colons* and other Europeans) who had capital to cultivate the land took over villages, using peasants from Spain or Italy. Dispossessed villagers became labourers on new estates on lands they formerly owned (see Chapter 6, below). In 1863 Napoleon III, ruler of France, in an attempt to reconcile various interests, reversed the policy of dividing village lands and recognized the rights of cultivators to the land.[9] Whereas the Arabs of Algeria were generally despised, the French, including De Tocqueville, thought that the Kabyles could be assimilated, as they appeared less devoted to Islam. Such thinking merely reflects the French policy of divide and rule.[10]

However, the colonial factor must not be pushed too far. For reasons other than imperialism François Ier had endowed the first Chair of Arabic at the Collège Royal in 1538. This was followed, much later, by the creation of other Chairs of Middle Eastern languages by the Convention at the end of the eighteenth century. Subsequent developments may have led Victor Hugo to say, in the preface to *Les Orientales* (1829), that Oriental studies had never before been promoted to such an extent and that whereas in the age of Louis XIV people were Hellenists now they were Orientalists. Indeed, there is a long tradition of investment in Oriental languages by European nations, including the French, the Spanish, the Italian, the British and the Dutch. Unlike these nations, the Germans were not motivated by colonial considerations and are particularly important for their efforts, especially in Qur'ānic studies. It does not really matter too much to know who were first in the field. For what matters is not the volume of the output, but its quality. To keep things in perspective it must be recognized that despite the increasing importance given to Middle Eastern languages by European nations from the seventeenth century onwards, these languages, essential for a proper understanding of Islam based on original sources, remain the preserve of a minority.

For his perception of some aspects of Islamic civilization the general reader of previous centuries who did not belong to this privileged minority often depended on travellers' accounts of the Middle East (chapter 5). The cultural background and preoccupations of these travellers varied enormously. Their presentation of Islam depended, to a large extent, on what they were seeking to find in the region – knowledge about Islamic communities and their beliefs and practices, spiritual/poetic inspiration, aesthetic pleasure, sexual satisfaction or the mere satisfaction of their curiosity. Those selected here are not tourists who spend a few days in the Middle East, have no understanding of the cultures of the countries they visit and who are often misled by locals spinning stories for foreigners and lacking a strong Islamic background themselves. Generally speaking, many of those selected have spent enough time in these countries and have documented themselves before travelling. Lane, for example, learnt Arabic in England and took steps on arrival in Egypt to improve his knowledge of it, rather like today's good British students of modern languages during their year abroad. A few of the travellers may have even raised the reader's expectation that they would somehow study the problems of actual contemporary life in Middle Eastern countries. This is not always the case. It is not implied that they had no contact at all with nineteenth-century Middle East. Lamartine, for example, not only met people of the area but he also had Europo-centred plans for their future. He cannot, however, be judged solely by his imperialist designs. That would indeed be a demonstration of rhetorical techniques! To some travellers, both men and women, the Middle East was a place for sexual encounters. To Isabelle Eberhadt, for instance, Algeria was what Egypt was to Flaubert, except that the latter, who forms part of the French literary canon, is more often quoted. His encounter with an Egyptian prostitute does not mean that he provided a model of Oriental woman to the rest of his century. For in *Voyage dans la Basse et Haute Egypte* (1802), Vivant Denon has a drawing of an unveiled

Egyptian woman with a literary description of her which may have set an early precedent for the general nineteenth-century representation of the Oriental woman as a strongly sensual creature. The drawing certainly points to Eugène Delacroix's 'The Death of Sardanapalus', which forms part of the Louvre collection, Paris. It was painted in 1827 even before he travelled to the East and was partly inspired by Byron. This means that perception of the Oriental woman is often based on a mixture of reality and fantasy.

However, the sexual activities of travellers and Orientalist painters are not a major preoccupation of this study which is more concerned with what new insights writers can offer into the world of Islam. The visions of Lamartine and Nerval can be offset against the reality of Egypt described by Edward Lane, Antoine Clot and J.B. Saint-Hilaire. The notion of France's 'mission civilisatrice' no doubt permeates the thinking of Clot and Eusèbe de Salles. But Saint-Hilaire's account of Muḥammad 'Alī's land reforms is quite convincing. At the same time it must be recognized that some of the writers do not fit easily into the category of travellers: their presence in Chapter 5 is for convenience alone. Edward Lane and Lucy Garnett, for example, are noteworthy for their anthropological observations. The latter is particularly important because, as Billie Melman has pointed out in *Women's Orients: English women and the Middle East, 1718-1918*, she was the first ethnographer to have devoted a whole study to women in a Middle Eastern country, based on field work in Turkey. But the majority of travellers are not to be seen as anthropologists setting out on their journeys to do field investigations. Some of them could nevertheless make valuable contributions in different spheres: the abbé Toderini could have taught Renan a thing or two about Islamic science and made him tone down his outrageous remarks on the subject. Whereas in the seventeenth and eighteenth centuries travellers paid scant attention to the Arabian peninsula, they now went to the Yemen and other parts of Arabia, even if

J.L. Burckhardt and R. Burton found safety in disguise when they visited the holy cities of Makka and Madina. The general reader would probably be grateful to the latter because they reveal to him, sceptical but curious as he is, something that goes beyond the nineteenth century—pilgrimage, a central aspect of Islam, which appears less mysterious now. Little by little the mysteries of the East, of Islam in particular, were being unravelled.

Perhaps the greatest of these mysteries was the harem (Chapter 4). For a long time the reader had to make do with Montesquieu's male sexual fantasy in the *Lettres persanes* (1721) or the not too reliable account of harem life in Turkey by Lady Mary Wortley Montagu three years before. The fascination of the harem continued into the nineteenth century when some key elements in the image of the Muslim East were conveyed by Romantic poets such as Byron and Hugo: splendour, cruelty, sensuality and despotism. A different image also appears in *Don Juan* (1822) where the hero, disguised as a woman, is confined to a harem. There is mention, in Canto VII, of ladies of the harem whose 'education led/Doubtless, to that of doctrines the most true/Passive obedience'. Unlike Byron, Hugo never travelled to the East. Yet in *Les Orientales* there are frequent allusions to the Sultan's harem where capricious sultanas and jealous concubines are locked up, far from the gaze of the outside world. In 'Les Têtes du Sérail' shouts are heard when the Turkish Sultan is indulging in his pleasures at the expense of 'our sisters, our daughters and our wives'. The anthology helped other writers to turn their attention to the East, but it stressed appearance and the picturesque rather than reality.[11]

But why stick with fantasy when realistic accounts are available? Already in the latter part of the eighteenth century, Dr. Alexander Russell had initiated a movement towards more realism in his narrative of the harem in Aleppo. Would women writers such as Sophie Poole, Emmeline Lott and Lucy Garnett try to offer readers an even greater dose of realism prevailing in the harems of Egypt and Turkey and help to demystify them or would they continue the tradition of Lady Wortley Montagu? Would the nineteenth century be more successful in restoring her soul to the Muslim woman after the powerful condemnation of half the Muslim population launched by Montesquieu? Granted that there was a certain misogyny stemming from some *aḥādīth* and which continued in medieval Arabic literature, including the *Arabian Nights*, were women outside the harem passive like those of Byron's creation? Were they helpless, even in Egypt? The question of women in Islam is a burning issue. A whole 'industry' on this subject has sprung up in recent years: some are about women in the Qur'ān and the *Sunna* and others are about the representation of Muslim women in Western literature (chapter 4). Interesting as these studies are, few set Muslim writings side by side with Western writings on women: such a juxtaposition might enable one to draw conclusions on the extent and origin of prejudice against Muslim women. One of the questions I therefore wish to ask is: how is the depiction of Muslim women different from that of previous times?

Although this study concentrates on French and English writings, some awareness of the contribution of other European nations to the dissemination of knowledge about Islam, especially the Qur'ān and the Prophet, seems appropriate (chapters 1 and 2). It is essential to discuss European writers' perceptions of the sacred text and of the life of the person who transmitted it. After all, there would be no Islam without the Qur'ān and the Prophet. Muslims want to know how the two central elements in their lives are viewed by European commentators. Spanish translations of the Qur'ān from the fifteenth to the seventeenth century are known to exist, beginning with Yça Gidelli's translation of 1456.[12] In their studies in Islam both Reland and Sale made use of Morisco sources written in Spanish. For part of his description of the Islamic creed in *De religione mohammedica libri duo* (1705) Reland used a manuscript in Spanish in Arabic characters. Although he had access to much more authoritative Arabic texts he preferred this source perhaps because he thought that in his work of popularization his readers might find that Western articulations of some Islamic beliefs were more accessible.[13]

Reference is made in chapters 1 and 3 to the work of German Orientalists such as Theodor Nöldeke, J. von Hammer-Purgstall and Gustav Weil. The reader's perspective is certainly widened by another German writer who was no Orientalist but who addressed a wider audience. That was J.W. von Goethe (1749-1832) in whom one may see a happy amalgam of various European reflections on Islam. Although the poet did not travel to the East, his only *hijra* being from Karlsbad to Italy in 1786, his interest in Islam lasted over a long period, having obviously found a source of inspiration in it for his poetry. Like Boulainviller in the early eighteenth century, he was fairly well informed about it through his reading of some of the better authors such as Tavernier, Chardin, d'Herbelot and Sacy.[14] Using part of this textual information but avoiding Boulainviller's polemical agenda, he wrote a poem on Muḥammad in 1773 entitled *Mahomets Gesang*, which he intended to be part of a tragedy on the Prophet's life. The poem was not developed and it remained only as a fragment. Nevertheless, it depicts a very positive image of Muḥammad, all of whose successes are represented as subordinated to the immovable purpose of the reformer: he leads his followers to God and no temptations can turn him from his path (p. 124). Following the publication in 1812 of a translation by Joseph von Hammer-Purgstall of the *Divan* of the Persian poet Ḥāfiẓ, Goethe published his own *West-Ostlicher Divan* in 1814. These were troubled times in Europe, caused by wars and the dynastic and political changes brought about by Napoleon. So Goethe sought refuge in what he believed was the calm serenity of the East! The poem *Hejira* in the first book of the *Divan* reflects this mood in the following lines: 'Thrones are shattering, Empires quaking;/Fly thou to the untroubled East,/There the patriarchs air to taste!/What with love and wine and song/Chiser's fount will make thee young.'[15]

By Chiser, Goethe means al-Khiḍr, the character alluded to, though not specifically mentioned, in the Qur'ān in *Sūra* 18: 65. The latter is given a significant role there as a servant of God when he attempts to elucidate the mysteries of destiny for the benefit of man. In a different context he is credited with having found the fountain of life and drunk thereof to become immortal: his name actually means the green one, that is, his knowledge is fresh and green. It is in this role that he interests Goethe. In the 'Book of Paradise' of the *Divan*, Goethe has a section on 'Elect women' among whom he places a new character called Zuleika, who is not mentioned as one of the inhabitants of Paradise by Tradition.[16] In a letter to Zelter dated 3 May 1820, Goethe shows his admiration for the mythology and manners of Islam. He says that these give scope for 'a kind of poetry which suits my age'.[17] But then he talks of Muslims' 'absolute abandonment to the unfathomable will of God'. Although this is a simplistic interpretation of the complex question of destiny in Islam, at least it reflects recognisably popular beliefs. Goethe's treatment of Chiser (the hermit in Voltaire's *conte* Zadig) and destiny in Islam is less objectionable than Flaubert's treatment of the Queen of Sheba in *La Tentation de Saint Antoine*. A Muslim reader familiar with Islamic teaching on her may find Flaubert's portrait of the Queen altered beyond recognition. Flaubert's character is the seducer who promises endless sexual pleasures to the hermit.

As background to the discussion on the Qur'ān and the Prophet in the eighteenth and nineteenth centuries some reference to the current debate on the subject might also be useful. Although some scholars such as Hugh Kennedy accept the more traditional accounts of Islamic history, a 'school' of Orientalists operating from Britain and the United States, consisting mainly of Patricia Crone, Michael Cook and John Wansbrough but attracting more attention than others, seems to have emerged in the last decades: these scholars have recently been joined by G.R. Hawting and J.P. Berkey.[18] Their intention is to renew modern studies in Islam and Hawting even says that he aims to treat Islam in the same way as the other monotheist religions and to do justice to it as part of that tradition (p. 10). My own standpoint is traditional, although I do not reject, for example, some historical development in Islam regarding the doctrine of the uncreated Qur'ān which became more firmly established in Sunnī Islam about 849 after the failure of the 'miḥna' in 833.[19] This does not mean that everything in Islam dates from the ninth century onwards. How could justice be done to it if its Prophet's role is reduced to virtually nothing, if it is argued that the pagan Arabs attacked in the Qur'ān were all monotheists, that Islam arose not in Makka, but in the Fertile Crescent, after the Arab conquests, and that it was formed from the interaction of Arabs and conquered peoples? The notion of a gradual elaboration of Islam through inter-faith seminars seems highly anachronistic. This would turn it into a purely human creation – a point made against Judaism and Christianity also by the authors of anti-religious clandestine texts in the eighteenth century. Even to-day it is often difficult for a Muslim to put forward his point of view in writing as he is often accused of betraying the bias inherent in an 'insider'. Apparently, the 'outsider' has some special intuition which guarantees objective assessments! Be that as it may, deconstructing the Qur'ān by tracing its material to various sources and environments and applying literary techniques to it and other early Muslim sources to build up the highly speculative and controversial theory that the Qur'ān dates from two centuries after Muḥammad is part of the Eurocentric tendency that requires every non-European work to be cast in the same mould as European literature. Moreover, the fact that only some Qur'ānic verses are inscribed on the Dome of the Rock, which dates from 691, is no evidence that the Qur'ān could not have existed before: the whole Qur'ān could not possibly be inscribed on a building.

Despite painstaking efforts, great erudition and the use of Syriac, Greek and Armenian sources by some Orientalists, it is often difficult for them, as it is for scholars in other fields who use different sources, to achieve the desired originality. From medieval times onwards one comes across Western writings - including some of those discussed in this book, by Vertot, Muir, Sédillot and Gobineau – where prevails the notion that Islam is a Christian heresy, that nearly everything in it is derived from Christianity or Judaism and that Muḥammad is its author. The same conclusions reappear now, albeit under a different guise. *Plus ça change*! Other modern non-Muslim scholars of Islam prefer to use more traditional Islamic sources. I am more in sympathy with them and with an earlier Orientalist like Simon Ockley, Thomas Adams Professor of Arabic at Cambridge in the early eighteenth century. He convincingly argued that Islamic history should be based on Arabic and not Byzantine sources. The accounts of Muḥammad, derived from Arab authors whether Muslim or Christian, paint a generally more favourable picture of him than those of European writers of the eighteenth and nineteenth centuries who have clerical connexions. Some of his qualities are well brought out in the nineteenth century which, however, remains ambivalent towards him on the whole.

On the other hand, modern revisionist historians dealing with the origins of Islam sometimes use archaeological and epigraphic material. But their theories, more often based on an elaborate source hunting machinery, appear highly controversial and sensational. Perhaps the pursuit of originality in such areas is an illusion after all. It certainly proved to be the case in the nineteenth century when the Orientalist Garcin de Tassy made a dramatic announcement that he had discovered an unknown chapter of the Qur'ān, which was published in the *Journal Asiatique*. It did not take long for the 'discovery' to be exposed, although its author made some significant contribution to Islamic studies later. He and Lane made the work of the Qur'ānic commentators al-Bayḍāwī and the Jalālayn more accessible to a wider public. Renan's view that Islam was the only great world religion to have been firmly based on history is now being challenged by modern scholars, but one of the results of a research that aims to be innovative gives the impression that nothing is known for certain about the origins of Islam, which are reshrouded in mystery. Although Lane and other writers of the period may be faulted for their fragmentary reading of the Qur'ān, they at least concentrated on the text itself and helped in a small way to spread its message. Their part in a reassessment of Islam, particularly by the Christian Church, was, however, far from being negligible. The views of De Tocqueville and Renan on the Qur'ān have been included in Chapter 1 for the sake of thematic unity. Their views on other matters relating to the world of Islam are given in separate chapters.

Some modern Orientalists are now claiming that it is not clear what is meant by Islam or what it means to be a Muslim. J.P. Berkey takes an extreme position on this matter: he even suggests that Muḥammad himself would not have understood the question![20] The fact that individuals – be they a jurist in Baghdad in the ninth century or a sufi mystic in Cairo in the fifteenth – may give different answers to the question does not mean that Islam undergoes a radical change with location and century, even if some variation in customs may occur at a local level. A region's Islam has to meet the criterion of *ijmā*ʿ (consensus) to be acceptable to the vast majority of Muslims. There are core beliefs and practices which constitute the heart of Islam: these have stood the test of time because there is *ijmā*ʿ about them. How come that at the beginning of the eighteenth century Adrian Reland, Professor of Oriental languages at the University of Utrecht, had a clear understanding of what Islam was about? In book 1 of *De religione mohammedica (1705)*, translated as *Of the Mahometan religion* (1712), he accurately describes the six articles of the Muslim creed – that is, the belief in God, His angels, His books, His prophets, the Last Day and the decree of God regarding good and evil – and their practical complement as reflected in the five pillars. These descriptions of the essence of Islam are in harmony with what is laid down in the Qur'ān in *Sūra* 4: 136 and elsewhere and therefore fit 'my' Islam which happens to be the Islam of the millions of Muslims throughout the world. Naturally, all aspects of a religion such as Islam cannot be summed up in just a few lines.

When it comes to the diffusion of Islamic culture in the nineteenth century (chapter 3) one may detect not so much an Eurocentric as a 'Gallocentric' tendency, that is, the notion that every literary production must conform to French taste with its high standards – a taste which, it should be pointed out, took a long time to evolve, if one remembers the coarseness of French medieval farce, for example. Betraying French chauvinism, Sylvestre de Sacy no doubt exaggerates Arab failings in literary taste. Yet it should be pointed out that his *Chrestomathie arabe* is a monument to Arab cultural achievement. In his choice of extracts Sacy displays remarkable perception. For instance, the space he devotes to al-Maqrīzī's *Khiṭaṭ* in the *Chrestomathie* is amply justified. Maqrīzī's masterpiece is the single most important and influential source for the study of the urban history of Cairo. His extended association with Ibn Khaldūn may have provided him with the methodological and theoretical framework to rationalize and organize his data on Cairo. The reputation of the *Khiṭaṭ*, written between 1418-42, has lasted for more than five centuries. One has to wait until the *Description de l'Egypte* (1809-28) for a similar survey of Cairo and Egypt.[21] Barbier de Meynard, for his part, manages to bring to the attention of French readers the contribution of Zamakhsharī to Islamic civilization and to remind them of their own La Rochefoucauld.

Readers wanting information on the political thought of the French concerning Algeria in the 1830s and 1840s could easily bypass travellers. A personality from the world of politics and diplomacy such as De Tocqueville could certainly provide it (chapter 6). However, such readers are in for a shock, since the ugly faces of colonialism and racism will stare at them without any ambiguity for the first time perhaps. De Tocqueville had become interested in Algeria and Islam even before he became a member of the Chamber of Deputies. It turns out that his interest in Islam was merely a springboard from which to launch his programme for the strengthening of French Algeria. A great believer in French domination in Africa and in the rhetoric of France's civilizing mission more than in the implementation of that mission, he was not unaware of the nefarious effects of French colonial rule on Algeria. Like Lamartine, his prophecy of European military triumph over the world of Islam came true. His more pragmatic approach contrasts with the clearly theoretical discourse of Gobineau. There is some logic in linking the career diplomat Gobineau with the statesman De Tocqueville who was briefly his Minister of Foreign Affairs in 1849. They carried on a correspondence over a number of years – from the 1840s to the 1850s. In it they exchanged fascinating views on the Islamic world. Gobineau became notorious for the controversial speculations on the classification of races in the *Essai sur l'inégalité des races humaines* (1853) which had polemical aims. The criteria he uses to determine racial superiority – cultural and scientific – were bound to put the Arabs at a disadvantage in a period of decline. Even the achievement of the greatest of the Arabs – Muḥammad – in the seventh century is diminished. The *Essai* will always rouse strong emotions. But it must not be allowed to detract attention from the stimulating perspectives Gobineau opened on other Muslim societies, particularly Persian, and on Islamic theology in his subsequent works. Never since the days of Jean Chardin at the end of the seventeenth century have such thoughtful responses been made on Persia, despite the fact that in his writings meant for publication, Gobineau generally refrained from making an evaluation of the contemporary situation prevailing there.

Renan fully deserves a whole chapter devoted to himself because of his standing in French intellectual life. Writing in the *French Studies Bulletin* in summer 1999, Giles Banderier thought that the publication of Renan's *Correspondance* by Jean Balcou would widen our knowledge of one of the best writers of the century, but deplored the fact that he had been relegated to the background. The relegation certainly does not apply to Islamic studies where he has been critically assessed, albeit only partially, in recent years.[22] If his reputation suffers even more than Gobineau's among Muslims, he can be said to have brought it on himself by some of his unacceptable remarks, especially on the dichotomy he perceives between Islam and science. However, rhetorical devices have been used against him by modern polemicists who conveniently leave out his contribution to the assessment of the Qur'ān, the Prophet and Islamic/Arabic[23] philosophy. With regard to Islamic science, if he had pointed out its decline in his own times, no outcry would have been raised. What a pity that such a gifted person should have made so little effort to document himself on the subject!

To do him justice and to get the perspective right, a whole range of texts written by Renan from 1848 to 1883 should be examined. One should not judge him solely by his controversial remarks on the Arabs and Islam, which may have been prompted by the publication of Gobineau's *Essai*. In his century responses to Renan came from Jamāl al-Dīn al-Afghānī and Gustave Lebon (see Chapter 7, below). There was an even better yardstick by which his pronouncements on the supposed opposition of Islam to science could have been assessed. He could also have been subject to a type of peer review. The Professor of Hebrew, who was not averse to reproducing extracts from other writers in his own works, need not have gone beyond the steps of the Collège Royal to learn a little about astronomy, for example. He should at least have consulted the work of another distinguished member of the Collège. The Professor of Astronomy there, J.B. Delambre, Secretary of the French Royal Academy of Sciences and a Fellow of the Royal Society, London, had published a history of astronomy in the Middle Ages. In his *Histoire* (1819), Delambre shows that al-Battānī (d. 929), author of *al-Zīj al-ṣabī* (The Sabaean Tables), studied and translated by C.A. Nallino in 1893, sometimes copied Ptolemy, but that he made a detailed and complete calculation of the ecliptic such as is nowhere found in Ptolemy or anyone else. He says that the discovery of the movement of the sun's apogee was largely due to the Arab astronomer.[24] In his view the most useful service done to trigonometry by al-Battānī and fellow Arabs was to substitute the calculus of sines for the calculus of chords. With regard to Ibn Yūnus (d. 1008), author of *al-Zīj al-Kabīr al-Ḥākimī* in 1007, he points out that the latter introduced tangents in trigonometrical calculus and that this useful innovation, generally believed to be due to Regiomontanus, took place only six hundred years after the Arabs, whose works he regrets 'have not been sufficiently diffused'. He mentions that Ibn Yūnus's work was studied and partly translated by Caussin de Perceval in 1804. Delambre's partial evaluation of the Arab contribution to astronomy has been continued by scholars such as C.A. Nallino, S.H. Nasr, G. Saliba and others.[25]

Notes

1. For example Norman Daniel, *Islam and the West: The making of an image* (Edinburgh, 1960) and Edward Said, *Orientalism* (1980).

2. Cicero, *De Oratore*, and Quintilian, *Institutio Oratoria*, both available in Loeb Classical Library translation (London, 1948, 1921).

3. Sharafuddin's and Hopwood's books have been reviewed by me in *Journal of Islamic Studies*, Vol. 6, No. 2, 1995, pp. 320-321; Vol. 12, No. 3, 2001, pp. 382-385 and my review of Haddad's book appears in the July issue, 2003, of *French Studies*, Vol. 57, No. 3, pp. 402-403

4. See Albert Hourani, *Islam in European thought* (Cambridge, 1991), p. 130.

5. See the paper entitled 'The postmodern age' by Z. Sardar in *Christian-Muslim Relations* (London, 1991), p. 68. In *Modern Trends in Islam* (Chicago, 1947), H. Gibb recognized the impossibility of avoiding the introduction of a very large subjective element into the discussion (p. xii). He presumably included both parties in the subjective discussion.

6. In this section I am indebted to Albert Hourani's *A History of the Arab peoples*, pp. 260-287.

7. See my review of Iradj Amini's book, *Napoleon and Persia:Franco-Persian relations under the First Empire, Journal of Islamic studies,* May 2000, pp. 246-248.

8. See D. Hopwood, *Sexual encounters in the Middle East*, p. 87

9. Hourani, pp. 270-271.

10. Hopwood, p. 91.

11. See the article entitled 'Quelques notes sur l'Orient dans l'oeuvre poétique de Victor Hugo' by Achira Kamel in *La Fuite en Egypte. Supplément aux voyages européens en Orient*, ed. J.C. Vatin (Cairo, 1989), pp. 157-158.

12. See the article on Spanish translations of the Qur'ān from the fifteenth to the seventeenth century by Consuelo Lopez-Morillas, entitled 'Lost and found? Yça of Segovia and the Qur'ān among the Mudejars and Moriscos', in *Journal of Islamic Studies* (1999), vol. 10, pp. 277-292.

13. Reland used a Morisco manuscript, now shelved in Cambridge University Library as Dd. 9. 49. Sale mentions in the 'Preliminary Discourse' to his translation of *The Koran* and in his comments on *Sūra* 3: 55, that he handled an apocryphal gospel of Barnabas, 'a forgery of some nominal Christians but interpolated since by Mohammedans'. In his comments on *Sūra* 7: 21-22, he actually quotes from the Morisco manuscript, now in Australia. The text is a piece of religious propaganda subversive of Christianity. I am grateful to Professor L.P. Harvey for his valuable suggestions regarding Reland and for drawing my attention to Sale.

14. See Goethe's *Poems*, selected and edited by H.G. Atkins and L.F. Kastner (London, 1902).

15. See *West-Eastern Divan*, tr. by Edward Dowden (London, 1914), p. 1.

16. Dowden, p. 178. It seems that European writers often do not manage to get right the names of the four women who, according to Tradition, are in Paradise. Cf. Nerval, below.

17. Atkins, p. 213.

18. See P. Crone and M. Cook, *Hagarism* (Cambridge, 1977), P. Crone, *Meccan trade and the rise of Islam* (Oxford, 1987); J. Wansbrough, *Qur'ānic Studies* (Oxford, 1977) and *The sectarian milieu (*Oxford, 1978); G.R. Hawting,

The idea of idolatry and the emergence of Islam (Cambridge, 1999) and J.P. Berkey, *The Formation of Islam* (Cambridge, 2003).

19. Although the notion of the Qur'ān being uncreated and eternal is present in *Sūra* 85: 22, for example, it led to fierce debates and the imprisonment of Aḥmad ibn Ḥanbal, its champion, from 833 to 835. The Abbasids persecuted those who denied that the Qur'ān was created until the Caliph al-Mutawakkil (847-61) allowed Muslims to believe what they wanted.

20. Preface, p. ix.

21. Nasser Rabbat gave a stimulating lecture, to which I am indebted, on 'History, the City, and Criticism: Maqrīzī and his book on the *Khiṭaṭ*' at the Oxford Centre for Islamic Studies in May 2001.

22. H. Djait, *L'Europe et l'Islam* (Paris, 1978); Said, op. cit.; O. Leaman, *Averroes and his philosophy* (Richmond, 1988, 1998) and A. Hourani, *Islam in European thought* (Cambridge, 1991).

23. D. Gutas feels that calling Arabic philosophy 'Islamic' and consequently seeing it as 'essentially linked to the religious and spiritual fact of Islam' injects an overpowering religious dimension to it which was not there. He rejects the view that Islamic philosophy, theology, and mysticism are closely related and that their common inspiration and origins are to be found in the Qur'ān and the *ḥadīth*. He calls this Islamic apologetics. Gutas's point that the philosophers wrote in Arabic, the language of Islamic civilization, although they were not all Muslims, is valid. He could have made the same point about 'Islamic' and 'Arabic' science, since some of the contributors to it were non-Muslims. However, it does not mean that Islamic philosophy and science never existed. Moreover, it is often difficult to avoid the use of these terms. See 'The study of Arabic philosophy in the twentieth century', *British Journal of Middle Eastern Studies*, May 2002, pp. 16-19.

24. In his article on al-Battānī in the *Encyclopaedia of Islam*, 2nd ed., pp. 1104-1105, C.A. Nallino says that the astronomer determined with great accuracy the obliquity of the ecliptic and definitely exploded the Ptolemaic dogma of the immobility of the solar apogee by demonstrating that it is subject to the precession of the equinoxes.

25. See S.H. Nasr, *Islamic Science. An illustrated study* (Westerham, 1976) and G. Saliba, *A History of Arabic Astronomy* (New York, 1994). Saliba rejects the view that Arabic astronomy simply acted as an intermediary that passed the Greek tradition to Europe during the twelfth century and then receded into oblivion. He insists on the creative productivity that had begun as early as the ninth century simultaneously with the translation activity and which continued to develop well beyond the fifteenth century (p. 247).

CHAPTER 1

Some European studies of the Qur'ān in the Nineteenth Century[1]

The Crusades brought the West into close contact with Islam, but the period between 1096 and 1270 saw only one attempt to introduce the Qur'ān to Europe. That was by Peter the Venerable, Abbot of Cluny (c. 1094-1156) who apparently commissioned a team of translators, including an English man, Robert of Ketton, and Hermann of Dalmatia. The translation, in Latin, was really by Ketton and was completed in 1143 but was only printed in 1543 by T. Bibliander in Basle. It seems to have encouraged the publication of several translations into French, Latin and English in the seventeenth and eighteenth centuries. The translation by André du Ryer, a French consul to Egypt, used by Montesquieu in the *Lettres persanes* (1721), appeared in 1647. Alexander Ross published an accurate translation of du Ryer's *L'Alcoran de Mahomet* in London in 1649. But perhaps the most important work on the Qur'ān in the seventeenth century was that by Lodovico Marracci who published the *Alcorani textus universus* in Padua in 1698, a Latin translation together with the Arabic text and commentary. He also included with it the *Prodromus ad Refutationem Alcorani* which he first published in 1691. No less significant was the appearance of George Sale's translation in 1734, prefaced by a substantial 'Preliminary Discourse'. Sale made an impact not only on the eighteenth but on the nineteenth century as well. Similarly, the translation by the French traveller, C. Savary, *Le Coran*, published in 1783, was widely used by the French in the nineteenth century, despite the appearance of the translation by Albin Kazimirsky in 1840 which ran into many editions. Of course, translations of the Qur'ān into various languages continued uninterrupted in the twentieth century.

Kazimirsky, an interpreter at the French embassy in Persia, also published an Arabic-French dictionary in 1860, but he is really known for his translation of the Qur'ān which, however, is not outstanding. For example, he continues to mistranslate *Sūra* 2: 62, taking this line to mean that Jews, Christians and Sabeans will be saved, translating the verb *āmanū* by the present tense, instead of the perfect.[2] So in what ways can the nineteenth century be said to have contributed to make the Qur'ān better known in the West? One of the interesting features of the period is to be seen in the systematic practice of some writers who chose to focus attention on excerpts from the Qur'ān rather than on the whole text. Such a practice was not unknown before. But whereas Antoine Galland (1646-1715) left his translation of *Sūras* 1 and 2 and his commentary on *Sūra* 3 unpublished,[3] Joseph Marcel, a member of the Institut d'Egypte and Head of Napoleon's printing press there, published extracts from the Qur'ān in 1798 under the title 'Exercices de lecture d'arabe littéral à l'usage de ceux qui commencent l'étude de cette langue'.[4] Marcel selected five short *sūras*, including *Sūra* 1. He reproduced the Arabic text in clear *Naskhī* style and gave a good literal translation of each *sūra*, stating the number of verses it contains. As his title suggests, the text and translation were meant to be a teaching aid to those embarking on the study of classical Arabic. He therefore did not turn his translation of *Sūra* 1, for instance, into a scholarly exercise. For unlike Galland, he makes no use of the commentators who suggest that the words 'against whom Thou art wrathful' refer to Jews and that the phrase 'those who are astray' in the last line refers to Christians. The other *sūras* chosen by Marcel, 97, 109, 110 and 112 are easy to memorize because of their brevity and are often used by Muslims in their daily prayers. Marcel also inserted the words of the call to prayer among his excerpts.

Nineteenth-century writers did their best to draw the attention of a wider readership to some sections of the Qur'ān. Their concentration on certain *sūras* only seems to have been prompted by the realization that the average Western reader might find it difficult to take in the whole of the Qur'ān at one time. In the preface to his *Selections from the Kuran* (1843), Edward Lane, whose contribution to the dissemination of knowledge about Islam is highly significant, actually tried to explain why he thought study of the Qur'ān was so neglected in Britain. The European public was fairly familiar with two of the criticisms he puts forward: (1) the arrangement of the contents of the book tires the most patient of readers and (2) it abounds with passages which are unintelligible without explanations. However, the third factor invoked by Lane might produce bewilderment: apparently, the Qur'ān, which is a code of moral, civil and criminal law is a prohibited book as it is unfit for the perusal of a modest female! It should be pointed out that no category of readers has ever been prevented from reading the Qur'ān. It may well be that Lane was thinking not so much of the Qur'ān as of sensual descriptions of paradise found in popular Arabic texts.

If Lane openly acknowledges his debt to Sale in the title of and in the preface to his *Selections from the Kuran*, he does not miss the slightest opportunity to point out Sale's errors and highlight his own achievement here or to refer the reader to his translation of the *Arabian Nights*. In his translation of the Qur'ān, Sale had referred to a number of Arab commentators such as Zamakhsharī, Jalāl al-Dīn Suyūṭī and Bayḍāwī. But with the exception of Bayḍāwī (d. 1286), his sources were all consulted at second hand. Lane was among the first writers to point this out, criticizing Sale for not acknowledging the extent of his debt to Marracci and claiming, with some justification, that Sale merely mentioned the names of the Arab authors taken from Marracci without consulting the original authorities (p. v). There is perhaps less justification in Lane's suggestion that Sale's errors were partly due to a lack of knowledge which could only be obtained by residence among Arabs or other Muslims (p. iv). Lane's criticism of Sale, interesting as it is, does not by itself suffice to show the progress being made in Qur'ānic studies in the nineteenth century. However, Lane's contribution can be seen from his use of the well-known fifteenth- and sixteenth-century Qur'ānic commentators, the Jalālayn, that is, Jalāl al-Dīn Mahallī (d. 1459) and Jalāl al-Dīn Suyūṭī (d. 1505). Unlike Sale, Lane is not guilty of name dropping: he did consult the Jalalayn and so the general reader is given an insight into the thinking of two important Qur'ānic commentators hitherto only available to Arabists. In his translation of *Sūra* 96, the first *sūra* revealed to Muḥammad according to Muslims, Lane has incorporated, in brackets, remarks made by the Jalālayn into the text which becomes clearer to the reader: 'Recite [commencing thus] in the name of thy lord who hath created [all creatures] who hath taught [the art of writing]'.[5] As Lane says, the Arabic commentary also mentions that the first person who wrote with the pen was Idrīs.

Another example of the use of the Jalālayn, in the preface to the *Selections*, is given in Lane's translation of and commentary on *Sūras* 22: 39-40 and 2: 256. Lane's objective here is to show the contrast he perceives in Qur'ānic attitudes towards religious tolerance at various stages in the rise of Islam. He points out that unprovoked war is clearly contrary to the letter and spirit of the Qur'ān, but that war against the enemies of Islam who have been the first aggressors is enjoined as a sacred duty. At the same time Lane is implicitly critical of Muḥammad. For he says that when the opposition of his enemies had become so great as to threaten the lives of himself and his followers and the latter were sufficiently numerous to take up arms in self-defence with a fair prospect of success, Muḥammad proclaimed that God had allowed him and his followers to defend themselves against the unbelievers (p. 70). However, the following italicised words from the commentary of the Jalālayn on *Sūra* 22 which was revealed at Makka shed light on the Muslim attitude to war: "Permission is granted unto those who fight, *that is unto the believers to fight*, because they have been treated injuriously *by the unbelievers* ... turned out of their dwellings unjustly, *for no reason* save their saying, our Lord is God *alone*." The interesting point Lane makes is that the following verse proclaiming religious tolerance 'Let there be no compulsion in religion' (*Sūra* 2: 256) was revealed in Madina after *Sūra* 22: 39-40.[6] Again, the commentary of the Jalālayn provides the reader with the necessary context. They wrote, as reported by Lane, that this verse was 'revealed concerning those of the helpers of Medina who had children whom they desired to compel to embrace Islam'.[7]

In the *Selections* proper verses of the Qur'ān are generally arranged according to theme and historical chronology, especially as regard the prophets. After quoting the opening *sūra* and the first six lines of *Sūra* 2 which he calls 'premonition', Lane focuses on God and His attributes and creation. Particular emphasis is placed on *Sūra* 112 and *Sūra* 2: 255, the 'throne verse'. In the case of the latter, we see some continuity with the eighteenth century in the tendency to emphasize 'purple' passages of the Qur'ān. While observing that the 'throne verse' is one of the most admired passages by Muslims and non-Muslims alike, Lane has to acknowledge that his translation, like Sale's, perhaps does not come up 'to the dignity of the original' (p. 102). The reader learns from him that it is recited at the close of the five daily prayers, though not by all Muslims, and is often engraved on an ornament of gold or silver which is worn as an amulet. Despite Muslim veneration for this verse, it is not certain that Lane is accurate in his remark which may not have been based on personal observation. His comment on *Sūra* 65: 12 about the creation of seven heavens by God provides him with an opportunity to promote his translation of the *Arabian Nights* as he reproduces note 2 of his Introduction to the translation. Similarly he refers the reader to note 21 of his Introduction when he mentions Muslims' belief in three different species of created beings: angels, *jinn* and men. On the whole, it could be argued that Lane succeeded, to some extent, in his aim of popularizing the Qur'ān by frequently associating it with a popular work of the imagination like the *Arabian Nights*.[8]

At any rate Lane who used French works such as La Roque's *Voyage dans la Palestine* (1717) and Sylvestre de Sacy's *Grammaire arabe* (1810) in the *Selections* had a more positive attitude to the Qur'ān than C.E. Oelsner, a diplomat who represented the interests of Frankfurt with the Directory. Oelsner's 'mémoire' entitled *Des effets de la religion de Mohammed* was published in Paris in 1810. It purported to trace the impact of Islam on Muslim nations during the first three centuries of the *Hijra* and had been 'couronné' by the Institut de France in 1809. Like many writers attempting to evaluate the impact of Islam, Oelsner has some observations to make on the Qur'ān. Referring to *Sūra* 4: 166-169, he thinks that it gives sound, lofty and worthy ideas of the Supreme Being, especially those concerning the unity of God, His providence, wisdom, justice and kindness. However, Oelsner is critical of a book which he says resembles Caesar's Testament in that it can be adapted to circumstances. As he puts it, one first receives permission to defend oneself, then to attack, except during the first two and last two months of the year and soon no period is considered sacred.[9] Oelsner seems to appreciate the beauty of the imagery, especially that of *Sūra* 24 (although he is not specific about which line), the subtle and witty, even comic, remarks found in other *Sūras*.[10] Against these, he argues, must be set the 'loud monotony of the *sūras*'. In short, he is ironical at the expense of this 'immortal' work so imposing in the outstanding results it achieved. For, in his view, an eloquent work in which fiery and well-balanced sentences do duty for sound logic is vastly inferior to that of Demosthenes and Bossuet.[11] Oelsner was not able to rid himself of Eurocentric tendencies, of the temptation to assess the Qur'ān by European criteria. He did not seem to realize that Bossuet had contributed little in stimulating French responses to Islam.[12] In fact, Bossuet had been so negative that he set the tone for some of the unfavourable responses emanating from different categories of French writers later.

It would appear that France's colonial objectives in the nineteenth century went hand in hand with her interest in Islam which was further enhanced by conquests in Algeria. In this connection it must be pointed out that the distinguished political thinker and statesman, Alexis de Tocqueville (1805-59) wrote two *Lettres sur l'Algérie* in June and August 1837 in the *Presse de Seine-et-Oise*.[13] His private correspondence, too, sheds some light on his thought. With regard to Islam itself, it was perhaps De Tocqueville's cousin and childhood friend, Louis de Kergorlay, who provoked his curiosity about it by the letter he sent him on 18 March 1838.[14] Rather surprisingly, Kergorlay, quoting St. Paul's epistle to the Romans (III, 28) about man being justified by faith quite apart from success in keeping the law, found it similar to a verse of the Qur'ān. That led him to draw some false conclusions. One was that both St. Paul and the Qur'ān taught that to be saved one needed faith without good works. The other was that such a doctrine must have developed in a religion founded by the sword, that is, Islam, and that it did not develop in another based on persuasion, that is, Christianity. This cliché led to another false conclusion, namely that the importance of faith is exaggerated in Islam in order to make it easier for believers without morality to be admitted into it: in his own words 'c'est élargir la porte, pour y faire entrer plus de monde à la fois' (p. 26). Kergorlay, of course, gave a caricatural reading of Islam. While God is always at the forefront in the Qur'ān, He is often associated with the practice of good works, as in *Sūra* 64: 9, for example. Kergorlay's misrepresentation did not kill his friend's interest in Islam. On the contrary, it seems to have prompted him to spend some time reading the Qur'ān.

Writing back to Kergorlay on the 21 March 1838, De Tocqueville told him that he had been reading Muḥammad's biography and the Qur'ān and that reading the Qur'ān was most instructive because the eye sees clearly in it all the threads by which the Prophet held and still holds his followers.[15] De Tocqueville thought the Qur'ān was a complete course on prophetic art and urged Kergorlay to read it. But he did not understand how Christophe de Lamoricière, who was to be made a general in Algeria in 1844, could think it was a progress on the Gospel. He argued that there was no comparison between the Gospel and the Qur'ān, the latter being simply a clever compromise between materialism and spiritualism. In his view, Muḥammad pandered to the coarsest human interests in order to introduce a number of refined ideas so that mankind might walk suspended between heaven and earth. De Tocqueville reinforces Kergorlay's caricature by claiming that the following doctrines are to be found on every page of the Qur'ān: salvation is through faith alone, the first of all religious duties is to obey the Prophet blindly and holy war is the first of all good works. The idea of salvation through faith alone shows Kergorlay's undoubted influence on De Tocqueville, while the remaining 'doctrines' reveal De Tocqueville's own simplistic and erroneous misconception of Islam. *Sūra* 5: 92 for instance, commands the believer to obey God and the Messenger.[16] There is no question of blind obedience to the Prophet, while holy war is not one of the pillars of Islam. De Tocqueville is rather vague about the violent and sensual tendencies of the Qur'ān: he claims these are so obvious that they cannot escape the attention of any man of sense. He acknowledges that the Qur'ān marks a progress on polytheism in that it contains clearer and truer notions of the divinity and that it has a wider and clearer grasp of the general duties of man. But he concludes that it is perhaps more harmful because it rouses man's passions more than polytheism which does not have the same hold on the masses.

It is not to be imagined that De Tocqueville's strictures on Islam were confined to his private correspondence. For he made a number of observations on it in a text entitled 'Notes sur le Coran' at about the same time (March 1838). These notes, based on Savary's translation of the Qur'ān, form part of the 'Ecrits et discours politiques' and have been published in volume III of the *Oeuvres complètes*. In these notes, De Tocqueville commented on *Sūras* 2 to 18 (which he calls chapters) or rather he often reproduced translations of the verses with comments here and there. Oddly enough, what De Tocqueville calls chapter 1 has nothing to do with the opening *sūra* of the Qur'ān. Under this item, he chose to make general remarks, repeating what he said in his letter to Kergorlay about the need to obey the Prophet as one obeys God and about faith being constantly superior to good works. However, he mentions the splendid images of God to be found in the Qur'ān without giving any example, and the Qur'ān's link with the Old Testament. In his remarks on *Sūra* 2, as on other *Sūras* such as 4, 5, 9 and 11, De Tocqueville is selective to the point of caricature. His main objective seems to be to paint Islam as a religion rewarding violence and war. He claims that in *Sūras* 11 and 14 the idea is to get the Arabs acquainted with all the prophets whom people refused to believe and to frighten them with the portrait of the horrible punishments which God meted out to such people for unbelief. This leads him to make sweeping statements about the Qur'ān: one of these is that in much of it Muḥammad is more interested in getting people to believe in him than in laying down moral rules. In his note on *Sūra* 9, he claims that everything that relates to war is precise, whereas everything relating to moral teaching, except alms-giving, is vague and confused. His reading of *Sūra* 4 is slightly more acceptable in that De Tocqueville mentions laws governing inheritance, marriage and suicide. But his remarks contain no reference to Qur'ānic teaching on the kindness Muslims should show towards parents, relatives, orphans, the needy, neighbours and travellers, which is clearly mentioned in line 40. The rest of the 'Notes' is full of complaints about the lack of moral teaching in the Qur'ān.

However, De Tocqueville seems conscious of Savary's shortcomings as a translator of the Qur'ān and of the weakness of his own perceptions. For in his 'Notes du voyage en Algérie' of 1841, published in *Voyages en Angleterre, Irlande, Suisse et Algérie*,[17] after remarking that the Arabs use classical Arabic in writing, he says that Savary's translation is elegant but not faithful. He laments the fact that no good translation exists, pointing out that it is essential to translate at the same time the five or six major commentaries which help towards understanding the Qur'ān. In his view, the Qur'ān is a collection of day-to-day matters about which one understands nothing unless the insignificant affairs which gave rise to them are explained. He feels that the first scientific work of the government should be to have both text and commentary translated as best as possible and that this would be better than to spend 500,000 francs on a Scientific Commission which has no practical utility. De Tocqueville was probably unaware that the works of some of the great commentators of the Qur'ān were in fact being popularized in France at the time he was writing. For instance, the Orientalist Garcin de Tassy, a Professor at the Ecole de langues orientales, demonstrated knowledge not only of the Jalālayn but also of Bayḍāwī, though not of earlier commentators like Ṭabarī.

In his desire to show originality, Tassy had hoped to create a sensation by publishing in the *Journal Asiatique* of 1842 what he called a 'Chapitre inconnu du Coran'. He says in the introduction that he found this unknown chapter in the *Dabistān-i-madhāhib* (The school of sects), a Persian work written in India about the middle of the seventeenth century by a Muslim from Kashmir named Muḥsin Fānī. He seems to have much sympathy for the Shī'ites who arouse great interest because he claims that 'Alī's rights to the caliphate could not be challenged. He states that the Shī'ites reproach the Sunnites with removing from the Qur'ān a 'chapter' dealing with 'Alī, in which the persecution to which he was later subjected is miraculously foretold. Tassy's statement is sensational but groundless, as the definitive text of the Qur'ān is the *Muṣḥaf 'Uthmān*, the official version recognized by both Sunnites and Shī'ites. His final point is that despite the destruction of copies of the Qur'ān with variants by 'Uthmān,[18] the Shī'ites claim to have preserved the chapter. Tassy craves the indulgence of fellow Orientalists for his translation of the text which does not contain vowel signs as a help to reading. The Arabic text of the unknown chapter is reproduced, followed by a translation.

There is nothing wrong with the translation. What is wrong is that the text looks like a fraudulent piece of propaganda from an extreme sect on ʿAlī's behalf. Tassy does not say how this unknown *sūra* would fit in the Qur'ān and where and when it was revealed. The apocryphal lines start with an appeal to believers to believe in the two lights (Muḥammad and ʿAlī) sent by God who warns them about the punishment of the Day of Judgement. Needless to say, there is no basis in Islam for a belief in two lights which proceed from each other or for the suggestion that verses were revealed by God to ʿAlī. God is then made to say that He will restore to ʿAlī his rights on the Day of Judgement and that He is aware of the attempt to deprive him of these. Other verses refer to ʿAlī's piety and his being honoured above the whole of Muḥammad's family. More specifically Shīʿite in appeal is God's announcement to the Prophet of a progeny of just men who will not oppose His commandments. Tassy says in a parenthesis that this is a reference to the twelve Imams and that the reference in the phrase 'my kindness and pity will be on them, living or dead' is to the twelfth Imām, called Mahdī. Moreover, God's wrath is reserved for those who will act like tyrants towards them after their tyrannical behaviour towards ʿAlī. Contemporary writers rejected Tassy's 'discovery' with contempt.[19]

A futile attempt at originality should not be allowed to undermine the efforts Tassy made elsewhere towards an understanding of the Qur'ān in the nineteenth century. For Tassy's contribution in that respect was far more significant than that of Noel Desvergers whose achievement in other fields of Islamic studies was outstanding.[20] In his work called *Arabie* published in 1847 in the series 'L'Univers. Histoire et Description de tous les peuples', Desvergers, a member of the Council of the Société Asiatique and a Vice President of the French Geographical Society, included a section entitled 'De l'Islamisme et du Coran'. In it he made some scathing remarks on the Qur'ān which, in his view, contained an incoherent and confused code, a collection of sermons inspired by the events of one day but rejected the next day, truncated stories borrowed from Christian holy books, couched in a dense style, the beauty of which escaped the French while its concision was such that numerous commentaries were needed by the Arabs themselves. To Desvergers few books could be less interesting than the Qur'ān and few could defy analysis more than it.

As if to challenge this view, Tassy produced his *L'Islamisme d'après le Coran* in 1874, a work divided into four parts and containing a preface. The second part is a translation of the texts of the Turkish scholar Birgili (1522-73) about the principles of religion. Tassy first published the translation in 1822 as 'Exposition de la foi musulmane'. The preface itself is not very promising. Apart from including a misreading of Voltaire with whose writings on Islam Tassy is not very familiar and who is merely seen as throwing scorn on Islam and the Prophet in his play *Mahomet*, it is critical of the fact that the Qur'ān is not arranged according to the chronological order of its revelation. Instead of showing taste and discernment, it went on, the compilers drew together the verses ending with the same rhyme by placing first those clearest in meaning, then the less clear and finally those which are obscure. In this confused collection are found religious precepts, moral and civil, biblical narrative, Arab traditions, allusions to contemporary events, abrogated and abrogating verses, all lumped together amidst countless repetition. However, Tassy maintains that such defects cannot obscure beauty of thought in the original, which is brought out by the charm and harmony of the style. Although he accepts that European translations make tiresome reading, he still uses Savary's translation, but not blindly, and he proposes to give fragments relating to religious doctrine which will enhance appreciation of the work and its true principles.

In the first section entitled 'Doctrine and duties of the Muslim religion', Tassy lists a large number of themes picked out from the Qur'ān, establishing at the same time a sort of hierarchy among them. Topping the list is God. There are abundant quotations from the Qur'ān, stressing the unity of God and celebrating His attributes as creator, dispenser, master of the world and the centre of everything.[21] Like many other European writers, Tassy does not fail to translate the 'Throne Verse'. After mention of God come angels (35: 1) then inspired books. In the translation the Pentateuch is described as the light and the rule of the pious (21: 48-49) while the Gospel is described as the touch of faith and a book that enlightens and instructs those who fear the Lord (5: 49). Tassy naturally devotes more space to what is said about the Qur'ān. The way he has arranged references to it contributes to create a more positive image of Islam's Holy book than his preface does. The reader learns *inter alia* about a book in which shines knowledge that guides the believers and grants them divine mercy (7: 52). The Qur'ān is a book wherein is no doubt, a guidance to the Godfearing who perform the prayer and give to the poor part of what God has given them and who have faith in the hereafter (2: 2-4). It is God's work, confirming the truth of the scriptures preceding it (10: 37). Among the verses that compose it some contain clear precepts that form the basis of the work, while others are ambiguous. No one knows its interpretation save only God. Those who have a deep knowledge of science will say: 'We believe in the Qur'ān. All that it contains comes from God' (3: 7).

Whereas Lane placed the Prophets alongside divine books, Tassy chose to treat them separately. But like Lane, he presents

Abraham, Jesus and Muḥammad in chronological order, although little is said about Moses. Abraham is the head of the believers, a man of pure faith and no idolater, showing thankfulness for God's blessings and in the world to come he shall be among the righteous (16: 120-122). Tassy carefully notes that no difference is made between God's messengers by Muslims (2: 285) despite what might appear as a contradiction in line 253. His presentation of the prophets accords well with Islamic teaching on the subject.

Under the headings 'Justification by faith' and 'Worship of the one God', Tassy reproduces lines purporting to prove that Muslims, Jews, Christians and Pagans who will believe in God and who will have practised virtue will be exempt from fear and will have a reward from their Lord. These lines are meant to translate *Sūra* 2: 62 and 5: 69. But they are not a faithful translation of the Qur'ān where there is no mention of Pagans. The use of the future 'will believe' is not justified by the Qur'ānic text. Under the heading 'Sanctification', there is a reference, broadly based on *Sūra* 39: 74, to man being put on earth in order to gain the eternal abode. Further from the meaning of the Qur'ānic text, *Sūra* 10: 23, is the idea that man will acquire earthly pleasures at the expense of his soul. This idea reflects more faithfully that of Ibn Khaldūn (quoted by Tassy) who in the introduction to the study of history, book 1, Chapter V of the *Muqaddima*, stated that those who live sober lives discharge better their duty towards God; they discharge it more piously than those accustomed to pleasure and abundance, as there are few pious people among the latter.[22] However, Tassy is truer to the spirit of the Qur'ān when he mentions that on the Day of Judgement no soul for another shall give satisfaction, and no intercession shall be accepted from it (2: 48) and that evildoers will have no intercession save those who have received a promise from the All-Merciful (19: 87). He also adds in a note that Muslims believe that on that day prophets and saints will be able to intercede with God on behalf of believers who have sinned. In his desire to throw a bridge between Islam and Christianity Tassy translates verse 46 of *Sūra* 7 as 'a barrier shall rise between the chosen and the damned' and says that this is what Catholics mean by purgatory.[23] A closer parallel is drawn by Tassy between Catholics and Muslims who believe that the prayers and alms of the living are useful to the souls of the dead. It is not clear what Muslims he has in mind when he says that Muslims follow Catholic practices such as veneration for tombs, relics and pilgrimages.[24] However, there is nothing controversial in Tassy's portrayal of paradise based on the Qur'ān. If he shows awareness of Christian reproaches against the apparently sensual pleasures of the Islamic paradise, he insists that such pleasures are meant to be taken allegorically.

Tassy includes a quotation from the Qur'ān about the soul: 'They will ask you concerning the soul. Say: The soul was created at the command of my God but you have no knowledge given unto you except a little' (17: 85). For the sake of clarification, he reproduces a quotation from fellow Orientalist Sylvestre de Sacy (*Journal Asiatique*, x, 344) who follows Bayḍāwī's interpretation that in this line is a reference to the spirit that invigorates and animates man and that is produced without pre-existent matter. But Tassy did not use Bayḍāwī at second hand elsewhere in his work. For in the third section entitled 'Eucologue musulman' where he is giving an account of Muslim prayer, he quotes the commentator directly. He seems well informed about what he calls '*sūras* that are used in prayer'. By this, he means the short *sūras* 105 to 113. With regard to *Sūra* 109, he reproduces accurately a comment of Bayḍāwī to the effect that the *Sūra* was revealed when the Quraysh said to Muḥammad: 'Worship our gods for a year and we shall worship your God for a year' (p. 232).

The other information Tassy obtained from Bayḍāwī was a tradition of the Prophet to the effect that reading this *sūra* was as meritorious as reading a quarter of the Qur'ān and that it drove away evil spirits and preserved one from unbelief. He is quite right in saying that most commentators agree that *Sūra* 110 was revealed before the capture of Makka and that it foretells the Prophet's death. As he says, Bayḍāwī informs the reader that when 'Abbās, Muḥammad's uncle, heard it being recited by his nephew, he began to weep. As far as *Sūra* 108 is concerned, Tassy relied on the Jalālayn to report on the circumstances surrounding its revelation, that is, 'Āṣ, son of Wā'il, gave Muḥammad the name of 'Abtar' (one without posterity) when he lost his son Qāsim. The last line of the *Sūra* means that it is rather the Prophet's opponent, who will be '*abtar*', because Muḥammad has received from God 'Kauthar', abundant prophetic graces.

It seems that Tassy had paved the way for Jules La Beaume to publish his study, *Le Koran analysé*, in 1878. Although he relied on Desverger's *Arabie* in a number of instances in this work, La Beaume had obviously not been put off by the latter's remark about the Qur'ān being unfit for analysis. Hardly any study exists in the nineteenth century which gives a lengthier account of the contents of the Qur'ān than *Le Koran analysé*, although the book achieves far less than it promises. It would have been quite useful for the nineteenth-century reader to learn that 95 *sūras* were revealed at Makka and 19 at Madina, La Beaume not attempting to distinguish between *sūras* completely or partly revealed in Makka and Madina. His analysis is arranged according to eighteen themes starting with 'Muḥammad' and finishing with 'Progress'. Based on Kazimirsky's translation, La Beaume's work perpetuates some of its errors. Thus under the heading 'Jews', he reproduces Kazimirsky's translation of *Sūra* 5: 64 as follows: 'The Jews say: the hand of God is tied up; may their hands be tied up to their necks; may they be cursed for their blasphemy.' He also adds the translator's note in which it is claimed Muslims believe that on the Day of Judgement Jews will appear, because of this curse, with their right hands tied to their necks. There is, of course, no such belief among Muslims. Under the heading 'Christians', La Beaume uncritically reproduces the translation of *Sūra* 2: 62 as: 'Those who believe, Jews, Christians, Sabeans shall have their reward with their Lord' while a few pages later under the heading 'Religion',[25] he also reproduces, but without comment, the translation of *Sūra* 3: 85 as: 'whoever desires another religion than Islam, it shall not be accepted of him, in the next world he shall be among the losers'. La Beaume does not seem to realize that *Sūra* 3: 85 clarifies *Sūra* 2: 62 where it is inappropriate to use the present tense 'believe'. He is misled by Kazimirsky's literal translation of *Sūra* 3: 55: 'Jesus, I shall make you die and raise you up to Me' which Yusuf Ali translates as: 'Jesus, I will take thee/And raise thee to Myself'. (In Kazimirsky, the line is 48.) This leads him to conclude that the line gave rise to numerous discussions between Muslim commentators on the grounds that it contradicts *Sūra* 4: 157 and that Kazimirsky is right in saying that the reference is not to a particular, but general circumstance. But there is no contradiction between 3: 55 and 4: 157. For in Islamic teaching, Jesus is not dead and will die only after the destruction of the Antichrist (Dajjāl). 3: 185 makes it clear that every creature, including Jesus, will taste death.[26] With regard to 4: 157: 'They did not kill him (Jesus), nor crucify him, he was assimilated to them', La Beaume translates the last phrase as 'a man who resembled him was put in his place' which is literally correct. This gives him the opportunity of saying that the legend was not invented by Muḥammad, but was current among the Manicheans, the Marcites and other heretics. He refers the reader to Marracci's *Refutation*. With regard to the miracle of the clay bird raised to life by Jesus by God's leave (3: 49), La Beaume points out that it is quoted from an apocryphal Gospel. According to Yusuf Ali, the miracle is mentioned in apocryphal Gospels.[27]

Following Kazimirsky, La Beaume makes under the heading 'Worship' pertinent remarks on some *sūras* such as 113 and 114. As he states, these are known as the 'preservative' *sūras*, because they begin with the phrase: 'I take refuge with the lord'. But instead of saying that Muslims who recite them believe that they are guaranteed divine protection from bodily and mental pains he says the verses are carried by them as amulets. While it is true that the carrying of amulets is a current practice with some Muslims whose veneration for the Qur'ān is unbounded, La Beaume makes no distinction between superstitious Muslims and others. As far as *Sūra* 36 (Yā Sīn) is concerned, La Beaume strikes the right note by describing it as a prayer for the dying. Although under 'Dogma', he mentions the notions of original sin and redemption which are not acceptable in Islam, in his comment on *Sūra* 2: 38, he represents Islamic belief correctly by suggesting that in Qur'ānic teaching, unlike what happens in Brahmanic and Christian teaching, no expiatory victim is required. On the contrary, Qur'ānic teaching immediately gives an intimation of reconciliation between God and man.

Now and then, La Beaume is tempted to quote his authorities inappropriately. Thus to the translation of *Sūra* 64: 15 'Your wealth and your children are only a trial and with God is a mighty wage', he appends the following excerpt from Ibn Khaldūn: 'Muḥammad has said that all children are born with the same natural disposition: if they become Jews or Christians or worshippers of fire, the fault lies with their parents' (*Muqaddima*, i, 259). The quotation from Ibn Khaldūn seems to have no bearing on the verse. Yet *Le Koran analysé* contains interesting observations elsewhere on other topics such as the condition of women in Islam, moral teaching and human progress. Perhaps one of the most stimulating remarks comes under the heading 'Democracy'. The political implication in *Sūra* 42: 38 'Those who harken/To their Lord, and establish/Regular prayer; who (conduct)/Their affairs by mutual consultation;/who spend out of what/We bestow on them/For sustenance', is skilfully brought out by La Beaume. He gives it a certain contemporary resonance by linking it with the name of Khayr al-Dīn (d. 1889) who, he says, shows that this verse condemns absolutism. Indeed, the principle of consultation (*shūrā*) in all matters concerning the community is explicitly proclaimed in the Qur'ān. La Beaume referred to *Réformes nécessaires aux états musulmans*, the French translation of the introduction, made under the Tunisian political reformer's supervision in 1868, of *Aqwam al-masālik fī ma'rifat aḥwāl al-mamālīk* (1867).[28]

The behaviour of some autocratic Muslim rulers of the past did not therefore prevent La Beaume from appreciating the democratic processes laid down in the Qur'ān. Equally remarkable is the ability of another Frenchman – Tassy – to grasp some of the fundamental principles of the Qur'ān. Whereas modern Orientalists are trying to suggest that there is no such thing as authentic Islam or that there are countless Islams, Tassy chooses to call his work *L'Islamisme d'après le Coran*. He is thus asserting that Islam has to be based on the Qur'ān. Where he perceives local deviations from Qur'ānic teaching, he does not hesitate to say so and in terms that are not offensive to Muslims. Indeed, the fourth part of his book is called 'Mémoire sur les particularités de la religion musulmane dans l'Inde'. He castigates certain practices born out of the contact of Muslims with Hindus. As he says, the numerous pilgrimages to tombs of saints, some of whom are not even Muslims, are usages that are contrary to the spirit of the

Qur'ān, but have become established through contact with Hindus. If he had taken some account of *Ḥadīth* as well, Tassy would have made an even greater impact.

A quite different personality with a deep interest in Islam and the philology of Arabic was Ernest Renan. As Renan's comments on Islam were wide-ranging, it is not surprising that they include some on the Qur'ān in the *Histoire générale des langues sémitiques*. He claims that if biblical traditions appear in the Qur'ān different from what they are among the ancient Hebrews it is because the Arabs relied on popular stories, narrated orally and nearly always apocryphal. The result was that the stories in the Qur'ān sound more like rabbinical than biblical tales. Renan does everything to devalue the Qur'ān and its divine inspiration by suggesting that certain parts of it were 'written' during the Prophet's lifetime but that it was doubtful whether they had been written by the Prophet himself. The idea of a multiple authorship of the Qur'ān has not been heard of before. Renan refers to *Sūras* 68: 1 and 16: 1-5, to 'prove' that Muḥammad did not mind people believing that he could read by divine grace without having learnt to read. Basing himself on De Sacy, he finds *Sūra* 29: 44-48 very curious and almost unintelligible. Renan has unnecessarily complicated the meaning of verse 48. The fact is that before the Qur'ān was revealed to him, Muḥammad did not preach eloquent truths as from a book, nor was he able to write or transcribe with his own hand. If he had these gifts the 'talkers of vanities' could have legitimately accused him of speaking not from inspiration, but from other people's books.[29]

The mode of 'composition' of the Qur'ān strikes Renan as something peculiar, unmatched by any other example. It is neither a book written with a logical connection between parts, nor a vague text delivering its final message gradually nor the late assembly of the master's teaching in accordance with what the disciples remembered. The last remark suggests Renan was thinking of the way the Bible was written. The Qur'ān, he thinks, is rather a collection of the preaching, or even the orders of the day of Muḥammad, still bearing the date and the name of the place where they appeared and traces of the circumstances that provoked them. Indeed, the Qur'ān generally 'gives solutions to and rulings upon specific and concrete historical issues, but it provides, either explicitly or implicitly, the rationale behind these solutions and rulings, from which one can deduce general principles'.[30] At the risk of contradicting himself, Renan admits that each *sūra* was written down after it had been read by the Prophet. He could have added that the latter caused his disciples to memorize them. He could have used this information to show the authenticity of the Qur'ān. But instead he uses lack of order as evidence of its authenticity.[31]

Renan's interest in the Qur'ān in the *Histoire générale des langues sémitiques* is really literary and linguistic and this leads him to pre-Islamic times. He states that Islam was not the cause, but the effect of the reawakening of the Arab nation, a reawakening that took place at least a century before Muḥammad. Thus the Arabic language appeared with its learned and refined form in a distinctly original poetry as early as the sixth century. Renan is struck by the poetical activity and intellectual refinement of that period as witnessed by the *Mu'allaqāt* (Golden Odes), the 'suspended poems' written by Labīd, Imru'l Qays and others before Islam, and the *Kitāb al-Aghānī* (Book of songs). Indeed, the *Aghānī* of Abu'l Faraj al-Iṣfahānī (897-967) reveals the whole of Arabic civilization from the *Jāhiliyya* (times of ignorance) to the end of the third (ninth) century. Renan observes that the last *sūras* of the Qur'ān, the poetic elegance of which he admires, have the same rhythm as ancient Hebrew and Arab poetry. Because of their naïve conviction and spontaneity he prefers them to the first *sūras* which he says are full of politics and controversies and are written in prose.

Towards the end, the *Histoire* lays great emphasis on the impact of the Qur'ān on the Arabs. Renan claims that by giving to Arabia an authorized text recognised by everyone the Qur'ān played the role of a true grammatical legislation. In support of his stance, he refers to *Sūras* 16: 103 and 26: 195 and makes the Prophet say that the Qur'ān is written in the purest Arabic. This is a slight exaggeration, as no superlative appears in the Qur'ānic text. Renan further exaggerates by claiming that the Arabs are so preoccupied with language that the language of the Qur'ān became like a second religion to them, a dogma inseparable from Islam. He believes few idioms received such a solemn consecration. Quoting Pocock's *Specimen historiae Arabum* (1650), he attributes to Muslims the belief that the Qur'ān is the language of Ismā'īl, revealed again to the Prophet, the language that God will use with his servants on Judgement Day. Renan's conclusion about the Arabic language is foolhardy, as he proclaims that the composition of the Qur'ān ends the history of Arabic, that from about 650 the language has not varied in its literary and classical form and that the Arabic written in his own times by educated people in all countries is no different from what came out of the 'Uthmānic recension. While it is true that written Arabic is classical and the same everywhere, it is also true that countless spoken dialects differing from the written Arabic exist. Renan may well suffer from the obsession with a fixed language which afflicted French grammarians from the seventeenth century onwards. He does acknowledge the influence of Arabic grammar on the production of regular treatises on Hebrew grammar, ending up with the witty remark that because readers altered the meaning of the text with their misreading, grammar proved to be the remedy to the incorrections which threatened to alter the word of God! On the question of variant readings of the Qur'ān, Renan was rather superficial. For he does not mention the attempts of Ibn Mujāhid (859-935) to secure uniformity of the text in the tenth century.[32] Basing himself on a tradition whereby Muḥammad had been taught to recite the Qur'ān according to seven *aḥruf*, that is, sets of readings, Mujāhid wrote a book entitled 'The Seven Readings'. His conclusion was that the set of readings of each of seven scholars of the eighth and ninth centuries was equally valid, but that these seven sets alone were authentic. These sets accepted by Ibn Mujāhid represented the systems prevailing in Madina, Makka, Damascus, Basra and Kufa, each set having two slightly different 'versions'. Although all are accepted in principle, in practice only one of the fourteen versions, that of Ḥafṣ bin Sulaymān of Kufa, is now widely used.[33]

The *Vie de Jésus* (1863) provides further perspectives on the Qur'ān. As Renan's aim there is to reject the supernatural and to continue in the tradition of Voltaire who sought to humanise Jesus in the 1760s, he often likens Jesus to Muḥammad and the New Testament to the Qur'ān. Starting off with the idea that the Qur'ān presents in its disjointedness the different periods of Muḥammad's life and that the chronological order of its parts has been established, he tries to distinguish between the early and later *sūras*. He thinks it reasonable to suppose that a religious founder, that is, Muḥammad, begins with moral aphorisms (as Jesus did) and practices popular at the time, that as he matures, he indulges in a calm, poetic eloquence free from controversy, but in the face of opposition, ends up with polemics and invectives. Renan does not single out the Qur'ān in his criticism, since he claims that a reading of St. Matthew's Gospel will reveal a similar gradation in the division of speeches. He finds no lengthy exposition in Jesus's speeches which he describes as types of *sūras* in the Qur'ānic manner (4: 82-83). In the Preface to the *Vie*, he maintains that the

Gospels have a weaker historical basis than biographies of the Prophet such as Ibn Hishām's which can be relied on in some parts: their writers are no better than those biographers of Muḥammad who rely on *Ḥadīth* which is less historical than the Qur'ān and more legendary.

Despite their shortcomings and prejudices and despite the colonial atmosphere permeating some of their texts, European writers projected certain views of the Qur'ān in the nineteenth century which cannot be ignored in any evaluation of the relations between Islam and the West. However controversial and damaging to the Church Renan's utterances may have been, he was a major figure whose influence was never in doubt.[34] If, like other Frenchmen before, he preferred the poetry of the Qur'ān to its contents, at least he was helping to establish a crucial point about it – its authenticity. He and other nineteenth-century writers often gave a fragmentary reading of the text, but by their insistence on thematic and stylistic analysis and on certain key passages such as the 'throne verse' their contribution to a reassessment of Islam, particularly by the Christian Church, was far from being negligible.[35]

Notes

1. The research for this topic does not claim to be exhaustive, being primarily based on French and English sources. In the introduction mention was made of the Spanish contribution to Qur'ānic studies. For the German contribution to Qur'ānic studies, especially that of Theodor Nöldeke, winner of the prize of the Académie des Inscriptions et Belles-Lettres in 1857 for 'a critical history of the text of the Coran', see Bell's *Introduction to the Qur'ān*, revised and enlarged by W.M. Watt (Edinburgh, 1977), p. 175. An enlarged German version of the award-winning work published in 1860 as *Geschichte des Qorans* became the foundation of later European studies of the Qur'ān.

2. One of the few writers to have given a correct interpretation of this verse was Adrian Reland, Professor of Oriental languages at the University

of Utrecht from 1701-18. In the second book of his *De religione mohammedica* (1705), Reland points out that the verse does not mean that everyone can be saved according to his religion. It means rather that all those who believed in God and did good work before Muḥammad's message was proclaimed will be rewarded. Its implication is clarified by *Sūra* 3: 85 which means that after the proclamation of Islam salvation can be obtained only through it. In *Le Coran* (Paris, 1985), i, 75, Si Hamza Boubakeur made a stimulating commentary on *Sūra* 2: 62 which he has also well translated. Oddly enough, he uses the present tense to translate *āmanū* and the identical words of 5: 69, although he adds that this verse has been abrogated by 3: 85.

3. See 'L' Alcoran de Mahomet' in Bibliothèque Nationale, Fonds français, mss. 25, 280, f.1.

4. See *Arabic Tracts* (Alexandria, 1798), pp. 1-10.

5. Lane, *Selections*, p. 60.

6. In fact, *Sūra* 2 was the first to be revealed in Madina, the day after the *Hijra*, that is, 16 July 622, except verse 281, revealed at Minā.

7. Sale, though quoting Jalāl al-Dīn Suyūṭī, is rather vague in his comment that this passage was directed to some of Muḥammad's proselytes who, having sons that had been brought up in idolatry or Judaism, would oblige them to embrace 'Mohammedism by force'.

8. For a different view, see Leila Ahmed, *Edward W. Lane* (London, 1978), p. 189.

9. The sacred month of pilgrimage and truce is Dhu'l Ḥijja and the other sacred months are Dhu'l Qa'da, Muḥarram and Rajab. Oelsner's last comment is baffling.

10. Oelsner indicated in a parenthesis that by 'comic remarks' he is referring to *Sūra* 22: 15 'If any think that God/Will not help him/(His Apostle) in this world/And the Hereafter, let him/Stretch out a rope/To heaven and cut (himself)/ Off.' In his commentary on this verse Hamza Boubakeur quotes Zamakhsharī, *Kashshāf* (Beirut, 1947), 3: 28 for an ironical interpretation. He also points out that the meaning depends on the old Arab expression *Madda sababan ilā-s-samā'* which is used metaphorically to imply 'trying the impossible'. He further adds that the same image is found in modern local dialects of North Africa and Jordan. The idea of the verse is simple. Islam will grow and the Prophet will continue his mission, whatever is said or done to stop him, even if people tried the impossible. See *Le Coran*, ed. cit., i, 1113.

11. In his *Mahomet et le Coran* (Paris, 1865), J. Barthélémy Saint-Hilaire who also reproduced excerpts from Savary's translation, spoke of the effect the dynamism of the thought and imagery and the warmth of the expression had on people: their emotions were roused even before their intelligence was convinced (p. 188).

12. In the *Discours sur l' histoire universelle* (1681), Bossuet had summed up Islamic history in four sentences.

13. See Alexis de Tocqueville, *Oeuvres complètes*, ed. J.P. Mayer (Paris, 1962), vol. III, 'Ecrits et discours politiques', p. 11.

14. *Correspondance d'Alexis de Tocqueville et de Louis de Kergorlay*, vol. XIII in *Oeuvres complètes*, ed. cit., pp. 25-26 (letter no 158).

15. Letter no. 159, vol. XIII, p. 29 of the *Correspondance*.

16. A point well understood by Jules La Beaume who reproduces Kazimirsky's translation of *Sūra* 33: 36 where there is an injunction to the believer not to disobey God and the Prophet. For a fuller account of La Beaume's work, *Le Koran analysé* (1878), see below.

17. Published in volume V of the *Oeuvres complètes*.

18. Tassy's remark is too laconic to make sense. What should be understood is that when several copies of the Qur'ān, often full of inaccuracies, circulated in various countries of Islam, the Caliph 'Uthmān bin 'Affān deemed it necessary to put an end to this anarchy which could create divisions among Muslims. So he borrowed from Ḥafṣa, the Prophet's widow, the prototype copy of the Qur'ān established under Abū Bakr and gave it to a committee of experts with a view to making a recension of the text. A definitive corpus was thus established and incomplete or faulty versions were discarded.

19. In the *Journal Asiatique* of December 1843, Mirza Alexandre Kazem Beg, Professor of Oriental languages at the University of Kazan, wrote an article entitled 'Observations sur le Chapitre inconnu du Coran'. He pointed out that there was only one Qur'ān containing 114 *sūras* without variants (variants refer to manner of reading and not to text) and that Tassy's 'chapter', apart from a few words on behalf of 'Alī and his posterity, was nothing but a compilation of a few excerpts stolen from the authentic Qur'ān (pp. 399, 423). Tassy capitulated, acknowledging that he was far from maintaining the authenticity of the chapter which was, however, not apocryphal but simply a literary curiosity removed from oblivion. With little conviction, he argued that it was not improbable the chapter formed part of 'Alī's copy of the Qur'ān. La Beaume argued that since Muslim theologians were not stirred by Tassy's 'discovery', it would be useless to maintain that it was worth anything, op. cit., p. 322.

20. In 1841, he published a monumental edition of sections of Ibn Khaldūn's *History*, under the title *Histoire de l'Afrique*, with Arabic text and French translation. He also published chapters of Abu'l Fidā's *Al-Mukhtaṣar fī akhbār al-Bashar* with translation and notes as *Vie du Prophète Mahomet* in 1837.

21. For example, *Sūras* 7: 52, 3: 104, 4: 80, 112: 1-4.

22. *Les Prolégomènes d'Ibn Khaldoun*, traduits et commentés par M.de Slane (Paris, 1863), 3 vols.

23. This verse actually reads: 'between them (paradise and hell) is a veil and on the walls will be men who will recognize everyone by his marks'. Some traditionists believe that there is a zone between paradise and hell where believers whose sins are balanced by their virtues wait for God to decide their fate. In that sense, the question of purgatory arises. But the word *a'rāf* itself does not mean 'limbo' in Arabic: it means walls, heights. See *Le Coran*, ed. cit., i, 490.

24. Perhaps he is thinking of certain Muslims in India who frequently visit the tombs of saints. See 'Mémoire sur les particularités de la religion musulmane dans l'Inde', *L'Islamisme d'après le Coran*, p. 296.

25. Under this heading, La Beaume reproduces *Sūra* 17: 56 and draws attention to Kazimirsky's remark that this verse is against the invocation of saints.

26. See the note on verse 55 by Hamza Boubakeur, *Le Coran*, i, 213.

27. See Yusuf Ali's note 390 on this verse. *The Holy Qur'ān* (1946), i, 135.

28. See Albert Hourani, *Arabic thought in the liberal age. 1798-1939* (Cambridge, 1988), pp. 84-88.

29. See Yusuf Ali, *The Holy Qur'ān*, ii, 1042, n. 3478 on verse 48.

30. Fazlur Rahman, *Islam and modernity* (Chicago, 1982), p. 20.

31. W. Montgomery Watt shows the authenticity of the Qur'ān through the preservation of what he calls 'varying and even contradictory deliverances'. See *Bell's Introduction to the Qur'ān*, p. 56.

32. The generally accepted view in Islam is that the variants relate not to the written text which is definitive, but to the manner of reading. See, for example, *Al-Qur'ān al-Karīm*, translation and notes by Dr. Salah ed-Dine Kachrid (Beirut, 1984), pp. XXII-XXIV.

33. See Watt, op. cit., pp. 48-49.

34. See H.W. Wardman, *Ernest Renan. A critical biography* (London, 1964), p. 80.

35. It is worth noting that the Vatican Council declaration on Islam in 1965 actually uses words and expressions taken from the Qur'ān. More extensive and equally sympathetic to Islam, but not well publicized, is the declaration of the Anglican Church on Islam at the Lambeth Conference, 1988. One of the most significant points of the Anglican declaration is the recommendation that Muslims should be allowed to define their beliefs themselves and not in terms of stereotypes imposed by the West.

CHAPTER 2

Perceptions of the Prophet in some French and English texts

In previous centuries, as in the modern period, the life of the Prophet fascinated Western writers who had some interest in Islam. The further back we go in time the more current is the use of the terms 'Mohammedanism, Mohammedan, Mahometism, Mahomet' and their variants to describe Islam. That may have been because in the case of some earlier religions such as Zoroastrianism, Buddhism and Christianity it was deemed appropriate to focus on their founders – Zoroaster, Buddha and Christ. Even to-day, however, Pope John Paul II, who has some favourable comments to make on Islam in his book *Crossing the Threshold of Hope* (1994), actually calls a chapter 'Muḥammad' when he means Islam, whereas another chapter is called 'Judaism'. For long periods the focus was almost entirely on the man Muḥammad. The further we turn to the past the more negative is the view of him. In the Middle Ages and the times of the Crusades he is perceived as the promoter of a religion of superstition and fanaticism. In the thirteenth-century *Roman de Mahomet* by Alexandre du Pont, for example, the 'impostor' Muḥammad appeared like a brigand; he had the devil in him, committing all sorts of reprehensible acts. Such negative views were strengthened later when European countries were at war with the Ottoman Empire – by Michel Baudier in *L'Histoire générale des Turcs*

(1625) and by Bishop Bossuet in *Discours sur l'histoire universelle* (1681). Some three centuries before the positive statements of Vatican Council II on Islam in 1965, Bossuet could claim that he was speaking in his own name and not on behalf of the Roman Catholic Church, when he pronounced Muḥammad to be a danger to the whole of Christendom. He added that the 'false' prophet gave victories as the only sign of his mission as he laid the foundation of the empire of the Caliphs. Here was some weak attempt to examine the role of Muḥammad in history. This historical perspective was completely lacking in Louis Moréri's article 'Mahomet' in the *Grand Dictionnaire historique* (1683). Moréri offers a caricature of the early years and upbringing of Muḥammad. Humphrey Prideaux was perhaps more significant. In *The true nature of imposture fully displayed in the life of Mahomet* (1697) which was translated into French, he tried to justify the idea evident from his title. He also showed some understanding of Muḥammad's teaching, namely that he did not claim that he was introducing a new religion, but simply reviving an old one. He, however, had a negative impact on Pierre Bayle. In the article 'Mahomet' in the 1702 edition of his monumental *Dictionnaire historique et critique* (1697), the latter recognized his debt to Prideaux for the suggestion regarding Muḥammad's 'imposture'. Fortunately, he managed to get rid of the image of the legendary Muḥammad to concentrate on the historical figure. Above all, Bayle took great care to stress his teaching, pointing out that Muḥammad did not pander to loose morals. More learned than Bayle but also more hostile was Barthélemy D'Herbelot. In the article 'Mahomet' of the *Bibliothèque orientale* (1697), D'Herbelot refused the title of 'prophet' to Muḥammad and denounced his imposture and ignorance. Instead of discussing his achievement as legislator and social reformer, he laid stress on Muḥammad the warrior. So one cannot conclude that there was a significant evolution in attitude towards Muḥammad by the end of the seventeenth century: only Bayle gave a rather balanced evaluation of the Prophet.

Would the eighteenth century – the Age of Enlightenment – make any difference? At first it seems that French writers wished to maintain the French tradition of the seventeenth century with some of them making their assessment of the Prophet not in full-length biographies but in shorter texts such as a *Dissertation*, a *Discours*, a 'Notice' or a chapter of their books devoted to him. Sometimes they would discuss Muḥammad's role in history through some work which, judging by the title, does not appear to be directly linked to the Arabs or Muḥammad (see below). In view of its search for wider horizons and its sensitivity to non-European cultures, it would be surprising if the Age of the Enlightenment, for all its scepticism, did not provide the reader with some stimulating insights into the status of the Prophet and with the appropriate background to reflections on him in the next century. But as perceptions of Muḥammad in clandestine manuscript literature of the eighteenth century have been discussed in *Images of Islam in eighteenth-century writings* (1996), the emphasis here will be primarily on published texts.

For instance, the abbé de Vertot (1655-1735), a member of the Académie des Inscriptions et Belles Lettres, read a 'Dissertation sur l'auteur de l'Alcoran' at the end of a session of the Académie on the 14 November 1724. It is full of the clichés that came to be associated with Muḥammad from the Middle Ages, that is, he preached Islam by the sword, favoured loose morals and his book was lacking in divine inspiration and originality. These clichés reached a wider readership since the *Mercure de France* of December of that year gave a full account of the 'Dissertation'. The readers of the *Mercure* learnt from Vertot that the illiterate Muḥammad had dealings with people who were even more ignorant and that the wealth that he acquired through marriage enabled him to increase his standing among the Makkans. The 'Dissertation' stressed Muḥammad's alleged hypocrisy: all the austerity he affected in his external conduct, including his retreat to a solitary place, masked his true intention of studying the contents of the Old and New Testaments and of drawing what might suit his project of founding a religion. The self-contradiction of the abbé is glaring. For he is reconstructing the picture of an illiterate Muḥammad who reads the Bible! Even those who have doubts about Muḥammad's illiteracy at least recognize that he was 'unscriptured'.[1] While many Western writers refer to the assistance Muḥammad is supposed to have received from a Jew and the Nestorian monk Sergius, Vertot invents a story about Muḥammad closeting himself with these two men over a period of two years.

Muḥammad's hypocrisy and licentiousness are repeatedly stressed in the 'Dissertation' which is reproduced at the end of volume 1 of the *Histoire des chevaliers de Malte* by Vertot.[2] He devotes a number of pages to Muḥammad at the beginning of the later work. Like Bossuet, Vertot is interested in the origins of Islam. But the 'infidel' Persians of Bossuet's *Discours sur l'histoire universelle* have become the barbarians who were being challenged by the Roman Emperor Heraclius. The greater challenge, however, was provided from the deserts of Arabia by 'one of those restless and ambitious men who seem born just to change the face of the world' (p. 4). The change to the face of the world is not meant as a compliment. Here Vertot differs from Voltaire who in works like the *Essai sur les moeurs* (1756) sees in the change clear evidence of Muḥammad's impact on world history. Muḥammad is in Vertot's view the most skilful and dangerous impostor who appeared in Asia. To listen to the academician, it was marriage to a rich widow (Khadīja) that fostered Muḥammad's ambition for glory and independence. But to Muḥammad wealth without domination proved insufficient. To achieve his aim, the best method seemed to be the setting up of a new religion, 'a device used by many an impostor before' (p. 5). It does not occur to Vertot that Muḥammad never proclaimed that he was setting up a new religion. Muḥammad before his 'revelations' is represented as a voluptuous man who, however, abandoned his licentious companions to assume the appearance of one who had turned over a new leaf. To Vertot these 'revelations' were nothing but epileptic fits which the clever impostor passed off as ecstatic trances. Much of this account rests on hostile medieval images of the Prophet. In his attitude to Muḥammad, Vertot gives the distinct impression of wishing to contradict Bayle who, in the article 'Mahomet' of the *Dictionnaire historique et critique,* had rejected the idea that Muḥammad condoned loose morals.

Nevertheless, Vertot feels the need to redress the balance slightly in favour of Muḥammad by mentioning his qualities. To do this, he relies on Ibn 'Amīd, that is, George El-Makin (1223-73), the Arab historian whose world *History* was translated by Erpenius into Latin in 1625 as *Historica saracenica*. The *Historica* which begins with Muḥammad's birth was translated by Vattier into French in 1657 as *Histoire mahométane*. The picture of Muḥammad that emerges is of a man with noble bearing, gentle and modest looks; he was also persuasive and quick-witted. He lacked none of the qualities required of a party leader: in accomplishing his designs he displayed a firm spirit and courage that triumphed over the greatest dangers. What strikes Vertot above all is that Muḥammad excelled in a type of Oriental eloquence consisting of parables and allegories with which he bedecked his speech. He sees this eloquence reflected in what he calls the bombastic and figurative style of the Qur'ān where Muḥammad attempted to imitate the sublime features of the beginning of Genesis and the pathos of the true Prophets. At the risk of contradicting himself Vertot now says that Muḥammad did not claim to have founded a new religion, but to purify what was corrupt in older religions. He refers to Muslims' belief that Muḥammad was the last of the prophets, but falsely attributes to him the claim that he was greater than Moses and Jesus. The discourse ends on a negative tone. Muḥammad apparently borrowed from the Jews the principle of the existence and unity of God in order to consolidate his religion. The Christians provided him with the example of fasting, the frequent use of prayer which he fixed to five daily,[3] charity towards the poor and forgiveness of one's enemies. Vertot insinuates that to propagate his errors the clever impostor spoke a few truths and even put on an air of great virtue. The only evolution he sees in Muḥammad is that after having been a robber he became a conqueror.

Does the image of the Prophet change at all in a text written by a former member of the Académie française? Admitted to the Académie in 1695, but expelled from it in 1718 for his criticism of Louis XIV in the *Polysynodie*, the abbé de Saint-Pierre (1658-1743) published the *Discours contre le mahométisme* with his *Ouvrages de politique* in 1733. The abbé puts forward the then novel idea that Muḥammad was a fanatic of good faith for some time and that he would never have succeeded in converting his wife, his relatives and neighbours to believe in the truth and reality of his visions if he had begun as an impostor. Muḥammad was the first to be deceived and that made him more disposed to deceive others. According to the abbé, Muḥammad recognized his errors afterwards, but he refrained from undeceiving others. So from being a fanatic he became an impostor in order to exploit the errors into which he had made his followers fall and there was nothing remarkable about this. Saint-Pierre, of course, does not explain how Muḥammad continued to deceive millions of people after his death.

Two factors which he emphasizes in his attempt to account for the rise of Muḥammad and Islam are climate and imagination. As the climate of Arabia is particularly hot, the imagination of the Arabs is consequently more fertile. Imagination in hot countries represents more vividly the good and evil to come and whoever has the talent and the eloquence to portray to the ignorant great future evil can make them believe in it. The persuasive Muḥammad had a natural advantage in depicting the delights of an eternal Paradise and the woes of Hell, because no men could be more ignorant than the Arabs! Saint-Pierre forgets that the temperate climate of Europe does not prevent Virgil, Dante and Milton from representing the torments of Hell so vividly. He attaches so much importance to climate that the region which is more likely to foster various types of fanaticism is deemed to be that which is most affected by the sun. Unlike Vertot, Saint-Pierre finds in Muḥammad's patriarchal religion no trace of Christianity, but a coarse mixture of the old paganism and Judaism.

How does Muḥammad proceed, considering that the good faith of this fanatic is short-lived? According to the abbé, Muḥammad begins by having dreams in which he thinks he is talking to the angel Gabriel. He ends up by believing that his dreams are revelations. This insistence on divine revelation induces him to lie. He then decides to exploit the illness of those whom he has made ill. Saint-Pierre is convinced that Muḥammad is the first to fall sick and that his illness would not have been contagious, if it had not been an illness. The surprising comparison that he makes is between Muḥammad on the one hand and Descartes and Malebranche on the other. Though the two French men surpassed Muḥammad a thousand times in knowledge, they would never have had the power of persuasion to convince the ignorant Khadīja about Gabriel's revelations. As Saint-Pierre puts it, the ignorant Muḥammad 'made ill by his visions, easily does with his contagious disease what Descartes would never have been able to do with his great mind, through lack of surprise and fear' (p. 123). From imaginary prophethood, Muḥammad passed on to real imposture. Saint-Pierre sees hypocrisy everywhere in Islam, arguing that Muḥammad was not the only hypocrite. For example, Abū Sufyān, his former enemy, who became converted to Islam, won his confidence and gained much through hypocrisy.[4] According to Saint-Pierre many of Muḥammad's disciples realized that he was only a man like themselves. But seeing that they could become richer in declaring him to be a Prophet, they favoured his imposture and became impostors in their turn, although they recognized that his religion was reasonable and led men to justice and good works. It is only indirectly that the reader is given a fleeting glimpse of the fundamental teaching of Muḥammad who apparently imagines in a dream that the Angel shows him repeatedly how to avoid Hell and obtain Paradise by renouncing idolatry, observing justice, fasting, practising charity and going on pilgrimage.

Because of his impact on Voltaire reference may also be made to a lesser known writer, Jean Antoine Guer (1713-64), who published a two-volume study entitled *Moeurs et usages des Turcs, leur religion, leur gouvernement civil, militaire et politique* in 1747. At the beginning of volume 1 attention is at first concentrated on Muḥammad. He is made to appear like an ambitious opportunist who, by corrupting religion and making it pander to the basest instincts of his followers, caused it to gain ground rapidly. When his eloquence failed, he used force to win over adherents to his cause. To this conventional view of the Prophet, Guer adds a personal note in the form of an original comparison between Muḥammad and Cromwell, which was to be taken up later by Voltaire in the *Remarques pour servir de Supplément à l'Essai sur les moeurs* (1763). Whereas

Voltaire finds Muḥammad as fanatical as Cromwell but greater than he, Guer finds him less enlightened than the 'English usurper', his mind less cultivated, his politics less subtle, his eloquence less flexible and his designs less profound. According to Guer, Muḥammad was as brave and as courageous as Cromwell. But what established a common trait between the two impostors was the concealed hypocrisy which raised them to a high level of power. But the most original aspect of the comparison between the two figures is the role played by their respective wives who were both useful and necessary to their husbands. Whereas Khadīja proclaimed Muḥammad's revelations and his mission, Cromwell's wife worked ceaselessly to show the devotion and zeal of her husband to the public cause. Both helped to promote the cause of their husbands by winning them friends or revealing the machinations of their enemies.

Fuller and certainly more controversial accounts of the life of the Prophet also exist in the eighteenth century. Nowadays one does not hear much of Jean Gagnier (1670-1740), Laudian Professor of Arabic at Oxford from 1724. In 1723, he edited, in Arabic, some chapters on the biography of Muḥammad, extracted from the *Mukhtaṣar Ta'rīkh al-Bashar* (*the Concise history of Man*) of the Arab historian Abu'l Fidā' (1273-1331) together with a Latin translation of it under the title *De vita et rebus gestis mohammedis.* Fully aware that he would not 'satisfy the curiosity of those who could not read Arabic or Latin', he discarded Abu'l Fidā' and used instead the unreliable Muṣṭafā Jannābī (d. 1590), the author of a *History* dealing with Muslim dynasties known as *Ta'rīkh al-Jannābī.* He thus transformed a fairly scholarly work of 160 pages into a popular two-volume novel purporting to be a biography, where he gave free rein to his liking for the marvellous, indulging in lengthy descriptions of the miraculous events said to have accompanied the birth of Muḥammad or said to have been accomplished by him. The image of the historical Muḥammad became impaired in the process: not a word is said about him as legislator or even the victorious leader of men. Gagnier claimed that his purpose was not to depict Muḥammad as he really was, but to acquaint European readers with what orthodox Muslims say about him. If he had been genuine he would have known that Muslims prefer the biographies of Ibn Isḥāq, al-Wāqidī, Ibn Sa'd and al-Ṭabarī to Jannābī's (see below). Although he also pays homage to Muḥammad's personal qualities as described by Abu'l Fidā', the main aim of Gagnier's *Vie de Mahomet* (1732) was polemical: to refute Henri de Boulainviller's *Vie de Mahomed* (1730). The verdict of posterity, however, has been in favour of Boulainviller (1658-1722). One may wonder why there has been such a revival of interest in him in our times.

Norman Daniel felt that there was 'considerable charm' in Boulainviller's work.[5] Its significance, however, has nothing to do with charm. Boulainviller has been better understood by Diego Venturino who has devoted four important studies to him and the Prophet in the last decade: in 1992 Venturino wrote a doctoral thesis on Boulainviller's religious and political thought, published an Italian translation of the *Vie de Mahomed* and an article on him. In 2000 he published another paper on Muḥammad.[6] Boulainviller has also been discussed by Ann Thomson in an article published in 1997.[7] His biography of Muḥammad at first circulated in manuscript under the title *Histoire de Mahomet et de ses premiers successeurs.*[8] It was read by contemporaries such as Mathieu Marais as part of Boulainviller's anti-religious works: Marais thought that it should be handled with care because of some indirect criticisms of the Christian religion it contained.[9] In fact, in the manuscript Boulainviller unambiguously states that Muḥammad attacked Christian doctrine (f. 148) and that he established a religion not only in harmony with what his countrymen knew and felt and according to the prevailing customs of the land but that it satisfied general human ideas, so that he won over to his way of thinking more than half of humanity in less than forty years (f. 165).

Two traits, in particular, mark Boulainviller's polemical use of Muḥammad against Christianity. One is that he feels it necessary to proclaim loudly that he does not know Arabic and that he has not been able to have access to Arab sources. Yet his documentation, based on Orientalist European sources, is extensive: in his manuscript and published texts he shows familiarity with the works of Pococke (the elder), d'Herbelot, du Ryer, Marracci, Reland and Ockley whom he quotes. The other trait is that as a sop to Christian feelings he now and then feels the need to describe Muḥammad as an impostor and to be negative towards the Arabs. This is particularly evident at the beginning of book i, where the Arabs are portrayed as being more destructive than the Goths and hostile to science. However, this unpromising start is soon set aside.

The impostor gives way to the new legislator whose chief characteristic is the gift of persuasion by which he brought over to his religion not some coarse men but the most sublime heroes of their times in valour, generosity, moderation and wisdom (p. 133). Muḥammad's doctrine was far from being a mystery which cannot be explained. Moreover, he achieved conversion without any miracle. By his oblique reference to a mysterious doctrine in the printed text, where the attack has been slightly toned down, Boulainviller is making an indirect attack against Christianity, as Marais suggested. Muḥammad's eloquence was such that he could defy men and angels to compose anything to equal what he had given the public, that is, the Qur'ān. It should be pointed out that Boulainviller's approach is not only to attack Christianity but also to tell his readers what he thinks Islam is about. He is often alive to its spirit, grasping well Muḥammad's teaching against *shirk*, that is, association, since an infinite being has no need of another power to produce an effect (p. 135). This leads him to challenge the fundamental basis of Christianity such as the doctrines of the Trinity and the Incarnation. He says that Muḥammad condemns the Trinity because 'Christians admit a generation in the Divinity – generation which is obviously useless if it produces the same God' (p. 135).

Boulainviller does his best to dissociate Islam from the stereotypes with which it was linked, but cannot himself help reinforcing some of these. Thus he claims that the dying Muḥammad, on being consulted by his disciples about what was most essential in the teachings he had left them, recommends peace and among the means of preserving it was a permanent attention to cleanliness and the precaution to enclose and keep their wives separate. With regard to cleanliness there is a reference here to what Western writers often reproached Muslims with doing, that is, spending all their time washing themselves. As he himself asks, what link is there between Muslim men's jealousy towards their wives and their attention to cleanliness with peace and calm? Ignoring the context in which separation of men and women takes place in the Muslim world, Boulainviller suggests that the seclusion of women, practised in all the Orient, is an assured means of excluding them from political intrigues and preventing the storms they have often caused in the world. Pleasing their husbands alone will lead to domestic peace. Separation will ensure peace and tranquillity and that in turn will allow man to 'jouir de lui-même par préférence à ses autre biens'. It seems that Boulainviller was anticipating the Rousseau of the *Rêveries du promeneur solitaire* (1776-78) with the notion of man finding enjoyment in himself instead of relying on the external world.

The second book of the *Vie de Mahomed*, perhaps because of its greater daring, seems to justify the attention given to

Boulainviller by contemporary scholarship. Muḥammad is portrayed there as God's instrument in punishing the wicked Christians of the Orient who destroyed religion by their quarrels and mutual animosity – a notion current with writers such as Grotius.[10] Above all, he succeeded in bringing knowledge of the unity of God from India to Spain. This was a point Voltaire was to take up later, in the *Essai sur les moeurs*. Boulainviller rejects Western caricature of Muḥammad as a seducer of men through polygamy and the promise of a sensual paradise. It is a complete travesty of the man to suggest that sexual licence was used by him to produce a work as great and as solid as Islam (p. 168). He must have had great talents to be able to hold sway over such a large part of the world. Like other prophets, Muḥammad was not sent by God to teach new or mysterious doctrines giving rise to challenges. He is made to look on bishops, priests and all the clergy as a body of men who make religion serve their passions and greed: they are the source of all the disputes that divided Christianity then. The most mysterious doctrine – a suggestion first made in book i but now rendered more explicit – is the Incarnation which turns a man into God by the union of two incompatible natures. Muḥammad believed that the words of Christ and his disciples had been distorted to give them a meaning he never intended. The whole dogma is thus made to rest on a misunderstanding. Muḥammad, on the other hand, established the doctrine of the unity of God as the basis of all truth in religion and the need to fear and love Him: to do this one had simply to make a proper use of the reason He has given us. Thus Muḥammad preaches a rational religion in which Boulainviller sees no trace of mysticism, thus ignoring completely the existence of Sufi elements in Islam. Its truths – the unity and supreme power of God – can be demonstrated by simple human reason. Boulainviller has turned Islam into a religion very close to eighteenth-century deism. It is nevertheless close to Christianity as well, since it teaches resurrection and the Day of Judgement (p. 234). Muḥammad's moral teaching too is similar to that of Christ. At times sounding faithful to Islamic teaching, Boulainviller argues that in Muḥammad's judgement the justice of God could never impute to anyone the sin he has not committed; there is therefore no original sin in Islam and no need for any atonement. Muḥammad's fundamental teaching, however, consists of belief in three principles: the first is the existence and unity of God, exclusively of any other power; the second is that God, universal creator, justly rewards virtue and punishes vice not only in this life but also in the hereafter and the third is that God, pitiful towards men who go astray through lack of a teaching that could show them the truth, has personally elevated Muḥammad to be his Prophet. Only modesty (which Khadīja urged Muḥammad to overcome) prevented him from carrying out the designs of Providence. The above arguments go well beyond a plea for tolerance made earlier in the text when Boulainviller argued that reason should make us have mutual respect for the customs of every land because every nation has its traditions consecrated by habit. They may indeed have led Venturino to describe the *Vie de Mahomed* as the first openly pro-Islamic text generated by European culture.[11] Whether it is the first such text is open to discussion. But there is no doubt that it reflects a very positive image of Muḥammad on the whole. It shows how balanced French thought is. Single-handedly Boulainviller managed to refute all the Discours and Dissertations of previous writers against Muḥammad.

It is worth pointing out that Boulainviller does not always attempt to undermine Christian teaching. He claims, for instance, that Muḥammad's visit to Baḥīra may have laid the foundation for a kind of compassion he has always had for solitary people and monks. In any case, his travels contributed to his education, to his learning from the Persians the art of warfare and led to his acquiring knowledge that turned the camel merchant into an incomparable statesman and legislator superior to those produced by ancient Greece. Although he had earlier acknowledged his lack of Arabic he now claims to rely on Arab writers from whom he learnt that God wanted to educate Muḥammad gradually through the pains of hunger, thirst, fatigue and lack of sleep. There is even an occasional light-hearted witticism when he comments on Muḥammad's marriage to Ṣafiyyaḥ, a young Jewish woman Muḥammad married in 628.[12] The latter is made to say that Aaron was her father, Moses her uncle and Muḥammad her husband (p. 237). But Boulainviller failed to understand the nature of Muḥammad's marriages. He thought that the Prophet needed several wives as a distraction or as a relief from his labours. Long before his death Muḥammad was therefore forced to replace these faded beauties by younger wives. Boulainviller finds it hard to conceive how a Prophet who preached eternal truths which were revealed to him from time to time could have been so carried away by pleasures which are meant for persons with less serious projects. How astonishing, too, that a man with such designs, who needed peace to plan them, should have willingly opted for unrest and exposed himself to domestic troubles and jealousies! Such remarks have nothing to do with an anti-Christian stand: they are rather part of the traditional Western perception of the Prophet.

Later in the century, Claude Savary (1750-88) appended an abridged 'Life of Muḥammad' to his translation of the Qur'ān (1783). That guaranteed him a wider readership than a 'Life' by itself would have produced. Savary, who had some knowledge of Arabic, claimed that his biography was based on the best Arab writers and the authentic Traditions. He gave more importance to Abu'l Fidā' whose 'simple and faithful narrative' impressed him, although he did use Ibn Isḥāq, al-Bukhārī, Bayḍāwī and Jannābī at times. Savary was rather ambivalent towards the Prophet and certainly less well disposed towards him than Boulainviller, although he understood better than the latter the political dimension of some of Muḥammad's marriages: one in particular he discusses is Muḥammad's marriage to Umm Ḥabība, the daughter of Abū Sufyān who had already converted to Islam some years before (p. 135). Savary sounds plausible when he says that Muḥammad hoped that this alliance with the daughter of his former enemy would disarm him. The *Abrégé* starts off with miracles said to have occurred at Muḥammad's birth but subsequently dismisses alleged miracles such as an angel protecting Muḥammad from the rays of the sun in the desert. Savary adds that these made no impact on the learned Abu'l Fidā' who, despite being a Muslim, did not wish to turn his Prophet's life into a bad legend. He is scathing towards Gagnier and Marracci for spinning out these tales considered apocryphal by Muslims. Muḥammad is to be judged according to his words and deeds and not according to the visions of fanatics.

As Savary sensed, Muḥammad's Night Journey was, in Muslim eyes, a special case. Unlike Gagnier, Savary shows restraint in his account of this Journey in giving an abridged version of it based on the Traditionists al-Bukhārī and Abū Huraira while at the same time criticising Muslim theologians who have written volumes on the subject and indulged their wild imagination. His reliance on a canonical source such as al-Bukhārī enabled him to grasp one of the essential points of the Journey for Muslims. Western readers of his work could thus learn that Muḥammad after meeting several Prophets in various heavens finally took advice from Moses and God granted his plea to reduce the number of daily prayers from fifty to five. But Savary does not remain true to the spirit of Islam for long, since he argues that Muḥammad imagined the Journey simply to validate the new way of praying that he had established (p. 49).

While following Abu'l Fidā's account of Muḥammad's meeting in Bostra, Syria, with Baḥīra who warns Abū Ṭālib against the perfidy of the Jews, Savary claims that such knowledge as Muḥammad acquired instilled in him the desire to prophesy. Unlike Boulainviller, Savary at first makes Muḥammad rely on rhetoric and beautiful imagery rather than on reason to 'seduce' the Arabs. Later, however, he makes amends by arguing that the success of Islam was due to Muḥammad having preached a simple doctrine that reason could conceive easily (p. 239). He detects a trait of political expediency in Muḥammad whose success is mainly due to his diffusion of the Qur'ān over a period of twenty-three years: this wise precaution made him master of heaven's oracles and he made it speak according to circumstances. Where Boulainviller sees modesty, Savary sees sheer opportunism. So Muḥammad shrouds in mystery for three years his doctrine and his ambitious plans. When he could count on the blind obedience of new converts he would announce a new revelation. As long as he felt too weak to appear in broad daylight he did not order his disciples to take up arms. No sooner did he achieve some success than he made the order to fight the idolaters and the obligation to defend him to death come down from heaven.

Savary, it seems, wanted to make a distinctive contribution to the debate on Muḥammad's lack of learning. He at first suggests that Muḥammad pretended to be illiterate, relying on his natural eloquence to spread his message. Towards the end of the *Abrégé* he reproduced material to be found in Abu'l Fidā', which apparently confirmed his belief that Muḥammad could write. This material was a weak Tradition often used by the Shī'ites to strengthen their case about Muḥammad having appointed, in writing, 'Alī as his successor. According to it Muḥammad, who was suffering from violent pains near the end of his life, said: 'Bring me ink and paper and I will write a book for you that you may never err after me'. He is also made to say that it is not proper for people to quarrel before a Prophet. In the *Ṣaḥīḥ* of al-Bukhārī, the Tradition is attributed to Ibn 'Abbās who was prevented from writing it because of disagreement among the Companions. But it is not authenticated since 'Abbās had not witnessed the event personally. In any case, Sunnī Muslims who revere any genuine relic of the Prophet, would have piously preserved any material attributed to him if this had existed. It is a fact that he, like Emperor Akbar of India, did not write letters themselves but used secretaries.

At this point Savary's observations sound rather familiar. However, he tried to make his mark in an earlier episode, the details of which are recorded by Ibn Isḥāq. In 628, the Qurayshites sent an ambassador named Suhayl ibn 'Amr to make a treaty with Muḥammad. After having met some preliminary objections to the wording of the treaty, Muḥammad then dictated the following to 'Alī: 'These are the terms of the truce between Muḥammad the Messenger of God and Suhayl ibn 'Amr'. Suhayl objected to the expression 'messenger of God'. At his insistence Muḥammad told 'Alī to substitute Muḥammad ibn 'Abdullāh for Muḥammad, the Messenger of God, which he did. According to Savary it was Muḥammad himself who made the substitution by crossing out the words with his pen. No such information is to be found in Abu'l Fidā' or Ibn Isḥāq. Savary notes that at that moment Muḥammad forgot that he could neither read nor write.[13] He maliciously adds that this forgetting was a miracle. His explanation is that the feigned ignorance was simply a stratagem used by Muḥammad to impart a divine character to his book and that it is probable during the fifteen years spent in solitude he had acquired sufficient knowledge for his designs.

However, positive images of the Prophet do appear frequently in the *Abrégé*. One of these, as Savary shows, is connected with his ability to achieve conciliation. Savary points out that as Madina was divided between the tribes of Khazraj and Aws Muḥammad extinguished the flames of ancient hostility among them and preached unity and concord. At a secret meeting of seventy-five Madinan converts at ʿAqaba at the end of June 622, for instance, he invited them to swear allegiance to him and to choose twelve leaders among themselves to take charge of their people's affairs. They elected nine from the Khazraj and three from the Aws. To make his point Savary now relies on Ibn Isḥāq who, as he says, has recorded the names of the twelve leaders. He felt it important to quote the words of the Prophet, namely that the twelve were sureties for their people just as the disciples of Jesus (p. 60). After discussing the division between the Madinans Savary referred to that between the *muhājirūn* (the Makkan emigrants who went with Muḥammad to Madina) and the *Anṣārī* (Muḥammad's Madinan followers, the helpers). The first group claimed precedence for having been the first to embrace Islam, while the second thought this was due to them for having sheltered him. The dissension would have been calamitous, but Muḥammad managed to reconcile them. However, typical of Savary, he says that the latter made a verse (without specifying which) come down from heaven in *Sūra* 3.

Another highly significant episode occurring after the conquest of Makka in 630 is used by Savary to show how Muḥammad won over the leaders of the tribes. He says that everything gained during the war was sacrificed to win their affection. He does not actually refer to a recently revealed verse (*Sūra* 9: 60) introducing a new category of persons entitled to benefit from spoils used as alms such as the poor and the needy, and those whose hearts are to be reconciled, slaves and captives and debtors. He simply mentions that among others Abū Sufyān and his two sons Yazīd and Muʿāwiyah were given one hundred camels each, likewise ʿIkrimah, the son of Abū Jahl. As he points out, the *Anṣārī* who had been left out complained to the Prophet. But he did reproduce a version of Abu'l Fidā's text in which Muḥammad answered the complaints of the *Anṣārī*. Muḥammad criticised the latter because they were grumbling about the things of this world by which he had reconciled men's hearts that they may submit to Islam, while they already had the true faith which promised them eternal happiness. Savary adds that the *Anṣārī*, stung by this mild reproach, went away satisfied.

Savary also made some favourable comments on the Prophet's character. Basing himself on Abu'l Fidā', he had described the young Muḥammad, before the Revelation, as a man who roused people's admiration by the qualities of his intellect; he was the best at a reply, the most truthful in conversation, the most excellent for fidelity and the furthest of all from anything base so that his name among his countrymen in Makka became synonymous with the faithful. Savary had additional comments to make on Muḥammad's personality shortly before his death. He is critical of Arab authors who took delight in representing Muḥammad with all perfections of body and mind. He preferred 'Alī's account of him as recorded by Abu'l Fidā' who, he felt, was wiser and less partial than others. Savary attached greater importance to Muḥammad's personal and moral qualities than to his physical traits which are, however, listed. According to this account Muḥammad received from nature a superior intelligence, he had excellent reasoning faculties and an astonishing memory. He was just towards everyone: he gave equal treatment to a relative, a stranger, the powerful and the weak. He neither despised the poor for his poverty nor respected the rich for his riches. He listened patiently to the person who conversed with him and was not the first to leave. The conqueror of Arabia would often sit on the ground, light up his fire and himself prepare a meal for his hosts. Possessor of so much wealth he distributed it generously and kept for his household the bare necessity.

The public aspects of Muḥammad's life are presented with equal sympathy. In the course of it, as Savary tells his readers, Muḥammad had to endure disgrace, exile and proscription, but these only strengthened his resolution. The accumulation of protests and hatred from Christians, Jews and Qurayshites did not frighten him: his genius was meant to overcome obstacles. He created an order of brotherhood and this order united his countrymen. Not forgetting his French background, Savary turned Muḥammad into a general who offered his soldiers victory or martyrdom, rather in the manner of a Cornelian hero whose predicament gave him very little choice but to triumph over his enemy or to die for his country or religion. However, forgetting the wars of apostasy waged by Abū Bakr after the Prophet's death, Savary no doubt exaggerates when he claims that Muḥammad established his power on such a solid foundation that Arabia remained faithful to Islam and that his successors simply had to follow the path he had traced. In the final analysis, however, Savary ends on an optimistic note: Muḥammad's laws have survived the ruin of empires and the wise among the Orientals rightly confer on him the title of Prophet and consider him to be one of the greatest men that ever existed. Thus, the contribution of eighteenth-century French writers to an assessment of Muḥammad's biography proved rather more positive at the end than at the beginning of the century. What do later writers have to offer on the subject?

The life of the Prophet continued to fascinate those nineteenth-century European writers who had some interest in Islam. In a number of cases it was commented on by the same authors who had devoted their time to the study of the Qur'ān. A close link was perceived by Renan, for instance, between Muḥammad and the origins of Islam while other writers interested in different aspects of Islamic civilization could not help making a passing reference to the personality of Muḥammad himself. That was because he was often perceived as the 'author' of Islam's sacred book, Islam itself being identified with its 'founder' and being absorbed by him.[14] In the *Life of Mahomet* (1858) William Muir suggests that 'Mahomet and the Coran, the author of Islam and the instrument by which he achieved its success are themes worthy the earnest attention of mankind' (iv, 324). At the same time many French and English writers, whether they were specialists of Arabic or not, could not choose to remain indifferent to Islam and its Prophet when their constant presence was felt in many fields.

As more research was carried out into primary source material, often culminating in critical editions of early Islamic texts, nineteenth-century writers such as Aloys Sprenger (1813-93) and William Muir (1819-1905), as well as contemporary Arabists, including Montgomery Watt and Martin Lings, prefer to use older Arabic sources of the eighth, ninth and tenth centuries when compiling their biographies of the Prophet.[15] These sources include the *Sīrat Rasūl Allāh*, a life of Muḥammad by Ibn Isḥāq (d. 768) in the annotated recension of Ibn Hishām, the *Kitāb al-Maghāzī*, a chronicle of his campaigns by al-Wāqidī (d. 822), the *Kitāb at-Ṭabaqāt al-Kabīr*, a compilation containing material on Muḥammad and a biography of his chief Companions by Ibn Sa'd (d. 845), secretary of al-Wāqidī, and a section of the *Ta'rīkh ar-Rusul wa'l-Mulūk* (the History of the Messengers and the Kings, also known as the *Annals*) dealing with the life of Muḥammad, by al-Ṭabarī (d. 923). Not all of the source material was available to earlier Western writers in sound critical editions: some of these writers, however, despite the advice given later by Sprenger and Muir that Abu'l Fidā' should be rejected, deliberately chose to focus on him. Abu'l Fidā' was even deemed to be the best of the Prophet's biographers by Sédillot.[16]

Perhaps because of the concision of his extract dealing with the life of Muḥammad, Abu'l Fidā' seems to have enjoyed a high reputation among many eighteenth- and nineteenth-century French and English writers who were prepared to forget his late arrival on the scene.[17] Not only did the extract provide the basis for Gagnier's and Savary's biographies, but it was also translated by W.M. Murray into English in 1833 and by N. Desvergers into French in 1837. Murray, an episcopal clergyman, appended a preface, an introduction and an appendix to his translation which, like Desvergers's, was quite accurate on the whole. He acknowledges that Abu'l Fidā's work is necessarily compiled from older authorities. It should be pointed out that it does use Ibn Isḥāq's *Sīra*, for example. But Murray exaggerates by claiming that it contains all the leading facts and omits many fabulous and inconsistent stories and is therefore quite sufficient to give all the information on the subject: it 'will exhibit the meaning with sufficient correctness without being absolutely literal' (p. 38). Where Desvergers is happy simply to translate, Murray frequently uses an introduction and footnotes in the appendix in order to rewrite Abu'l Fidā', at the same time showing hostility to Muḥammad. For example, he finds the historian too discreet in his account of the Night Journey. So, like Gagnier some hundred years before, he says he wishes to rectify the situation. But he could only do this by reinstating the miraculous. This did not prevent him from claiming at the same time that he was giving the main circumstances of the affair which, in his view, was simply 'a piece of curiosity' (p. 174). His comment shows that he had obviously misunderstood the significance of a landmark in the development of Islam as a religion.

Murray was also not satisfied with Abu'l Fidā's account of the incident which occurred in 627, on the return from the expedition undertaken by Muḥammad against the tribe of the Banū Muṣṭaliq, and which gave rise to malicious gossip against

'Ā'isha. So to 'supply the defect', he gives his own account and says that Muḥammad pretended a revelation came from heaven. What he is referring to is *Sūra* 24, which cleared 'Ā'isha's name. He, however, saw in it a proof of Muḥammad's dexterity in dealing with his people. He then takes the opportunity to correct Gagnier, who had mentioned Muḥammad going to a cave in Mount Ḥirā, by pointing out that Abu'l Fidā's original has nothing about a cave. Murray is right about the omission of a cave in Abu'l Fidā': the reference to a cave is to be found in Traditions.

Having initially criticised some zealous Christians who 'suffered their prejudices to get the better of their judgement so far as to represent Muḥammad as a monster of wickedness, without allowing him a single virtue' (p. 1), Murray later claims in a footnote that Muslim writers have said enough to convince anyone of his duplicity, treachery, cruelty and ambition (p. 179). The emphasis henceforth will be on a cruel Muḥammad. Thus after victory at the battle of Badr (624) he showed something of his revengeful disposition in ordering some of his personal enemies and prisoners to be put to death, betraying the same implacable and inhuman disposition subsequently.

At times, however, Murray appears to soften his attack against Muḥammad, but what he really does is to suggest that the latter was shifting responsibility on to others. In 627, for instance, Muḥammad sought to punish the Jewish tribe of the Banī Qurayẓa, who were allies of the Aws, for their treachery. According to him Muḥammad sometimes affected humanity and impartiality in his conduct. So, in the above episode, he appointed Sa'd bin Mu'ādh as umpire to judge the case of his confederates. When Sa'd had decreed that the men should be slain, their property divided and the women and children made captive, he said that Sa'd had judged with the judgement of God. Many men were beheaded.

Murray also used Muḥammad's treatment of Abū Sufyān to make a point about his leniency towards former enemies. Before the conquest of Makka in 630 Abū Sufyān had converted to Islam and Muḥammad's uncle al-'Abbās sought a favour from the Prophet on his behalf. Al-'Abbās convinced Muḥammad who said: 'Whosoever enters the house of Abū Sufyān shall be safe.' Murray quotes these words to argue that though Muḥammad destroyed those whom he considered dangerous and troublesome, his general plan was to conciliate by kindness and persuasion rather than to resort to indiscriminate destruction of opponents. Wishing to do him justice, Murray stresses that Muḥammad prohibited his followers to fight or to exercise any violence at the taking of Makka. As he rightly says, Muḥammad was much displeased with Khālid bin al-Walīd when, contrary to orders, he slew many of the Banī Jadhīma. It would appear that Khālid's conduct was prompted by the Jadhīma's killing of his uncle.[18]

Unlike Savary, Murray casts doubt on the genuineness of 'Alī's description of Muḥammad as found in Abu'l Fidā', on the ground that Muslim traditions contain a great deal of fiction. Flattering as Muḥammad's mental powers and natural disposition are, he finds these improbable, granted that he was a man of great talents and that his general conduct was calculated to gain the respect of his countrymen. He dismisses as fictitious Muḥammad's offer of making amends to those he had hurt by suggesting that Muslim writers may have simply borrowed the idea from 1 Samuel 12. 3 and applied it to their Prophet. Seeing in him striking signs of pride and arrogance instead of justice in all his dealings, he challenges Abū Hurayra's account of Muḥammad living at subsistence levels, feeding on dates and water and depriving himself of a fire for months. As to Muḥammad's suppression of hunger he thinks that this may apply to some hermit, but not to him.

As was to be expected, Noël Desvergers seized the opportunity to project certain unflattering images of Muḥammad in his popularizing work, *Arabie*. The format of the book was probably a factor in preventing Desvergers from producing a coherent study of the Prophet. He was certainly less objective there than in his translation of Abu'l Fidā', although he did use the latter frequently. The result was that there was little new in his evaluation. Among the myths that he propagated was the myth that the Prophet had appointed ʿAlī to be his successor. He did not go into any depth on the question of Muḥammad's succession. Instead he stressed Muḥammad's indebtedness to Christianity. For instance, he used the episode of the early Muslims' flight from persecution in Makka to Abyssinia in 615 to show that Muḥammad had deliberately chosen a Christian country so that his disciples might help him bring his teaching into line with what they had learnt from Christian Scriptures. He no doubt exaggerates when he claims that Muḥammad closely followed the doctrines of the Man-God whose divine nature he recognised. As everyone knows, Islam denies the divinity of Christ, although it accepts the Virgin birth. Desvergers also claims that as long as Muḥammad was persecuted the divine moral teaching of the Messiah held sway with him. Later, however, he took his detailed prescriptions from Moses. As *Arabie* was meant for the general public its author felt they would be interested in Muḥammad's 'scandalous' marriage to Zaynab b. Jaḥsh. Without producing any supporting evidence he tells his readers that both Zayd b. Ḥāritha and his wife Zaynab recognised the impossibility of resisting the man who made Heaven speak whenever he wished.

A more balanced study of Muḥammad comes from the pen of Caussin de Perceval, Professor of Arabic at the Collège Royal and at the Ecole spéciale des langues orientales vivantes. His *Essai sur l'histoire des Arabes*, published in three volumes in 1847-1848, contains interesting views on Muḥammad, especially in volumes 1 and 2, volume 3 being dedicated to Arab tribes. He made good use of Arabic manuscripts available from the Bibliothèque Royale (Nationale), especially one entitled *Sirat* which is Ibn Isḥāq's, although he does not state this clearly. He frequently referred to the *Ta'rīkh Khamīs*, that is, the *Ta'rīkh Al-Khamīs Fī Aḥwāl Anfas Nafs*, a very late biography by the Turkish writer Ḥusayn b. Muḥammad b. Ḥasan who died in Makka in 1559. He also used Ṭabarī, Iṣfahānī, Mas'ūdī, Abu'l Fidā', Ibn Khaldūn, Pococke, Savary and Reinaud.

Despite an unpromising start with the suggestion that Muḥammad's imagination exalted by meditation and retreat could have persuaded him that he was the expected Prophet, Caussin felt that it would be an injustice to him to consider him merely as a successful and ambitious impostor. In his comments on the early life of the Prophet he sheds some new light on the name of the monk the latter met at Bostra. He says that in the *Murūj adh-Dhahab* of al-Mas'ūdī (d. 956) which was also used by Gagnier, the monk was known among Christians by the name of Jirjīs (George). Instead of the latter name Gagnier read Serjis and Caussin suggests that this reading made Gagnier identify Baḥīra with Sergius. Again, writing in a non-polemical manner, he corrects Savary who he thinks is mistaken in supposing that Muḥammad freed Zayd b. Ḥāritha after the latter had embraced Islam. As he says, the manumission and adoption of Zayd by Muḥammad took place before the first revelations: this information, however, is to be found in Ibn Sa'd's work,[19] not in the *Sīra*, edited by Ibn Hishām whom Caussin describes as the most esteemed of the biographers of the Prophet (iii, 331).

There are more significant aspects of Muḥammad's character and life which are highlighted by Caussin. He gives details of his marriage to Khadīja, but what interests him particularly is the fact that Muḥammad's changed circumstances did not make him become intoxicated with power. His modesty made him use his wife's wealth sparingly. Thus Muḥammad put in a good word for Ḥalīma, his former nurse, to whom Khadīja gave forty sheep. Although he later quotes the Tradition according to which Muḥammad is supposed to have asked for pen and paper shortly before his death, he doubts whether Muḥammad could read and write. However, he is convinced that Muḥammad learnt about the principal dogmas of the Jewish and Christian religions in the course of his travels and in the company of the Christian Waraqa, Khadīja's cousin.

With regard to Muḥammad's succession Caussin, although alive to Shīʿī claims on ʿAlī's behalf, shows great sensitivity to Sunnī Islam. He uses the information given in Ibn Isḥāq about Khadīja being the first person to believe in Islam and ʿAlī the first male believer, followed by Zayd b. Ḥāritha. But he dismisses the Shīʿī claim that Muḥammad uttered words suggesting that ʿAlī was his successor. As he says, there is no such reference in the *Sīra*, although soon after the *hijra* the Prophet instituted brotherhood between emigrants and helpers, took ʿAlī by the hand and said, 'This is my brother'. In view of the part played in Islamic history by Abū Quḥāfa, that is, Abū Bakr, Caussin is justified in proclaiming that the latter's conversion to Islam was more important than Zayd's.

Caussin himself is not particularly interested in the miraculous aspects of Muḥammad's life. For the benefit of those who are interested he mentions Gagnier's *Vie* where details of the Night Journey abound. Yet he understands perfectly well the importance of this episode: more clearly than Savary perhaps, he points out that it was only after it that the number of daily prayers was definitely fixed in Islam. This is indeed the case: Muslims have been required to pray five times a day since the *isrā'*, that is, since 619-620.

It is in his account of Muḥammad's life after the *hijra* that Caussin seems particularly well disposed towards the

Prophet. He speaks of a mosque laid from the first day on 'piety', referring to *Sūra* 9: 108. As he points out, the Prophet joined in the building to encourage the Muslims to work hard. He then draws attention to the covenant, based on reciprocal obligations, between the Muslims and the Jews, according to which Muḥammad guaranteed the latter religious freedom and peaceful enjoyment of their property. More importantly perhaps, the covenant stipulates that the Jews of the Banī 'Awf and other tribes and all those living in Yathrib (Madina) are one community with the believers and the contracting parties are bound to help one another against any attack on Yathrib. Caussin refers to the conversion of two learned rabbis to Islam: these were 'Abdullāh b. Sallām and Mukhayriq who claimed that the coming of Muḥammad had been mentioned in the Torah. He, however, adds that their example was followed by few of their brothers. As he points out, Muḥammad who could rely on the devotion of a large number of Muslims was not worried about the underhand opposition of a few Muslim hypocrites. He spared the Jews and he abandoned this policy of moderation towards them only when he recognised the stubbornness of their hatred. In Madina he continued to pray towards Jerusalem for some seventeen months as he had done at Makka.

Unlike other commentators, Caussin does not attribute the change of *qibla* (direction of prayer) to Jewish coolness towards Muḥammad, but he simply refers to Qur'ānic verses authorizing the change and to the temple of Makka being an object of respect to both Muslims and Arab idol worshippers. Like Murray, he mentions the killing of prisoners after the battles of Badr and Uḥud, while stressing Muḥammad's humanity, but he uses an episode at the latter battle to show how Muḥammad refrained from an initial inclination to wreak vengeance on the Quraysh who had mutilated the body of his uncle Ḥamza and recommended to his disciples never to mutilate the bodies of their enemies. In support of this stance Caussin quotes *Sūra* 16: 126-127, where the teaching is that there is more merit in enduring pain with patience.

As learned as Caussin was Aloys Sprenger, but his mentality was quite different: he was much less well disposed towards the Prophet. Aware that Ibn Isḥāq was highly esteemed among Muslims and among other European historians whom he criticised, he did his best to undermine his reputation.[20] Although he acknowledged the latter's faithful memory, refined taste and elegant style, he wanted him to be considered 'the father of Mohammedan mythology' (p. 69). Fortunately, he was refuted by William Muir who used Ibn Khallikān's *Biographical Dictionary* to vindicate Ibn Isḥāq's standing (*Life*, i, xci-xciii). Sprenger preferred Ibn Saʿd to Ibn Isḥāq: he thought that Ibn Saʿd had produced by far the best biography of Muḥammad. Curiously enough, he claimed that Sunnis were disgusted with Saʿd's impartiality, accusing him of Shīʿa bias. Ibn Isḥāq having included 'Ā'isha (the Prophet's future wife) among the Companions who accepted Islam about 614, Sprenger points out that as she was born at that time she could not have been converted simultaneously and urges readers to use the biographer with caution. Despite the slip made by Ibn Isḥāq, Sprenger used him often. As one of his aims was to show how much Muḥammad learnt from Christians he even distorts the meaning of Ibn Isḥāq in some cases. Thus, he quotes him as saying that Muḥammad had intercourse with ʿAbd al-Raḥmān, a Christian of Yamāma. What Ibn Ishaq actually wrote was that there was a rumour circulating among the rabbis of Madina to the effect that 'We have heard that a man in al-Yamāma called al-Raḥmān teaches you' (p. 140). In response to this rumour came the revelation in *Sūra* 13: 30 which includes the following: 'Thus have we sent thee amongst a people before whom other peoples had passed away ... yet do they reject Him the most Gracious.'

By omitting all reference to the context and the revelation Sprenger has attributed to Ibn Isḥāq thoughts that would have been far from his mind. He also used him to show that before the first revelations Zayd b. ʿAmr had considerable influence on the development of monotheist ideas in the Qur'ān where, according to Sprenger, all the sayings of Zayd were literally repeated. Ibn Isḥāq described Zayd as a man who had sampled Judaism and Christianity and was not satisfied with either of them (p. 103). He adds that when Zayd reached the country of the Lakhmites he was attacked and killed. Sprenger finds this conclusion very suspicious without saying why.

In part of *The Life of Mohammad* (1851) Sprenger tries to some extent to be positive towards the Prophet. He wants his readers to consider him from the perspective of the slaves of Makka who saw in Muḥammad their liberator and converted to Islam, although 'they were superstitious enough to consider his fits ... as the consequence of an inspiration' (p. 159). But he also has another agenda by which he attempts to show that Muḥammad improved his knowledge of Christianity at the same time, since slaves such as Zayd b. Ḥāritha and Bilāl were of Christian parentage. He makes laboured efforts to prove Muḥammad's sincerity. Whereas in his lecture on 'The Hero as Prophet' in 1840, Thomas Carlyle had without hesitation stated that Muḥammad was 'one of those who cannot but be in earnest; whom Nature herself has appointed to be sincere',[21] Sprenger chose a roundabout way to come to the same conclusion. Mindful of his German cultural background, he sees Muḥammad's affinities not with Cromwell but with Faust: Muḥammad's struggles, he suggests, bear a strange resemblance to the opening scene of Goethe's *Faust*. In both Muḥammad and in Faust he notes anguish of the mind, distracted by doubts: the anguish, however, is dispelled by the song of angels and is the voice of consciousness of their sincerity. It is not unadulterated sincerity since after the crisis they blasphemously sacrifice their faith and God to self-aggrandizement.

The story of the 'satanic verses' is told to prove Muḥammad's sincerity. As tradition has it, about 615 as he wondered what would induce the leaders of Makka to accept Islam a revelation came to him: 'Have you considered Al-Lāt and Al-'Uzzā, and Manāt, the third, the other?' (*Sūra* 53: 19-20). But immediately after them it is mentioned in Ṭabarī's *Tafsīr* that the Prophet's tongue slipped and by mistake he said the words below which were later corrected by Gabriel.[22] Ṭabarī mentions another version according to which Satan said these words in a way that people thought the Prophet himself said them. In the *Kashshāf* Zamakhsharī expressed the same view.[23] Rāzī rejected this story which is not to be found in the six canonical collections of *Aḥādīth*. The false verses were: 'these are the swans exalted, whose intercession is to be hoped for'.[24] The Makkans were delighted, but the true continuation of the *sūra* was soon revealed to Muḥammad. Later another verse which appears to refer to this episode was revealed: 'God annuls what Satan casts, then God confirms His signs (verses) (22: 52). In Sprenger's words, after having pronounced the satanic verses the following day Muḥammad 'repented and said the verses were prompted to him by the devil' (p. 185). However, by saying that Muḥammad himself rescinded the verses Sprenger is at the same time attempting to prove that the latter is the author of the Qur'ān. He goes on to say that by deviating from his conviction Muḥammad might have extricated himself from all persecutions and difficulties, but he disdained to gain this victory at the expense of his conviction. To Sprenger this was the strongest proof of Muḥammad's sincerity. He also refers to *Sūra* 80: 1 where the Prophet is rebuked for having shown impatience towards a blind man who had interrupted him ('Abdullāh b. Umm Maktūm) as further evidence of Muḥammad's sincerity.

Sprenger claims that towards the end of his career it was not conscience but his more sincere friends who saved him from compromise. He quotes Zamakhsharī's comment, on *Sūra* 17: 73 in *Kashshāf,* relating to the demands made by the Thaqifites to convert to Islam, which included exemption from prayers. According to Sprenger (pp. 186-187), Zamakhsharī said that the Prophet remained silent and 'Umar ibn al-Khaṭṭāb complained that the Thaqifites had filled his heart with contagion. But in Zamakhsharī there is nothing about the Prophet's silence and 'Umar, addressing the Thaqifites, actually said: 'you have inflamed the heart of our Prophet. May Allah inflame your hearts'.[25] Ibn Isḥāq says that Muḥammad refused the request. Sprenger even distorted the meaning of the verse beginning with the information that Muḥammad had almost been tempted away from that which was revealed to him by adding that 'at the right moment a friend reprehended thee'. The end of verse 73 simply says that they (the Thaqifites, presumably) would have made Muḥammad their friend.

As a distraction from a full-length biography of the Prophet perhaps, even if one cannot escape equally ambivalent images, one may look at Sédillot's chapter on Muḥammad in his *Histoire générale des Arabes (1854)*. Why does a writer whose preoccupations are primarily scientific feel it worthwhile to devote a chapter on the subject? It must be that he considers Muḥammad to be at the heart of everything. The chapter is not very scholarly, but Sédillot tries hard to do justice to him. In his view all the prodigious achievements of the Arabs are due to one man – Muḥammad who, inspired by Jewish and Christian ideas, founded a religion in which the supernatural was banished. The contradiction in his approach is clear: Muḥammad, he claims, considered that neither Judaism nor Christianity could achieve the project of political regeneration upon which he was meditating. So he decided to found a new one. But then Sédillot says that Muḥammad discussed with Khadīja, ʿAlī, Zayd and Abū Bakr the need to restore to the old religion of Abraham its original purity. Muslims indeed believe that their Prophet came to restore the religion of Abraham.

In the chapter Sédillot stresses the fact that Muḥammad acted upon people's minds through eloquence. Yet he insists that the battle of Badr (624) achieved more for Islam than all his eloquent preaching, as the believers were strengthened in their faith and the doubters got rid of their doubts. At the battle of Uḥud (625) against the Makkans the circumstances which led to the temporary defeat of the Muslims – the defection of the hypocrites and the disobedience of a body of archers – allowed Muḥammad to turn the defeat into a just punishment for disobeying his orders and made him opt for easier victories. Sédillot turns Muḥammad into a skilful politician who understood that his doctrine would perish if he allowed his disciples to become inactive. Hence war was the best option to sustain the fanaticism which he had aroused. The chapter, however, ends on a positive note. In Sédillot's opinion the moment when Muḥammad's triumph began was perhaps the most difficult period of his life as he needed the greatest circumspection to be alive to the feelings of his disciples. Muḥammad had to handle carefully those who had joined Islam through self-interest and those who had joined out of devotion. Sédillot thinks that not everything was praiseworthy in the immense task he had undertaken, but he invites the reader to consider the numerous obstacles Muḥammad had to face, the deep roots that idolatry had spread among his countrymen, the many improvements (he does not specify which) achieved through his authoritative speech. His conclusion is that one cannot but show admiration in the face of the outstanding results due to him.

The next chapter, called 'L'Alcoran', shows further aspects of the Prophet's character. Although he says that Muḥammad at first panders to the prejudices of his compatriots, referring to his fraudulent ecstasy and the old story of the dove, Sédillot defends him from the charge of barbarism and cowardliness. He argues that critics have failed to recognise historical truth and that Muḥammad did everything in his power to abolish hereditary vengeance then prevailing among the Arabs. The final impression that Sédillot leaves of Muḥammad is rather surprising: that of a tender-loving grandfather who allows his grandson to climb on his back during prayer and of the champion of maternal love which consists of simple words – that paradise is at the foot of the mother.

In the Preface to the *Life of Mahomet*, William Muir informs readers that his work was undertaken at the suggestion of the Reverend C.G. Pfander, 'so well-known as a Christian apologist in the controversy with the Mahometans'. Readers could therefore guess what was in store for them. The suggestion of Pfander, a German-born missionary of the Church Mission Society, that Muir should produce a biography of the Prophet 'suitable for the perusal of his followers' is almost a contradiction in terms. There is ample evidence to show that Muir failed in his objective of writing a book acceptable to Muslims, despite his use of early Islamic sources such as Ibn Isḥāq, Ibn Hishām, al-Wāqidī, Ibn Sa'd and al-Ṭabarī and his recommendation that the early Traditionists should be respected for what they have to say on Muḥammad. Muir's four-volume *Life* is even more detailed than Caussin's three-volume *Essai*. What distinguishes the Englishman from the Frenchman is his attitude above all. Where the latter remains fairly neutral the former is rather hostile to Muḥammad. Muir rejects completely the notion of his having received any revelation. He claims that because Muḥammad feared that in his 'pseudo-inspiration there should be even appearance of a human colouring' every sentence of the Qur'ān is prefaced by a divine command and 'Mahomet henceforth assumes the name of God' (ii, 75). He was critical not only of Muḥammad but also of Ibn Hishām. In volume 1, in which some 105 pages are devoted to a study of sources, Muir censures the latter (whom he otherwise appreciates) for omitting the story of the 'satanic verses' as it is to be found in Ibn Isḥāq and Ṭabarī.

Muir's unfavourable account of Muḥammad is particularly evident in volumes 2 and 3. How could Muslim readers like the story that he narrates about Khadīja's wedding to Muḥammad? Apparently, Khadīja, dreading her father's refusal of Muḥammad, got her father drunk and the old man accepted the marriage while he was under the effect of wine. Muir reproduced the story despite the reservation expressed by his source, Wāqidī. He adds that the tradition of Khuwaylid's prior death was invented to discredit the story of his drunkenness (ii, 23). Instead of emphasising Khadīja's support of Muḥammad he says that descriptions of a voluptuous Paradise in the Qur'ān were almost entirely confined to a time when he was living a chaste and temperate life with her (p. 143). Another story, based on Wāqidī and Ibn Sa'd, is given prominence to illustrate what he calls the origin of the law of female inheritance (iii, 197). After the battle of Uḥud the widow of Sa'd b. Rabī', who was killed in the battle, sought redress from the Prophet because Sa'd's brother had taken possession of the whole family inheritance and she needed her share of it in order to marry her two daughters. Muḥammad, moved by the tale, ordered Sa'd's brother to restore to his family their legitimate inheritance. Muir, who frequently quotes the Qur'ān at other times, in this instance prefers to rely on a story and relegates the Qur'ānic provision on inheritance, contained in *Sūra* 4, to a footnote.

Like Murray and Delaporte, Muir does not approve of the concise account of the Night Journey, as given in the Qur'ān. But unlike French biographers such as Savary and Caussin de Perceval he failed to grasp its significance to Muslims. Otherwise he would not have speculated that Muḥammad and his disciples might have been praying five times a day before they left Makka (iii, 37). If this were the case the Night Journey would lose much of its *raison d'etre*. However, there is nothing controversial in his information that in 624 Muḥammad, after having given alms, went with his followers to the *muṣallā*, that is, place of prayer, outside the city on the Makkan road. What is controversial is the suggestion that he cast off Judaism and its customs by replacing the fast of *'Āshūra*. Muḥammad promulgated, as a divine command, that Ramaḍān should be the annual fast from the end of 623. Without quoting any source Muir says that Muslims followed Jews in every practice: apparently, they at first fasted from sunset to sunset like the Jews and abstained night and day from all pleasures throughout the month. But Muḥammad 'checked this ascetic spirit' (iii, 48).

It is therefore not surprising that Muir's *Life* gives the impression of being written from an entirely Jewish, if not Christian, perspective. The few Jews who were persuaded to convert to Islam by Muḥammad are branded as traitors, but Muir accepts that they were of 'utmost service to his cause and constantly referred to as his witnesses' (iii, 36). He claims that Muḥammad's darker shades as well as the brighter aspects of his character must be depicted by the faithful historian. But he is not that historian. For he selects special episodes to darken Muḥammad's character without paying attention to the context in which these episodes take place. His aim is to show how cruel Muḥammad is to whole tribes and to individuals. So he describes a Muḥammad who exults with savage satisfaction over the dead bodies of his Qurayshite enemies at the battle of Badr, the purpose of which, according to him, was simply to win booty. In 628 Muḥammad subjects Kināna, the Jewish Prince of Khaybar, to inhuman torture for having concealed his tribe's treasures. Nor does he disapprove of the expedition against Umm Kirfa: the old woman's legs were tied to separate camels which were driven in different directions (iv, 13). Like many other writers, Muir prefers Muḥammad at Makka to Muḥammad at Madina. He argues that Muḥammad had no ulterior motive but the reformation of his countrymen at Makka: he may have been mistaken as to the means used to achieve his purpose, but he was of good faith. At Madina, however, Muir sees rapid moral decline and fierce fanaticism in him (iv, 317).

Yet, without conceding it, Muir actually paints the picture of a Muḥammad who evolves. For he sees some fine traits in him at the conquest of Makka in 630 – singular magnanimity and moderation. He says that it may have been in Muḥammad's interest to forget past injuries, but it nevertheless required a large and generous heart to do this (iv, 133). He adds that Muḥammad was duly rewarded, for the whole population of Makka adhered to him. Muḥammad also liberated prisoners from the Banī Tamīm, entertained them hospitably and sent the chiefs away with rich presents and provisions on their journey (iv, 174). There is also a grudging admission about the significance of the conquest of Makka, which is well brought out: amongst other things, Muḥammad now had control of the annual pilgrimage and custody of the sacred mosque. But in Muir's eyes the possession of Makka now 'imparted colour of right to his pretensions' (iv, 168). Muir, however, has a true appreciation of the action of Muḥammad in asking Abū Bakr to preside at public prayers in his absence. There is little doubt in his mind that by his nomination Muḥammad intended to signify the delegation of supreme authority to Abū Bakr, 'if not to mark him as his successor after his death' (iv, 265). The question of the succession is not as straightforward as Muir makes it appear, but his guess about Muḥammad's intention is not without merit. Muir finally concedes that Muḥammad conferred on his followers the benefit of the unity and infinite perfection of God and a special all-pervading Providence which became a living principle in their hearts and lives. But, as is typical of him, he also added that the benefits were purchased at a costly price (iv, 320).

Muḥammad was never far from the public view in France. For instance, J.T. Reinaud (1795-1867), a pupil of Sacy and his successor to the Chair of Arabic at the Ecole des langues orientales from 1838, produced a 'Notice sur Mahomet' which was published in the *Biographie générale* of F. Didot in 1860. It is true that this extract did not make a significant contribution to knowledge on the life of the Prophet, but it would have reached a general readership, which thus learnt that Islam was a religion for adventurers seeking booty. The account is oversimplified: it suggests that if one were victorious one could be enriched by the spoils while if one were killed in battle one went to Paradise. But later Reinaud modified his stand by declaring that it would be a grave mistake to think that people were attracted to Islam for love of booty or for other interested motives. No more convincing than Savary and without producing any new evidence, he says that Muḥammad learnt to read late in life and could write but imperfectly. According to him the only literary quality that Muḥammad acquired was the ability to express his ideas in a rhymed prose which was indigenous. Later, argues Reinaud, when Muḥammad admitted that he could not compete with Imru'l Qays and other poets of the pre-Islamic age he gave himself the title of *nabī al-ummī* (*Sūra* 7: 158) which he translates as popular prophet.[26] This interpretation of the above expression has not been heard of before and it is certainly inaccurate to say that the Prophet gave himself the title.

For the formation of the image of Muḥammad in the nineteenth century special credit should be given to writers who were not Arabists. The case of Barthélemy Saint-Hilaire is an interesting one. In *Mahomet et le Coran* (1865), a study he describes as more philosophical than historical in the 'Avertissement', he proclaims that it is based on articles published in the *Journal des Savants* where he reviewed the works of Sprenger, Muir, and Caussin de Perceval. Here he also used Gustav Weil's *Mohammed der Prophet* (1843). How he interprets his sources is the relevant question. In his summary of the biography of Muḥammad the main events are clearly presented and the reader is provided with a useful time-chart such as he does not often find among many biographers. Following in the steps of Renan whom he mentions, he too stresses the historicity of Muḥammad (p. 27). When he passes on to his character, he claims that he can easily prove that Muḥammad was the most intelligent and the most clement of contemporary Arabs and that the religion he preached, though inferior to Christianity, was of immense benefit to the races that adopted it. Moreover, Muḥammad must never be isolated from his milieu. Saint-Hilaire appreciates his kindness and moral rectitude and the fact that he listened more than he spoke. He dismisses Sprenger's account of Muḥammad's alleged epilepsy as irrelevant, since it explains nothing: besides, all people suffering from hysteria are not prophets. Although he says he will not make a forced comparison between Muḥammad and Socrates this is what he in fact does and he highlights the sincerity of both (p. 101). He later devotes a separate chapter to the question of Muḥammad's sincerity, drawing encouragement from Theodor Nöldeke's views on it in *Geschichte des Qorans* (p. 2).

Saint-Hilaire focuses on certain landmarks in the career of the Prophet. Thus at the first pledge at 'Aqaba in 621 when Muḥammad met twelve men of Yathrib from the tribe of the Aws and the Khazraj, he made them swear an oath which is famous in the Muslim world and which, in his view, deserves to be permanently remembered in history. As he points out, the new Muslims undertook to worship but one God, not to steal, not to kill their children, not to commit adultery and to abstain from slander. Muḥammad wants them to renounce idolatry and to correct their barbarous customs. With hindsight Saint-Hilaire says that one is inclined to laugh at these naïve undertakings, but bearing in mind Muḥammad's times he finds the venture admirable. Before coming to the *hijra* he reminds his readers that at the age of 52 Muḥammad has only ten more years in which to achieve all the great deeds that have immortalised his name. The first part of his career turned out to be the most difficult and the most eventful, for it laid the foundation of what was to follow. He says that most historians have acknowledged its stainless character, even Muir who became extremely severe towards Muḥammad immediately. As Muir would have wished Muḥammad dead at the time of the *hijra* because of his alleged cruelty thereafter, he deems it an extreme injustice because the man Muḥammad remained the same. Muḥammad may have yielded to political necessities rather than to his passions, but despite being placed under new circumstances he maintained the best part of his virtues (p. 114). He picks on one or two examples to illustrate Muḥammad's moderation in 630: he quotes Muḥammad's behaviour towards 'Ikrima, the son of Abū Jahl and another Qurayshite, Safwān, on their conversion to Islam. He finds such moderation very rare in victory after long battles and this respect for the vanquished is unusual among victors, even among the most advanced civilisation: if Muḥammad sometimes lapsed one may, without being too indulgent towards him, conclude that he had been driven by necessity rather than by coarse sentiments.

One of the last assessments of Muḥammad by French writers in the nineteenth century comes from P. Henry Delaporte. In his *Vie de Mahomet* (1874) Delaporte claims to have all the credentials to write a biography: he had been French consul in the Orient, knew Arabic, had access to written Arabic sources and had consulted the *ʿulamāʾ*. Despite his background he achieved less than he promised and the main body of the text is particularly disappointing. It is an endless series of battles with little commentary. Delaporte seems to have been so carried away by his love of the marvellous that, writing in the tradition of Gagnier, he devotes eight chapters of the book to the Night Journey and nearly every chapter is studded with a miracle. Two samples should suffice to give an idea of his way of writing. In 624 as al-Ḥārith of the tribe of the Aws went to attack Kaʿb b. al-Ashraf who had written verses against Muḥammad, he was wounded. Delaporte says that he was immediately cured by the latter's saliva (p. 81). In 627 when Saʿd b. Muʿādh died in the campaign against the Jews of the Banī Qurayẓa the angels are reported to have rejoiced at his entry into Paradise and even the throne of God shook with joy. In the *Kitāb al-Maghāzī* Wāqidī quoted the Prophet as simply saying that when the grave closed in on Saʿd God gave him blissful relief.[27]

Yet in the introduction one may find a rather fair evaluation of Muḥammad's impact on world history. Delaporte points out that the founders of great empires have left behind but a vague memory: Cyrus, Alexander and Charlemagne are good examples. Not so in the case of the 'legislator' of the Arabs. Perhaps unique in world history, Muḥammad belongs to the present by virtue of the still living creation of his genius. What makes Muḥammad's glory, in his view, what sets him apart from founders of world empires is that he has been able to impart to his work a force capable of reacting against the influence of factors that modify human institutions and lead to the decay of political creations; his law is living and strong after centuries. He reckons that if Muḥammad had only been a clever hypocrite who got Heaven to intervene as his ambition required his first step along that course would also have been his last: the good sense of the Arabs would have seen through his tricks, since one cannot deceive a people for long. Muḥammad, however, was driven by a profound conviction and truth on which his law was founded – the dogma of the unity of God and the immortality of the soul which may have been in a dormant state among these peoples but which needed reawakening. A doctrine free from abstraction, its principles clearly laid down, must have flattered Arab national pride and roused among this warlike nation the most impetuous passions, the spirit of domination and love of vengeance.

Some interesting points made by Delaporte are that Muslims were Muḥammad's Companions – *ṣaḥāba*, a word often recurring among Arab authors, as he rightly suggests – and not his subjects, so that the oath of loyalty was reciprocal and obedience conditional. From a purely religious point of view Muḥammad's character displays astonishing wisdom and power of reasoning, considering prevailing conditions and customs which must have influenced him. For while he recommends the strict observance of religious devotions to his followers he exhorts them not to give too much importance to external rites, in a passage where, in Delaporte's opinion, is summed up the purest moral teaching given by a man to other men (p. 30). This passage, in which the essential teachings of Islam are quoted by Delaporte, is probably made up of various parts of the Qur'ān which he has put together. He thinks that a ray of supreme wisdom must have descended on the Prophet when he uttered a sublime declaration of faith: after having read it one no longer wonders at the sway this man held over his contemporaries.

The work of the former consul is not, however, without its ambivalence. In the preface Delaporte had warned that he was not going to portray the Arabs with delicate feelings and subtle thoughts which can only characterise 'a more advanced civilisation' (p. 3). So, in the introduction, their leader is made to have founded a religion based on an error, a so-called divine mission. In support he refers to Voltaire, author of *Mahomet ou le Fanatisme*, as if this was the last word of his compatriot on Muḥammad. Worse still, stereotypes which had been associated with Muḥammad for centuries creep in. The 'Arab legislator' propagated his religion by violent means: in his hands the sword made more conversions than persuasion and it was the key to Paradise and Hell. Perhaps to modify his stance a little he admits that the 'armed missionary' (p. 20) wanted to conquer the world only in order to place it under God's command. Muḥammad was not cruel by design and Greek and Roman history do not show many examples of a similar moderation as Muḥammad's.

A more negative image of the Prophet is present in *Mohammed and Mohammedanism* (1889) by S.W. Koelle, a German missionary of the Church Mission Society and Professor of Arabic at Fourah Bay College in Sierra Leone. Again, it is a question of mentality, since the learned missionary uses Ibn Isḥāq, and often accurately, but still manages to be hostile to Muḥammad. Yet he is not uninteresting in some of his remarks. In tracing the development of Muḥammad as Prophet he at first finds an inward harmony between his Makkan and Madinan periods despite their outward dissimilarity. Later, however, he challenges the Muslim view that Muḥammad's public life was from beginning to end one congruous whole since he detects a radical change of principles in him: the ardent preacher, zealous reformer and austere Prophet of Makka pleading for mere toleration and bare recognition of his teaching is in reality the seed and precursor of a military commander and insatiable conqueror. In both places he is essentially the same man – only in Makka he is trying to succeed with his plan while in Madina he actually succeeds. Yet Koelle sees in Muḥammad a thoughtful and patriotic Arab who realized the full implication of Abyssinian and Persian domination of the Yemen over a number of years and who therefore concluded that he could rely on Arabs only for the security of his country. Few commendable traits in Muḥammad emerged after these preliminary observations.

Koelle does not believe that Muḥammad received any divine revelations. Thus the change of *qibla* was prompted by prudence: Muḥammad simply waited until the strength of his Arab following increased. Like Sprenger, Koelle insinuates that Muḥammad may have received from the *ḥanīf* (an Arab who, in pre-Islamic times, tended to monotheism) Zayd b. ʿAmr instruction in religious matters which, after the latter's death, he gave out as being derived directly from Heaven. He claimed that the Prophet said that people could pray for Zayd's soul. The Muslim view is rather different: Muḥammad praised Zayd, saying that on the day of the Resurrection 'he will be raised as having, in himself alone, the worth of a whole people'.[28] Because of Zayd's high standing in Islam Koelle goes to the length of suggesting that if Muḥammad had been motivated by religious objectives he should have followed him and Waraqa (Khadīja's Christian cousin) in embracing the religion of the man-God Jesus! (p. 53). Unlike Delaporte, he thinks that Muḥammad contented himself with mere formal worship and an external relationship with God. Besides, Muḥammad did not have the faintest idea of the development and growth of divine revelation. Otherwise, he could not have supposed that the religion of Abraham could be brought back again after thousands of years to re-occupy the place it filled before. No thoughtful man could regard it agreeable to the perfection of God first to reveal this religion, then replace it for so long by the Law and the Gospel and at last to send it back again by Gabriel to a Prophet in Arabia, thus altering his previous measures.

Every opportunity is taken by Koelle to show Muḥammad in an unfavourable light. With regard to the matter of the 'satanic verses', for example, he says that Muḥammad cuts a sorry figure by claiming to speak the words of God whilst he is uttering inspirations of the Devil: Muḥammad needs an angel to point out to him so gross a mistake. Koelle casts doubts about the wisdom of Muḥammad as a military commander. He chooses the battle of Uḥud to make his point. Like Muir, he recalls how before the battle Muḥammad had at first taken the advice of the experienced ʿAbdullāh b. Ubayy who thought that the Muslims should not leave Madina to fight the Makkans, but then listened to the promptings of others who wanted to fight. He says that Ibn Ubayy avenged himself by at once returning to Madina with three hundred men (p. 157). The Muslim point of view is that Ubayy turned back to Madina with three hundred of the hypocrites and doubters. But Koelle is ironical at the expense of Muḥammad who, in the words of Ibn Hishām quoted by him, later said that his uncle Ḥamza was among the inmates of the seven heavens.[29] He also quotes Ibn Isḥāq according to whom Muḥammad said that all those who had been slain in the path of God would rise on the day of resurrection with their wounds emitting blood of musk-like aroma.[30] He rejects the Muslim view that the defeat at Uḥud was due to the disobedience of followers: instead, he traces the defeat back to the rejection of the good advice of a man Muḥammad had 'supplanted' (p. 161). This point had been made before by Muir (iii, 159).

Koelle is also critical of Muḥammad's attitude towards Christians because in his later dealings with them he did not reciprocate the good treatment his followers had received from the people of Abyssinia when his followers sought refuge there from persecution. He would have wished Muḥammad to be enlightened on the all-important subject of Christianity: instead the latter tried to show its insufficiency and imperfection so as to enhance the superior claims of his own rival system.

He quotes Ibn Isḥāq fairly accurately to show that this was the aim of Muḥammad in 622 in his theological controversy with the Christians of Najrān (in Yemen) who sent a deputation, led by their Bishop, to him. There was another deputation from them in 631 when they sought to make a pact with the Prophet. A favourable treaty was signed: according to it, in return for the payment of taxes they were to have the full protection of the Islamic state for themselves and their churches and other possessions.[31] But in Koelle's view this treaty was imposed upon them and it was made under humiliating conditions – the Christians from Najran had to give way before Muḥammad's religious dictatorship and their civil rights and national independence had to succumb to the overbearing power of a political despot (p. 138). Koelle has his own interpretation of a later episode when Muḥammad sent messengers to a number of potentates, including the Roman Emperor Heraclius and the Negus of Abyssinia. His guess is that Muḥammad's letters may have made some impression on those recipients who lived near enough to have cause for apprehending that the Prophet might follow them up with measures of violence. Koelle therefore challenges the information given in Ibn Isḥāq, that these Christian leaders were fully convinced of Muḥammad's divine mission, as gratuitous invention.[32]

In *Victorian images of Islam* (1992), followed by *In Search of Muḥammad* (1998), Clinton Bennett offered readers interesting perspectives on Islam and the Prophet. By concentrating attention on the writings of six British Christians in the first book he was able to establish a neat – perhaps too neat – category of three writers with a conciliatory and another category of three writers with a confrontational approach.[33] My own strategy in this chapter, based on the feeling that many writers are never as clear-cut as that but are often rather ambivalent, has been different. I have deliberately set writings in French next to those in English. By this process it is possible to group them on the following basis: (1) those of clergymen or Christian apologists and supporters of Christian missions and (2) those of authors with no strong Christian commitment. In accordance with this classification Vertot, Saint-Pierre, Gagnier, Murray, Sprenger, Muir and Koelle would belong to the first category and Boulainviller, Guer, Savary, Desvergers, Caussin de Perceval, Sédillot, Saint-Hilaire and Delaporte to the second.

What should emerge clearly from the above classification is that the image of Muḥammad is more positive, on the whole, with the second class of writers. This is certainly the case with Boulainviller, Savary, Caussin and Saint-Hilaire. Sédillot and Delaporte appear rather ambivalent. It is worth mentioning here that knowledge of Oriental languages, especially Arabic, and periods of residence in the world of Islam, however desirable in writers, do not always ensure impartiality and sympathy towards the Prophet. Both Sprenger and Muir spent years in India, but it cannot be said that contact with Muslims there made them look favourably on the Prophet. However, because of their scholarly research into Arabic source material dealing with his biography and the fact that they passed the fruit of their labours on to others they cannot be easily dismissed.[34] Muir himself certainly profited from the investigations of Caussin de Perceval, although he lacked the balance displayed by the latter. However, a close analysis of the *Life* may surprise the reader: Muir does not appear as hostile to Muḥammad as his background would suggest. After all, towards the end of his book he did acknowledge, albeit grudgingly, that Muḥammad implanted in the heart of his followers the doctrine of the unity of God. More than a century before, Boulainviller was proclaiming the same message loud and clear. This shows that lack of Arabic has never been a bar to a deep understanding of

Muḥammad's teaching and achievement by those who were not prejudiced against him.

Guer stands apart from the other writers in his group. Lacking the stature of many of them he shares affinities, however, with writers of the other group through his insistence on Muḥammad's fanaticism and hypocrisy. In the eighteenth and nineteenth centuries these were among the favourite weapons used against Muḥammad by militant Christians. But in the final analysis, estimates of Muḥammad depend on the attitude of their authors. In the nineteenth century chronology appears almost meaningless in this connexion: there is hardly any difference between the beginning and the end of the period because the missionary zeal of a Murray against Muḥammad in the 1830s can be matched by that of a Koelle in the 1880s. Those who are free from this zeal and wish to take a more sober approach to Muḥammad's conduct during his military campaigns will stress context and view his acts against a background where he appears more moderate than other commanders. If Guer sees a Cromwell in Muḥammad, Saint-Hilaire sees a Socrates in him. It seems that such divergent views of the Prophet will always exist.

Notes

1. See the article 'Ummī' by R. Paret in the *Shorter Encyclopaedia of Islam* and W. Montgomery Watt, *Introduction to the Qur'ān* (Edinburgh, 1970), pp. 33-36. See also n. 13, below.

2. Published in 4 volumes in Paris in 1726 with Fontenelle's 'approbation', this work betrays the crusading spirit of the author who at the beginning refers to the first 'infidels' against whom fought the Knights of St. John and to the religion of these barbarians.

3. Vertot gives the impression that five daily prayers had been prescribed from the beginning of Muḥammad's preaching, whereas in fact they became established only after Muḥammad's Night Journey, that is, after 619-620. See Caussin de Perceval's remark, below.

4. There might be some basis to Saint-Pierre's comment on Abu Sufyan. For the latter, an inveterate enemy of the Prophet, may have shown some

opportunism in his late conversion to Islam. At any rate, the opponents of the Umayyads, from whom he descended, may have taken this view. But see Savary's comments, below, for a real understanding of Muḥammad's intention.

5. N. Daniel, *Islam and the West: the Making of an Image,* revised edition, (Oxford, 1993), p. 310.

6. D. Venturino, *Le ragioni della tradizione. Nobilita e mondo moderno nel pensiero di H. de Boulainvilliers* (Florence, 1992); *Vita di Maometto* (Palermo, 1992) and 'Un Prophète Philosophe? Une *Vie de Mahomed à l'aube des Lumières*', *Dix-Huitième Siècle,* no. 24, 1992, pp. 321-331 and 'Imposteur ou législateur? Le Mahomet des Lumières', SVEC, vol. 2, 2000, vol 2, pp. 243-262.

7. A. Thomson, 'L'utilisation de l'islam dans la littérature clandestine', in *La philosophie clandestine à l'Age classique,* ed. A. McKenna and A. Mothu, (Paris, Oxford, 1997), pp. 247-256.

8. Three complete copies are to be found at the Bibliothèque Mazarine, Paris, in Mss. 1946, 1947 and 1948. Mss. 1949 contains the first book only. I quote from the mss. and the printed text.

9. M. Marais, *Journal et Mémoires sur la Régence et le règne de Louis XV*, (Paris, 1863-68), ii, 213-214.

10. H. Grotius, *De veritate religionis Christianae*, 1627, tr. by Symon Patrick (London, 1680), p. 207.

11. D. Venturino, 'Un Prophète Philosophe?, p. 322.

12. W. Muir criticised Muḥammad for not observing the *'idda*, that is, the period of three months waiting required of Muslims before marrying a divorced or widowed woman. See the *Life of Mahomet* (London, 1858), iv, 69. So did S.W. Koelle in *Mohammed and Mohammedanism* (London, 1889), p. 183. Martin Lings notes that the seventeen-year-old Ṣafiyya, deeply pious since childhood, had not been happily married to Kināna who ill-treated her. At Khaybar she was given the choice of remaining a Jewess, but she chose Islam and the Prophet. See *Muḥammad* (London, 1983), pp. 268-269.

13. Aloys Sprenger makes some desperate attempts to prove that Muḥammad could read and write, but he, like Montgomery Watt in *Introduction to the Qur'ān*, remains unconvincing. One is sceptical about Sprenger's suggestion that the expression which may have been used by Muḥammad in reply to the angel: *mā anā bi qār'in*, which means 'I am not a reader', implied a refusal in Muḥammad's time. To make his case he relies on Shī'a commentators. In one instance, he even twists the meaning of Bayḍāwī with regard to the word 'ummīyūn' in *Sūra* 3: 20. He claims that Bayḍāwī explains 'ummīyūn' here as 'those who do not believe in the Bible and who are not of our (Jewish) religion'. See *The Life of Mohammad from original sources* (Allahabad, 1851), pp. 95-99. In his *Tafsīr* Bayḍāwī actually says 'those who have no book like the pagans'.

14. According to H. Djait in *L'Europe et l'Islam*, p. 28, this point was made before Voltaire's *Essai sur les moeurs*. Djait argues that Voltaire's historical perspective in the *Essai* allowed him to distinguish between the Prophet's contribution and later developments in Islam.

15. W. Montgomery Watt, *Muḥammad at Mecca* (Oxford, 1953) and *Muḥammad at Medina* (Oxford, 1956); A. Guillaume, *The Life of Muḥammad*, a translation of Ibn Isḥāq's *Sīrat Rasūl Allāh* (Oxford, 1955) and Martin Lings, *Muḥammad* (London, 1983). My quotations of Ibn Isḥāq are from Guillaume, despite some mistakes to be found in the translation.

16. In *Histoire générale des Arabes* (Paris, 1877), p. 82.

17. Apart from Jean Gagnier's edition of 1723, J.J. Reiske published in 1754, at Leipzig, an Arabic and Latin version of Abu'l Fidā's work under the title *Annales Muslemici.* A five-volume second edition of Reiske's work by I. G. Adler was published between 1789 and 1794. 'The Life of Muḥammad', equally divided between both versions, occupies some two hundred pages of the first volume which contains events up to the overthrow of the Umayyad caliphate, that is, from 661 to 750.

18. See A. Guillaume, *The Life of Muḥammad* (Oxford, 1955), p. 561, n. 1. Guillaume shows that this information is not given by Ibn Hishām, but that it is recorded in Ibn Isḥāq, according to Ṭabarī's history.

19. See Martin Lings, p. 38.

20. Sprenger attributes to Muslim authors the view that Ibn Isḥāq attempted to shape the biography according to Christian ideas, that he accepted traditions uncritically and that he was therefore not relied upon by early writers such as Bukhārī and Wāqidī. See *The Life of Mohammad*, p. 69, n. 1-5.

21. T. Carlyle, *On Heroes, Hero Worship and the Heroic in History* (London, 1841), p. 72.

22. See Ṭabarī's comment on *Sūra* 22: 52 in *Tafsīr* (Beirut, 1978), vol. 7, pp. 131-134.

23. See Zamakhsharī's comment on the same verse in *Kashshāf* (Beirut, 1979), vol. 3, p. 19.

24. See Malise Ruthven, *Islam in the world* (Harmondsworth, 2000), p. 44.

25. See Zamakhsharī's comment on *Sūra* 17: 73 in *Kashshāf* (Beirut, 1979), vol. 2, p. 460.

26. Montgomery Watt translates 'ummī' as non-Jewish, Gentile, native, that is, belonging to the Arab community. See *Introduction to the Qur'ān*, p. 34.

27. See Martin Lings, *Muḥammad*, p. 234.

28. See Lings, p. 73.

29. See Guillaume, p. 756, n. 613.

30. See Lings, pp. 324-325.

31. See Lings, pp. 324-325.

32. Guillaume reproduces extracts of Ṭabarī from the lost work of Ibn Isḥāq, which are omitted by Ibn Hishām. From these both Heraclius and the Negus appear to accept Muḥammad as a Prophet, the latter more clearly. See *The Life of Muḥammad*, p. 653, n. 3 and pp. 656-658.

33. See my review of *Victorian Images of Islam* in *Journal of Islamic Studies*, vol. 5, no. 2, 1994, pp. 292-294.

34. For other views of Muir see Jabal Buaben, *Image of the Prophet Muḥammad in the West* (Leicester, 1996), pp. 21-47 and Clinton Bennett, *Victorian Images of Islam* (London, 1992), pp. 103-127 and *In Search of Muḥammad* (London, 1998), pp. 111-120.

CHAPTER 3

The diffusion of Islamic culture by French scholars

Following the significant work accomplished by scholars such as d'Herbelot and Galland in the seventeenth and eighteenth centuries, the French continued to demonstrate their interest in the study of Middle Eastern languages. Their experiment with the 'Ecole de jeunes de langues', that is, the School for the training of young students in Arabic, Persian and Turkish who went on to serve as interpreters in French missions overseas proved valuable, if not entirely satisfactory.[1] The next step was to strengthen the systematic study of Arabic, Persian and Turkish in France. In this connection the Convention, the revolutionary assembly of France from 1792 to the rule of the Directory, created the 'Ecole publique des langues orientales vivantes' in 1795. The new School was to have a remarkable impact on Oriental studies in the nineteenth century.[2] Napoleon himself was particularly interested in the progress of Oriental literature. It would appear from a Report drafted in 1810 by Bon Joseph Dacier, Secrétaire perpétuel of the Institut de France responsible for the history and ancient literature sections, that the Emperor had guaranteed its future development.[3] This was partly achieved when Napoleon agreed that Oriental literature should be allowed to compete for the major prizes awarded by him.[4] Dacier mentioned various works in Arabic and Persian being edited by French scholars, but he dismissed Turkish literature, especially poetry and the novel, as being mere imitation of Arabic and Persian. In his view, only in modern history had the Turks produced original writers.[5] Dacier was not entirely complacent, for he was critical of an incomplete Arabic Grammar by Savary, the only thing useful in it being the dialogues in colloquial Arabic, while Ruphy's French-Arab abbreviated dictionary was of very limited use. He also mentioned the difficulties encountered in the production of a bigger, popular dictionary whose publishing costs were being met by the government.

It was not so much prizes awarded by Napoleon as other steps taken by the French government that favoured the development of Oriental studies. These included, according to Dacier, the assembling of countless and various Oriental block capitals which placed the imperial printing press at the head of typographical establishments in Europe and the creation of a new Chair of Persian by Napoleon at the Collège de France. This was in addition to the Chairs of Persian, Arabic and Turkish set up by the Convention, Venture de Paradis having been appointed to the Chair of Turkish, Langlès to that of Persian and Sylvestre de Sacy to that of Arabic. After 1803, Sacy was assisted by Dom Raphael Monachis, a Coptic monk who had been a member of the Institut d'Egypte and who was appointed by Napoleon.[6] Sacy was appointed to the newly created Chair of Persian at the Collège de France. Dacier claimed that France could boast having done for Arabic literature as much as the rest of Europe put together, although many works started in 1789 were not yet completed. He naturally mentioned Sacy's works, highlighting the achievement of Sacy in the *Chrestomathie arabe* (1806). As he points out, the *Chrestomathie*, which was primarily meant for students, also offered scholars a collection rendered more interesting by the fact that it contained mostly unpublished material and was well received in European and Middle Eastern countries of learning.

In his *Eloge* of Sylvestre de Sacy (1758-1838), the Duc de Broglie, a member of the Académie française, laid particular stress on the *Maqāmāt* of al-Ḥarīrī, edited by Sacy. The aim of this work was to place at the disposal of literature students and beginners varied and pleasant prose exercises and to help them acquire a deep knowledge of Arabic. Broglie felt that the three-volume *Chrestomathie* achieved this aim even better. As he put it, it was a huge anthology consisting of extracts borrowed from all branches of Arabic literature, from the most dazzling poets, the most remarkable prose writers, from the best critical and didactic works, methodically arranged in rising order of difficulty, enriched by commentaries, explanations, historical, literary and philological notes which are for scholars themselves genuine treasures. There is hardly any exaggeration in Broglie's appreciation of the *Chrestomathie* which truly represents a major contribution towards an appreciation of Islamic culture in the nineteenth century. Later on I hope to be able to demonstrate the freshness of its appeal to the serious reader. Before this a divergent view expressed by Edward Said in *Orientalism* should be mentioned, although this book is highly stimulating. Professor Said accused Sacy of having ransacked the Oriental archives and having doctored the texts he selected.[7] It would appear that this outrageous libel is without a shred of truth.[8]

It is unfortunate that Sacy allowed his scholarship to go hand in hand with colonialism and imperialism. Indeed, he was employed by the French Foreign Ministry from 1805 until 1829 when, for financial reasons, his post was abolished. His work included the translation of bulletins of the Grande Armée and the *Manifesto* of 1806 by which Napoleon hoped to excite 'Muslim fanaticism' against Russian Orthodoxy. At the time of the invasion of Algiers by the French army in 1830, Sacy translated its proclamation to the Algerians. His services were also used by other government departments such as the Ministry of Marine and the Ministry of War.[9] This was perhaps the price to pay when a French academic allowed himself to be lured by the enticements offered by his government which appeared to be protecting its investment.

Even more deplorable were some of the controversial pronouncements made by Sacy on the Arabs and their civilization. In the 'Avertissement' to the first edition of the *Chrestomathie* in 1806, he spoke of the difficulty and the expense of acquiring a sufficient number of copies of Arabic works by students and his desire to obviate the difficulty by publishing his anthology. There was nothing sinister here. Sacy was aware that some people might have wished him to publish a complete work instead of numerous extracts. But instead of justifying his choice on rational grounds such as variety of themes, styles and genres which were invoked by the Duc de Broglie, he came out with some typically French chauvinist remarks, namely that apart from chronicles or works devoted to a particular subject, that is, medicine and so on, few Arabic compositions had a sustained interest and were written with enough taste and critical spirit to warrant publication in full. He argues that in the rhymed prose and poetic extracts of his anthology, he frequently had to struggle against the daring, the eccentricity and the bad taste found in the thought and images of the original which he did not translate literally.[10]

In *De l'utilité de l'étude de la poésie arabe*, published in 1826 and reproduced from the *Journal Asiatique*, Sacy states that the Arabs are incapable of leading a story to a happy ending through ingenious incidents and that epic poetry, comedy and tragedy are unknown to them.[11] More objectionable perhaps is the remark reproduced from the *Journal des Savants* of March 1817.

After pointing out that the difficulty of translating Arabic poetry stems from descriptions, he says that these consist of countless details which, he claims, do not offer to peoples who have reached a higher degree of civilization the same interest and truth that they do to nomadic peoples living in deserts (p. 19). Among these details vividly captured by the nomads are the movement of eyebrows and exterior signs which Europeans conceal. So Arabic poetry could be more profitable if it were used as a means of casting light on biblical poetry and clarifying obscurities in the Old Testament.

Oriental inferiority with regard to literary expression is also illustrated in Sacy's *Discours sur les traductions d'ouvrages écrits en langues orientales*, published in the *Mélanges de littérature orientale* in 1833. With reference to the *Chrestomathie*, Sacy states that his inclusion of extracts from Arab writers was based on two criteria: (i) whether they were more interesting or were easier to introduce into French and (ii) whether they strayed least from French notions of taste, French mores and French ideas of decorum. However, it is in connection with the review of the book by his pupil L. Chézy who in 1805 translated *Laylā wa Majnūn* of the great Persian poet Jāmī (1414-92) as *Poème des Amours de Mejnoun et Leila* that the severest strictures against oriental taste are made by Sacy. Tracing the difference between Arab and Persian styles, he deplores in Persian poetry the lack of naïve charm, bold ideas and sublime descriptions characteristic of the nomadic, pastoral Arabs. Among the latter there are more witticisms, dazzling but false thoughts, original turns of phrase and far-fetched images: that is why it is more difficult to make Persian blend with the French language and satisfy a demanding French taste which is so precise, 'qui marche toujours le compas et l'équerre à la main'.[12] Sacy lays down rules to be observed by a translator intent not on guiding a beginner in the study of Persian, but on providing entertaining reading. The translator can take the liberty of making many excisions if he wishes to popularize the jewels of Oriental literature once they are cleared of the thorns that guard its approaches. Sacy gives a few examples of sentences that deserve to be suppressed because of their extravagance, adding that a literal translation of a Persian poem is not tolerable in French. So Chézy was justified in suppressing ridiculous scenes such as that involving Keis when, covered in a sheep's skin, he crawls to the ground to see his mistress. Here it is not a matter of a translator doctoring the text but rather his exercising an editor's right to remove what he considers bad taste.

Sacy's criticisms, harsh as they appear, do not mean that he adopted a negative approach towards Islamic civilization. For at the beginning of the *Discours*, he paid tribute to Arab achievement in science. He argued that the Arabs who were the disciples of the Greeks and our first masters in the mathematical sciences and in what he called the physical sciences such as chemistry, medicine, botany and in various branches of philosophy, must have made many discoveries after their long and patient studies. As Sacy put it, when Europe received the sciences from the Arabs, it found them at a level of development more advanced than when the Greeks left them (pp. 38-39). He stressed Arab contribution in the fields of astronomy, medicine and chemistry. What Sacy was arguing may have been common knowledge, but it was well worth saying. Even if contemporary Europe had made great strides in the physical and mathematical sciences which made Arab discoveries less relevant, he continued, the big gaps in the history of science could only be filled by a study of Arabic works. Such a balanced view could hardly be challenged.

In *De l'utilité de l'étude de la poésie arabe*, Sacy insisted that any defects found in Arabic poetry could not mask its real beauty. He is full of admiration for al-Iṣfahānī's *Kitāb al-Aghānī* (the book of songs), impressed by the immense erudition which this anthology displays and which, in his view, might suffice to present a panorama of Arab culture before Islam and during the most glorious period of the Caliphate, that is, the Abbasid period (p. 12). In the *Kitāb* are fragments of poetry which lend support to facts, which enhance style and entertain readers. While staking a claim for the study of Arabic poetry by those who choose Oriental literature as a career and who wish to be of use to their age, Sacy argues that Arabic poetry has as much right as Latin and Greek poetry. To him it does not matter if in questions of mythology or traditions of heroic times Greek poets have some advantage over Arab poets who only depict the concerns of pastoral life and tribal rivalries. What matters is that Arabic poetry provides scope for useful intellectual discipline and that it contains noble concepts that elevate the soul, lively impressions that rouse the imagination and true sentiments that blend the sensibility of the poet with his own. Sacy accepts that a Latin or French translation does not give a true appreciation of Arabic poetry. Besides, translations are only to be viewed as a help to its serious study. What is essential above all is a proliferation of Arabic texts and commentaries.

Sacy ended his *Discours* with the remark that the Société Asiatique (of which he became the first President) would be proud to have contributed to the publication of an edition of Abū Tammām's *Ḥamāsa* by Freytag and would welcome the edition of Maydānī's *Proverbs*, the *Majmaʿ al-amthāl*, and the publication of the complete texts of poets such as Mutanabbī and Abū Nuwās who are known only by fragments. He had himself set an example with his complete translation in 1810 of ʿAbd al-Laṭīf al-Baghdādī's *al-Ifāda wa'l-Iʿtibār* under the title of *Relation de L'Egypte* and his important edition of al-Ḥarīrī's *Maqāmāt* in 1822 which contributed to establish the latter's reputation in France.

It is clear from the above remarks that nothing in Sacy lends support to the idea of an Orientalist conspiracy to belittle Islam or its civilization. In fact there is nothing particularly Orientalist in Sacy's response to Arabic literature. For he is heir to a long-established tradition followed by the French who claimed superiority over other nations in matters of literary taste.[13] From the seventeenth century onwards the English, in particular, had been the butt of unfavourable criticism by the French in this respect. Rapin, for instance, claimed that the English surpassed the French in sublimity of thought and boldness of expression, but were inferior to them in matters of taste and form. Even those who were most well disposed to English literature attacked English taste. Prévost declared that the best English works often lacked a certain perfection in taste which was always present in French books. The French would concede that the English had genius sometimes, but taste never unless Englishmen followed the example of Addison and wrote in the French manner. It was this sense of superiority which led Rivarol to claim in *De l'universalité de la langue française* (1784) that France had provided her neighbours with a theatre, dress, taste, manners, a language and a new style of living.

Before Rivarol, Voltaire, particularly towards the end of his long career (1694-1778), had played a large part in upholding such a sense of superiority with his repeated denigration of English taste. If Shakespeare bore the brunt of his attack, Voltaire nevertheless made an important contribution in familiarizing his countrymen with the works of the English national poet and of countless other English writers. To achieve his aim, he resorted to a number of devices, one of the most significant being the use of extracts from various genres which he loosely translated, summarized, caricatured and commented upon in the *Lettres Philosophiques* (1734). There is some parallel between Voltaire, author of the English letters and Sacy, author of the *Chrestomathie*, although Sacy's translation of Arabic texts was much more accurate than Voltaire's translation of English texts and was devoid of any caricatural or polemical intentions. Thus there was nothing new, nothing showing a common Romantic concern in this use of fragments to popularize the culture of the Arabs.[14] But to appreciate the significance of the *Chrestomathie* in projecting images of Islam, a close account of it is essential.

Unlike Voltaire, Sacy provided the original texts of the works he was translating. Thus volume 1 of the 1806 edition of the *Chrestomathie* consists solely of the original of extracts from Arab writers, while volume 2 contains eleven translations and volume 3 contains eight translations with learned commentaries. The texts reproduced and translated range from the *History of dynasties* by Fakhr ad-dīn al-Rāzī (1149-1210) to diplomatic correspondence and proclamations in the late eighteenth century. As the *Chrestomathie* was intended *inter alia* to serve the needs of budding diplomats, the diplomatic material was published with the authorization of Talleyrand, Minister of Foreign Affairs. In all these texts, the authors' frequent references to the Qur'ān are pointed out by Sacy.

In the first extract from the *History* of the great Sunnī theologian Fakhr ad-dīn al-Rāzī two of the pillars of Islam – prayer and pilgrimage to Makka – seem faithfully observed by the Caliph Hārūn al-Rashīd who reigned from 786 to 809. He must have prayed more than five times a day, since his daily prayers amounted to a hundred *rak'as*,[15] whereas the five canonical prayers consist of a maximum of forty-eight *rak'as*. Apparently, he went on pilgrimage on foot – an act not accomplished by any other caliph. Moreover, when he did not himself go on pilgrimage, he would have it performed (in his name) by some three hundred people to whom he gave rich clothes and whose expenses he generously met. Pilgrimage can of course be made on behalf of someone else in Islam, but there is certainly much exaggeration here. After due allowance is made for the exaggeration, the reader is left with the impression that Hārūn was a pious caliph. He was also a patron of scholars, poets, legal advisers and grammarians. Sacy explains in a footnote that for the last category of persons, the text literally means someone skilled in reading the Qur'ān. He does not always explain why he departs from the text. Thus in the section on ministers of Harūn where he discusses the fall of the house of the Barmakides,[16] he narrates how Yaḥyā, the Barmakide, and a clerk went to a beautiful garden well stocked with trees and watered by fountains, in which were tables decked with all types of furniture and rugs. Sacy's intention clearly is to evoke the Islamic paradise. He actually quotes *Sūra* 56: 34 which literally means "on raised beds". The narrative continues with the story of a doctor who entered Hārūn's apartment in Baghdad called *qaṣr al-khuld*. It provides Sacy with another opportunity to refer his reader, in a footnote, to the abode of the blessed mentioned in the Qur'ān, that is, *jannat al-khuld* in *Sūra* 25: 16. He also mentions *dār al-khuld* the abode of the damned, *Sūra* 41: 28.

The second extract from Rāzī deals with the caliphate of al-Musta'ṣim (1242-58). In it the last of the Abbasid caliphs is described as a good prince, gentle in his manner, dignified in his speech and his morals. He was a pious man who knew the Qur'ān by heart, but he lacked judgement and knew nothing about the affairs of the empire. He had three children to whom he allowed complete liberty. One of Sacy's aims in selecting this extract was to illustrate the Sunnī-Shī'a conflict taking place in Baghdad. The text mentions the eldest son of the caliph, nicknamed Abū Bakr on the grounds that the plunder of a part of Baghdad occurred on his instructions. In a footnote, Sacy explains that the district of Karkh was inhabited by Shī'ites who had violent quarrels with the Sunnīs living in another part. Relying on Abu'l Fidā',[17] he claims that the caliph's son was given this name because he had acted against the Shī'ites as Abū Bakr, the first Caliph, had done against 'Alī, the fourth Caliph. There is little substance in this claim. The parallel which Sacy draws between the Caliph's troops plundering homes and committing atrocities and the soldiers entering the homes of the Jews, as in the Qur'ān, *Sūra* 17: 5, is rather forced.

The third extract entitled 'of the rights of sovereigns over their subjects' is directly inspired by the Qur'ān which is quoted verbatim as follows: 'O ye who believe, Obey God and obey the Messenger, and those charged with authority among you' (*Sūra* 4: 59). The text states that obedience is among the duties rulers may extract from their subjects. Before discussing whether this Qur'ānic injunction has been followed, the extract gives some insight into life under the first four Caliphs, laying particular emphasis on the ascetic austerity of 'Umar ibn al-Khaṭṭāb. It mentions the coarse cotton clothes and the shoes made of the bark of palm-trees that he wore and the fact that he walked on foot in the streets like any ordinary man, adding that these princes considered such behaviour as one of the duties imposed upon them by Islam. 'Umar's austerity is illustrated by anecdotal evidence. The austerity of the first Caliphs is contrasted with the profligacy of the Umayyad and Abbasid Caliphs. Despite the considerable power they enjoyed, the latter had to face rebellious subjects. Although the Abbasids reigned for more than five hundred years, they could not rival the Mongol dynasties as far as obedience of subjects was concerned. In short the later caliphs were simply interested in keeping up appearances and making sure that their names appeared on coins and were mentioned during Friday sermons. There is nothing strikingly new in what Sacy mentions, but the information is clearly presented for the benefit of the general reader.

Life in Egypt in the reign of the Fatimid Caliph al-Ḥākim (996-1021) is vividly portrayed in the fourth extract reproduced from *al-Khiṭaṭ* of al-Maqrīzī (d. 1442) who wrote a local history covering the period of the Mamluks from 1250 onwards. It is clear from the extract translated as *Description historique et topographique de l'Egypte* that Ḥākim's reign is marked by various forms of intolerance. Ḥākim had imprecations and curses against the first Companions of the Prophet written on the doors of mosques and shops and in cemeteries.[18] The target of sustained persecution, however, was non-Muslims. Although Sacy points out that some of the regulations against Jews and Christians had not been invented by Ḥākim, the latter bears responsibility for the humiliating treatment meted out to them. At first they had to wear belts around the waist and distinctive marks in their clothes. Then Jews had to have bells tied to their necks and Christians had to have crosses on entering the baths. In the face of persecution, many converted to Islam. People were beaten up for having played chess. Churches were burnt down and all that they contained and houses belonging to them were plundered. The type of conversion described above had nothing Islamic about it, of course, and the image of Islam appears very tarnished indeed.

It should be pointed out, however, that in describing the excesses of one fanatical caliph Sacy was not trying to score a point against Islam. There was no militancy in his attitude; his interest lay elsewhere. In a long footnote he starts off by explaining that *ribāṭ* means houses in general or hostels in particular and that endowments for mosques or churches were originally of that nature. But then he reproduces a long text of Maqrīzī with translation in which nothing is said about churches: it is almost a pretext to launch into a discussion of the *waqf* institution in Islam. The Maqrīzī quotation shows that pious endowments called *hubus* consisted only of houses and similar constructions at first, that the first Muslims, the Companions of the Prophet and their successors did not give lands as endowments.[19] The example mentioned is that of Ahmad ibn Ṭūlūn who did not make any land endowments to support the foundation of his mosque and other buildings. Land endowments became current following the practice of Abū Muḥammad Mardānī, but when the Fatimids came to Egypt from the Maghrib in 969, endowments of lands and villages became void. As Sacy remarks, the Maqrīzī text throws some light on a complex question.

In other parts of the extract, there is some account of variations in Islamic beliefs and practices current in Fatimid Egypt. At a time of shortages at the beginning of Ḥākim's reign a law was passed allowing people to begin and end the fast of Ramaḍān as they deemed fit, but no one who relied on the appearance of the moon for the beginning and end of the fast was harassed. In a footnote, Sacy points out that the suppression of the Sunnī practice of relying on the moon was one of the changes introduced by Jawhar, general of the Fatimid army of al-Muʿizz (953-75), who used astronomical calculations to determine the beginning and end of fasting during Ramaḍān. A reader's initial response could be that Islamic practices were being 'liberalized'. But the decision to suppress *tarāwīḥ* prayers in Egypt during Ramaḍān and allow variations in funeral prayers could never achieve *ijmāʿ*, consensus, in Islam. However, the discontinuation of the practice of cursing the first Muslims seemed to mark a step forward. Sacy is successful in evoking the Islamic usage of pronouncing blessings on them, although the blessing in the phrase 'may God be pleased with them' is not restricted to the first Caliphs.

Part of the proclamation allowing Muslims to follow in religious matters whatever opinions they hold suitable leads

Sacy to comment on the meanings of *ijtihād* and *mujtahid*. As he says, these are not to be taken in the Persian sense of *mujtahid*, since the first word means independent, rational interpretation derived from the Qur'ān and the *Sunna*, while the latter refers to one who uses all his intellectual faculties to seek truth in disputed areas. Equally sound are Sacy's comments on the *muṣallā* to which al-Ḥākim went to celebrate the end of Ramaḍān. He describes it as an open-air place to which people go, particularly on the occasion of the two festivals. Sacy may be right in saying that Muslims differ as to whether prayers should be said in a mosque or in the open air. However, he is not strictly accurate in suggesting that praying in the open air is more current among the Shī'ites, as Sunnīs also pray outside sometimes. Sacy's remark about open-air celebration can be verified by a glance at Maqrīzī's *al-Khiṭaṭ* which attracted much attention in the nineteenth century. Had a fuller text such as that of the Al-Furqan Foundation (1995), edited by Ayman Fu'ād Sayyid, been available, Sacy would have been able to offer more aspects of Fatimid Islamic civilization to his readers.

From another work by Maqrīzī dealing with dynasties reigning in Egypt, Sacy reproduces two letters about Tamerlane (Tīmūr). He says that these letters already appeared in a *Life of Tamerlane* by Aḥmad ibn 'Arabshāh (d. 1450), edited in Arabic by Golius. The first letter is by Tamerlane himself: it is full of threats and violent expressions which the great Asian conqueror uses to complain that his ambassadors to Syria had been killed. The second letter is a reply to it in which Tamerlane is treated as an 'infidel'. Why did Sacy include this material in the *Chrestomathie*? It seems that his aim was to increase his students' exposure to the Qur'ān in a rather indirect way. For Tamerlane glorying in the havoc he has wreaked and is capable of wreaking on nations substitutes himself for God who, in the

Qur'ān, punishes the wicked and protects the orphans. To strengthen his message, Tamerlane uses the Qur'ān eight times. The reply to him has recourse to the same source: in fact it contains ten references to the Qur'ān. All these quotations from the holy book, to which Sacy draws attention, are used out of context and are twisted to suit the purposes of the authors of the letters.

Islam is treated more seriously in a work by Khalīl Ẓāhirī (d. 1421), a Mamluk writer, translated as *Crème de l'exposition détaillée des provinces*. In the first book, Ẓāhirī draws attention to Egypt, specifically mentioned in the Qur'ān (*Sūra* 43: 49), and to its ruler whose authority extends over the sacred towns of Islam, Makka, Madina and Jerusalem – the destination for pilgrimages. His preference goes to Makka, the first place granted to man for divine worship and 'purged of all stains and profanation' (ii, 290). The Oriental flourish gives way, in book iv, to a more sober account of the relationship between ruler and minister. Ẓāhirī points out that in his choice of a minister to help him administer, the ruler is supported by the Qur'ān and the *Sunna*. But the emphasis is on the Qur'ān. In the story of Moses, God makes him ask for a minister chosen from among his family (*Sūra* 20: 30); in fact God gave Moses his brother Aaron as minister (*Sūra* 25: 35). The Prophet is also quoted as saying that if it pleases God to favour a man in charge of Muslim affairs He will give him a good minister to remind him of his duty if he forgets and that if God does not wish to favour such a man the opposite will happen. Sacy takes the opportunity to launch into a philological discussion of the word 'wazīr'. He uses the Qur'ānic commentator Wāḥidī (d. 1068) to explain it as 'refuge, aid' and shows that this is how it is used in *Sūra* 75: 11 'no place of safety'. Sacy gives two other meanings: (i) weight, burden and (ii) back. For the second meaning, he claims that the word comes from *azr* (back) and that it is in this sense that God, in the story of Moses, uses the expression 'Strengthen by his help my back'. He relies on al-Bayḍāwī's commentary on *Sūra* 20: 31. The interpretation of Sacy and Bayḍāwī seem rather far-fetched: the line really means 'By him increase my strength'.

The trials and tribulations of life at court are well illustrated in another extract from Rāzī's *History* by the story of the vizier Nejmoun, which is reminiscent of the story of Zadig and L'Envieux in Voltaire's *Zadig*. The minister's affection for Yaḥyā, the Caliph's son, gave rise to insinuations of homosexuality. As Nejmoun wore a ring on which were inscribed some letters envious people managed to give them a damaging interpretation. The Caliph, being made to read 'Nejmoun loves Yaḥyā', ordered that the vizier be put to death. However, he allowed the latter to appear before him and explain the meaning of the letters. Nejmoun read them as 'By the virtue of Ḥā Mīm 'Ain Sīn Qāf, deliver me', saying that they were the names of God taken from the Qur'ān. The story of the vizier enables Sacy to engage in a subtle discussion of Islamic theology in footnotes. He points out that as these Arabic letters on the vizier's seal had no diacritical point, they could be pronounced in various ways with various meanings. One reading could justify the accusation, while reference to the beginning of *Sūra* 42 (Ḥā Mīm 'Ain. Sīn Qāf) could justify the vizier. Sacy explains correctly that there are at the beginning of many *sūras* mysterious words whose meaning has been lost but which many commentators consider to be abbreviations. Hence commentators usually say that only God knows what they mean. He gives as example: Ḥā Mīm; Alif Lām Mīm As Sacy says, some commentators believe that these letters are monograms indicating various names of God.

In the 1826 edition of the *Chrestomathie*, Sacy widens the scope of his theological explanations in the story of the vizier Nejmoun who now gives the following reading of the inscription: 'In the name of Ḥā Mīm 'Ain Sīn Qāf, deliver me'. The Caliph liked his justification very much, gave him a fur coat and apologized to him. In an additional note, Sacy rightly says that to understand the vizier's answer one needs to know that when one reads the Qur'ān and one utters these monograms, one should name each letter by its name as if one were spelling it. He illustrates his remark by showing the reader how to pronounce the Arabic letters Alif Lām Mīm and Yā-sīn. At this point, Sacy reproduces the Arabic text of Bayḍāwī's *Tafsīr* and his translation of the commentary at the beginning of *Sūra* ii. Prominent in the commentary is the tradition reported by Ibn Mas'ūd, who had daily contact with the Prophet, that whoever reads a letter of the Qur'ān will do a good deed and every good deed will receive a manifold reward. One learns from Bayḍāwī that the aim of letters such as Alif Lām Mīm placed at the beginning of *sūras* is to draw people's attention. It is also to ensure that people's ears are struck by something miraculous in the composition of the Qur'ān. There is nothing unusual in the enunciation of letters by literate people, but some enunciation by an illiterate person like Muḥammad is remarkable. It is worth pointing out that Bayḍāwī's view that the Qur'ān is inimitable (the object of the introductory letters being to defend this inimitability) is also shared by Zamakhsharī in the *Kashshāf* and Ibn Kathīr in his *Tafsīr*. Sacy mentions the opinion of commentators that these letters are an oath formula by which God swears, as He swears by the fig and the olive tree. This remark applies particularly to Zamakhsharī.

Lighter in tone is the extract (reproduced in the 1806 edition) from the poem by Tantarani, a professor at the Niẓāmiyya college founded in Baghdad in 1067 by Niẓām al-Mulk, a vizier of the Seljuk sultan Alp-Arslān. In this eulogy Tantarani, a disciple of al-Ghazālī (1058-1111), spoke of the vizier as the glory of the human race, the champion of any victim of injustice.

What is striking in the poem is the far-fetched imagery and the style. Niẓām who offers hospitality and protection also makes the very mountains shake by the terror of his threats and his justice is compared to a cistern with waters ever pure. This type of imagery illustrates the point Sacy was making in his essays on Oriental literature. Here, however, is no surfeit of imagery which is held in check to satisfy the demands of French taste. Sacy offers a translation of some lines which is not completely literal. There is a sudden shift in the form of address. The address to the hero which is in the third person at the beginning suddenly becomes direct for the sake of emphasis when Tantarani writes: 'May you be showered with heaven's blessings without interruption, even more than those who have performed the sacred rites of pilgrimage at the Caaba.' The passage from indirect to direct speech is justified by an example taken from the Qur'ān, *Sūra* 1: 'Thee only we serve; to Thee alone we pray for succour.'

In the later edition Sacy provides extracts from a more famous writer, from the collection of stories (sessions) written in rhymed prose by al-Ḥarīrī (1054-1121). In a story of the *Maqāmāt*, translated as *Séance de Barkaid*, the hero Ḥārith narrates that he intended to leave Barkaid, but as it was already festival day, he could not leave the town. When the day came with its religious ceremonies, accompanied by all its pomp and splendour, he wore new clothes. Sacy explains in a footnote that the compulsory duties referred to in the text are the payment of *zakāt* at the end of Ramaḍān and the religious ceremonies inspired by devotion are the special prayers marking the end of fasting. He draws attention to the pun intended in the use of Barkaid which means (i) the place near Mosul and (ii) flashes of the festival. Without Sacy's help, the reader would not suspect that the phrase 'accompanied by all its pomp and splendour', literally 'accompanied by its cavalry and infantry' is actually taken from the Qur'ān, *Sūra* 17: 64 where God addresses Satan. When everyone was assembled on the *muṣallā*, a blind old man appeared, wrapped up in a cloak and he disappeared with an old woman.[20] Believing that she could introduce him to the old man, Ḥārith followed her. She invoked divine protection while the old man simply said: 'We belong to God and I put all my interest in His hands.' Sacy explains that the first part of the sentence comes from the expression 'We belong to God and we return to Him.' Although he does not specifically state that it occurs in the Qur'ān in various forms, he projects a faithful image of the Muslim who utters such words when he is confronted by death.

Another story by Ḥarīrī translated as the *Séance d'Alexandrie* is about the dispute between an old man (Abū Zayd) and his wife who claims that her husband did not redeem the many promises he made to her. But the judge ruled in his favour and advised them to bear misfortune with patience and trust in divine assistance. Abū Zayd claimed that the honour of men of letters is no longer safe from abuse and their most sacred rights are not respected. Sacy says that this line contains a reference to *Sūra* 9: 10. The parallel is rather forced, for the Qur'ānic verse really applies to polytheists who do not respect family ties and their promises to believers. However, when in the 1826 edition of the *Chrestomathie*, the hero says he kept quiet about what he knew of Abū Zayd, like the angel keeper of the register of men's acts conceals secrets in the fold of his book, the imagery may, more appropriately, be Qur'ānic in origin. Sacy says there is an allusion to *Sūra* 21: 104. There is, however, disagreement about the meaning of *sijjīl* in verse 104. Bayḍāwī, quoted by Sacy in Arabic, takes it to mean an angel or the name of a secretary of the Prophet. Ṭabarī (xvii, 99-100) and Zamakhsharī (iii, 22) also give the same explanation. But Si Hamza Boubakeur believes *sijjīl* meant a roll in the Prophet's time.[21]

Perhaps more interesting in the second edition of the *Chrestomathie* was the *Maqāmāt* of al-Ḥamadhānī (968-1010), in which the narrator tells stories of a trickster found in various situations.[22] The first narrative reproduced by Sacy as *Séance iii* is not particularly controversial. It is a monologue by a wanderer who utters thoughts that are full of Qur'ānic echoes. The extract described as *Séance viii* dealing with the adventures of Abu'l Fatḥ Iskandarī is more controversial. The protagonist offers his services to the inhabitants of a village threatened by floods. He exacts complete obedience from them in return for security from the floods. The price the villagers have to pay is heavy: a yellow cow has to be sacrificed to the torrent, a young virgin to himself and they have to offer a prayer of two *rak'as* behind him. The villagers did as Iskandarī wished: he warned them that they had to follow the ritual in every detail and that they would have to be patient, as the *rak'as* would be very long. The rogue stood up straight as a tree trunk at the first *rak'a* so that they had pains in their bodies. Then he prostrated himself and remained so long in that posture that they wondered whether he had not fallen asleep. But no one dared raise his head until he signalled to them to sit down and uttered the *takbīr*. After this, he prostrated himself a second time and beckoned to his companion to leave with him, while the gullible villagers remained prostrated. This *maqāma* represents of course a caricature of Islamic prayer in which there is no sacrifice of animals nor do Muslims utter the *takbīr* while prostrated. Its purpose is simply to entertain the audience by showing how easily gullible people can be tricked.

The satire against the same rogue posing as an imām in *Séance xx* is particularly strong. However, the beginning of the story is quite harmless, as 'Īsā Ibn Hishām, hears the call to prayer and considers it a duty to pray with the congregation. Having talked of the merit of prayer as a form of protection against adversity, he stands in the front row to begin the first part of the prayer. Then the imām moved towards the *miḥrāb* and read the first *sūra* of the Qur'ān according to the method of Ḥamza.[23] This was followed by a reading of *Sūra* 56. As this consists of 96 verses, 'Īsā was rather impatient, but he dared not leave, saying that he knew how rough people of that place could be if he left before the last salutation ending the prayer. Up to this point everything in the conduct of the prayer sounds authentic. Then the comedy begins as the imām (none other than Abu'l Fatḥ) bends his body in the form of an arch, affecting outward humility and devotion. 'Īsā thought the imam had fallen asleep while raising his hands in praise of God. But then the latter prostrated himself while 'Īsā looked for a way of running away. 'Īsā too had to remain prostrate until Abu'l Fatḥ gave the sign to sit down. 'Īsā said that after this the old rascal got up to begin the second *rak'a*. He read the first *sūra* which was followed by *Sūra* 101 about Judgement Day. Al-Ḥamadhānī wittily exploited the absurdity of the situation. For although *Al-qāri'a* consists of only eleven verses, the imām read it so slowly that it seemed to last as long as Judgement Day[24] and the congregation felt desperate. It would have been possible to leave after the prayers, but the imām requested all who loved the Companions of the Prophet to pay attention to him. He claimed that he brought them glad tidings from their Prophet, but that he would not reveal these until God had purified the mosque by making those who deny His messenger the title of Prophet leave. That was simply a trick on the part of Abu'l Fatḥ to stop anyone from leaving. He further claimed that the Prophet had taught him a prayer which he recommended him to teach the people. It was written on papers with an ink made of musk, saffron and other aromatic substances mixed in vinegar. Copies of the text would be available to anyone who wanted it and who would refund him the cost of the paper.

Soon silver coins were showered on him from all sides. All this has nothing to do with the Prophet and Islam. What Ḥamadhānī has succeeded in doing is to offer a tale of deception in which someone purporting to be a man of religion used his eloquence to trick gullible people into parting with their money, very much in the manner of Chaucer in the *Pardoner's Tale* (1387).

Contrary to what Edward Said thinks, the *Chrestomathie arabe* is not therefore made up of comparatively lifeless fragments arranged in tableaux.[25] Far from being dull, these are lively extracts catering for a variety of readers.[26] With their constant references to the Qur'ān and some of the Qur'ānic commentators like Bayḍāwī, to Islamic life and modes of thinking, they have or should have a particular appeal to readers, especially Muslim readers, who may see in them if not always, but quite often, faithful reflections of their culture, beliefs and practices. This may sound paradoxical, as Sacy's association with imperialism is no fiction. Even in the *Chrestomathie*, there is diplomatic material (extract xix in the 1806 edition) in the form of a proclamation from the Shaikhs of Cairo to the Egyptian people (written on Napoleon's instructions), suggesting that the French have always been, among European nations, the only friends of Muslims and Islam! However, this blatant piece of French propaganda does not loom disconcertingly large and does not detract from the merit of the rest of the anthology. Even Sacy's criticisms levelled at the Companions of the Prophet with regard to spelling in the extract (xvii in the 1826 edition) from Ibn Khaldūn's *Muqaddima* may be read as a kind of introduction to the more extensive studies on the Arab historian later in the century and in particular to De Slane's complete translation with commentaries of the text.[27]

Some ten years after Sacy's 1826 edition of the *Chrestomathie* the poet Lamartine did his best to acquaint French readers with some aspects of the Arab literary tradition. He engaged in a discussion on ʿAntar (ibn Shaddād), the model of the Arabic romance of chivalry, in his *Voyage en Orient* (1835) to which he added fragments of the romance. ʿAntar was first mentioned in Europe in 1777 in the *Bibliothèque Universelle des Romans* and introduced to European scholarship in 1819 by J. von Hammer-Purgstall (1774-1856).[28] Often discussed and partly translated in the *Journal Asiatique*, it deals with the heroic adventures of ʿAntar, the son of a Sudanese slave-girl, who was adopted into the tribe of the Banū ʿAbs for saving them at a time of great crisis. As the years passed ʿAntar the pagan became the champion of Islam.

In his entry dated 3 November 1832 Lamartine, who was on the outskirts of Jerusalem, sets the scene for his discussion of ʿAntar, blending religious and secular elements. He declares his preference for the sound of the *muezzin* calling the faithful to prayer to that of church bells. As the crowd of Arabs gathers around the olive tree, they smoke and tell desert stories, singing lines from the poem of ʿAntar. Although not understanding much of their Arabic, he could make out sounds of 'Allah, Allah'. He was so keen to listen to the words that he had extracts of the poem translated into Italian by his 'dragoman' which he in turn translated into French when he arrived in Lebanon. Lamartine's efforts to promote knowledge of Arabic literature among ordinary Frenchmen should not be dismissed on the grounds that he knew no Arabic. After all, even opera lovers who listen to their favourite arias in modern European languages cannot make out all the words they hear! Lamartine may well have been guided by the sounds of voices he heard and by the facial expressions.

Lamartine saw a deep affinity between Ariosto, Tasso and Arabic poetry and genuinely believed that the poem of ʿAntar mirrored the primitive traditions of the desert. As he states, the precise date of ʿAntar's birth is not known. He preferred the prose sections of the narrative to the interwoven lyrical fragments which he considered stilted and artificial like decadent literature: the puns and the imagery had more wit than soul. Yet Lamartine found ʿAntar more interesting than the *Arabian Nights*. That was because he thought it contained less of the marvellous, all the interest being focused on the heart of man and on the true adventures of the hero and his lady love or on adventures with an air of verisimilitude. He hoped that the reader would catch a glimpse of the beauty of the original through the imperfections of the selections he placed at the end of the volume.

French scholarship continued to pay tribute to Islamic civilization throughout the century. It was perhaps encouraged in the field of moral philosophy by the example of the English scholar Simon Ockley (1678-1720) who published a translation of a collection of one hundred and sixty-nine aphorisms by the poet al-ʿAmīdī (d. 1044) under the title of *Sentences of ʿAlī* in 1717. Whereas Ockley showed he had slightly polemical intentions in wishing to chastise the folly of Westerners who despise the wisdom of Eastern nations, Barbier de Meynard had no such intentions in publishing the *Aṭwāq al-dhahab* of Zamakhsharī (1075-1144) which he translated as *Les Colliers d'or* in 1876.[29] Meynard actually quoted the *Sentences of Ali* in one of the *Maxims*. The scholarly aim of Meynard can be seen from his reproduction of the original Arabic text, followed by translation and learned footnotes. All the Qur'ānic references are painstakingly traced by Meynard. Like Sacy, Meynard appealed to various types of readers. Some of them could draw a parallel between Zamakhsharī's hundred *Maxims* and those of La Rochefoucauld (1665). Despite the similarity in certain themes treated, there is no question of influence, as La Rochefoucauld had not read Zamakhsharī in the original or in translation. As Meynard points out in his Preface, Zamakhsharī knew how to assemble in his short, harmoniously-balanced maxims a large number of references to the sacred book, the traditions and proverbial phrases current with his contemporaries. Although the Arab writer is a well-known Muʿtazilite thinker, that is, a member of a rationalist sect believing in free will and the created Qur'ān, the moral teaching of his *Maxims* is such that it is acceptable to all shades of opinion in Islam.

A number of maxims deal with the foibles of humanity such as vanity and hypocrisy. Maxim ii seeks to lower the pretension of man who is born humble like an earthworm, but shows misplaced vanity by lauding his ancestors. In Maxim vii, man is advised to prefer obscurity to fame, since a highly-placed man inspires envy and hatred. His feeling of hatred is an evil that God punishes as He wishes. Meynard refers the reader to the Qur'ān, *Sūra* 22: 18, as the source of this maxim. But the parallel is rather forced, as the Qur'ānic verse applies to people who bow before God and others who have justly deserved punishment. Maxim vi, however, is directly inspired by the Qur'ān. It counsels man to shun publicity while doing good works or praying: it wonders why man raises his voice if he simply intends to satisfy a God who reads in the heart of the faithful, knows their thoughts and their most secret plans. As Meynard points out, the reference is clearly to *Sūra* 50: 16 which shows that God is nearer to man than the jugular vein.

Maxim vi is closer in thought to Maxim xxviii which states clearly that hypocrites incur God's wrath: they seek people's praise and rarely think of God. This is a direct echo of *Sūra* 4: 142 which reads: 'When they stand up to pray they stand lazily, showing off to the people and not remembering God save a little.' Meynard actually explains how he comes to use the word 'hypocrite' by pointing to one of the meanings of the verb *ra'a*. The maxim contrasts the hypocrite with the man who prays silently in awe of God. Then it digresses to talk of man's drowsiness when it comes to truth. Meynard draws the reader's attention to *Sūra* 18: 18, where God says of the sleeper in the cavern: 'Thou wouldst have thought them awake, as they lay sleeping.' Here it must be pointed out that though there is a linguistic affinity between the *ruqūd* (asleep) of the maxim and the same word in the Qur'ān, the meaning of the maxim seems to be different from that of the Qur'ān. The insistence on man's hypocrisy in the maxims is skilfully shown by Meynard. In Maxim li, for example, there is the idea that prayers and tears are motivated by hypocrisy and vainglory, that in the world most objects are beautiful in appearance and hideous inside and that it is difficult to find those who fear God as He deserves to be feared. Here Meynard demonstrates an intimate knowledge of the Qur'ān to which he draws the reader's attention. He notes that the Prophet had at first said: 'Fear God as He deserves to be feared' (*Sūra* 3: 102), but that judging the precept to be beyond man's capacity, he considered it to be abrogated (*mansūkh*) and replaced it by another verse: 'Fear God in accordance to what you can' (*Sūra* 64: 16). Meynard gives the impression that Muḥammad tampered with the revelation as he pleased. All that can be said is that the last verse brings piety to a human level and modifies the first verse which places piety on a superhuman level.[30]

Frivolity is denounced in Maxims iv and xxi. In both cases, Meynard has recourse to the Traditionist al-Bukhārī to clarify their meaning.[31] The first argues that man does not know whether he is worthy of punishment when he lets the helm of his robe trail on the ground and that he forgets that wearing long clothes or letting one's clothes lie about is a serious mistake. Meynard shows that in al-Bukhārī is a reference to the fact that a cloak left lying about burns in hell. This maxim ends with the witty observation that instead of man covering the earth with his cloak, it is the earth that will soon cover him with its gravel. Maxim xxi suggests that palaces will be useless to man, since the sight of death will make him forget all that is frivolous in him. After quoting *Sūra* 15: 99, where man is commanded to serve his lord until death (certainty) comes, Meynard refers to a *ḥadīth* quoted by al-Bukhārī where the Prophet is reported as saying that he has nothing in common with frivolity as it has nothing in common with him.

However, Zamakhsharī also betrays some of his prejudices in the *Maxims*. Philosophers bear the brunt of his attack in maxim xxiii: in his view, we can expect nothing from the ineptitude and absurdity of a man who poses as a philosopher and who turns nature into God. He is even fiercer in his satire of doctors, claiming that the trust put in them is a more serious disease than the disease from which man suffers. His advice to a patient is to raise his suppliant hands towards Him who can cure him if his illness worsens, for the cure, like the illness, depends on Him alone. Zamakhsharī claims that often a doctor's consultation or his remedies will kill the patient. The height of the prejudice is seen in the last line of the maxim: the patient should hate doctors, because many of them are materialists or worshippers of the cross in a church. Meynard explains that under the influence of religious prejudice, the practice of medicine and surgery was often considered an impure profession in the East and left to Greek or Syrian monks. Relying on Edward Lane's *Modern Egyptians* (1836), he observes that even in his time the influence of European civilization had not entirely succeeded in overcoming contempt stirred by fanaticism.

If Zamakhsharī is anti-medicine, he is not anti-science as such. On the contrary, high praise is bestowed on science in a number of maxims. In Maxim lvi, the advice given to man is that he should stick to a single science. As Meynard explains, science, par excellence, is that of which Qur'ān and *ḥadīth* are the base and the different sections of which are grouped together under the collective name of '*ulūm*'. In Maxim lxv, science appears difficult, but ignorance presents more difficulties. Again, science is used in the sense of religious science based on Qur'ān and *sunna*. But Zamakhsharī is no blind admirer of tradition. In Maxim xxxvii he exhorts man to walk in the path of religion under the banner of science, that is, dialectics, without remaining satisfied with traditions coming from various sources. To consolidate his attack against blind tradition, he uses some simple imagery: the scholar armed with proofs against his opponents is more formidable than the lion in his den; whoever follows theological precepts by simple imitation lies behind a door whose key he has lost. Zamakhsharī is dead against routine and he wishes God to condemn the man who treads such a path. With regard to the scholar's proofs, Meynard points out that the meaning of 'sulṭān' is derived from *Sūra* 10: 68 where Christians are accused of giving a son to God. He suggests, rightly, that Zamakhsharī was trying to draw a distinction between the *muqallid*, the blind follower of tradition and the *mujtahid*, the man of learning who draws conclusions through intellectual effort. He avoids a literal translation in the phrase 'God condemns the man who follows such a path', though he points out that it literally means 'God ties a rope around the neck of him ...' as in *Sūra* III: 5 which mentions Abū Lahab's wife burning with a rope of palm-fibre round her neck.

The blind acceptance of tradition is perhaps more wittily pilloried in Maxim xlii which starts with a play on the word *ḥanīf*. The reader is told that the *'ulamā'* combine the ḥanafī faith with the science of Abū Ḥanīfa and the gentleness of al-Aḥnāf. While he might be expected to know about Abū Ḥanīfa, founder of one of the Sunnī schools of law and the Ḥanafī faith, that is, true religion, such as that of Abraham, Meynard provides him with some useful and rare information about al-Aḥnāf, a disciple of the Prophet's Companions known for his patience and his earnestness. Zamakhsharī contrasts the true men of learning with others who look like remnants of straw floating on the surface of water. He suggests that the best way of describing those who are devoid of learning is to call them beasts of burden laden with books. In the phrase 'remnants of straw' is a reference to *Sūra* 23: 41, where the incredulous people of the Prophet Ṣāliḥ (not Moses, as mentioned by Meynard) are like waste carried away by the torrent. The phrase 'beasts of burden' is an echo of *Sūra* 62: 5, where there is an attack on those who have been loaded with the Torah and do not observe it: they are like an ass carrying books.

Maxim xl is striking with its fierce and witty denunciation of the venality of judges. To Zamakhsharī venality is a crime punishable by God. He is witty at the expense of the *qāḍī* who puts the interest of the prince before the rights of heirs when he is adjudicating on problems of inheritance. This man is called *qāḍī*, but his true name, according to Zamakhsharī, is *sāmm qāḍī*, that is, deadly poison. The sense of 'deadly', as Meynard suggests, derives from *Sūra* 69: 27 which reads: 'would to God that it (death) put an end (*qāḍī*) to every thing'. Meynard also suggests that the *qāḍī* who seeks to obtain the favour of the prince through flattery and gifts is common in the East, particularly in Persia.

Zamakhsharī does not always fulminate against the evil in man. Some of the maxims attach importance to man's qualities such as generosity and genuine piety. Thus Maxim xx describes all the qualities that help to make man agreeable to God, generosity being an innate virtue worthy of the highest praise. Meynard, at first relying on the 'Sentences of 'Alī' to stress the spontaneous nature of generosity, refers the reader to the varied manifestations of generosity outlined in the *Siyāsat al-Mulūk*, a moral and political treatise written by qāḍī Abu'l Najīb for Saladin, a Turkish version of which appeared in 1851. Maxim xxix warns the believer against the temptations of the devil, since in the words of the Qur'ān (*Sūra* 29: 83) evil spirits are sent to incite the unbelievers to commit sins. Only the believer, strengthened by the profession of faith, holds his ground in such circumstances. Indeed, as Meynard shows, the Qur'ān states that God will strengthen the believer in this life and the hereafter with the firm word (xiv, 27). The reference in the last phrase is to the Islamic profession of faith, a view which Zamakhsharī shares with other commentators such as Ṭabarī (xiii, 213-217). When this firm word penetrates deep into the heart through faith and reason, the believer remains steadfast in his belief. The message of Maxim xxxvi is that birth and honours are worth little, since true nobility is to be found in solid piety.

Two of the maxims stand out because of the way in which Zamakhsharī has recourse to direct preaching. In Maxim xxvi, he states that the man who has shunned iniquity will be calm in the pangs of death. This man will be welcomed by the supreme king; angels will proclaim to him eternal bliss and the sight of the throne of God. Happy is the believer who loves good and takes delight in it, who hates evil and turns away from it with horror. The whole of the maxim, as pointed out by Meynard, is a mosaic of different passages taken from the Qur'ān. Maxim xli urges man not only to show the greatest zeal in observing the divine laws, but also to follow the *sunna* of the Prophet and moral precepts derived from it. It acknowledges that divine laws may be superior to other laws, but such a consideration should not stop the Muslim from observing the *sunna*, from considering it as a guide and from following its moral teaching and studying it assiduously, taking care not to violate it. Here Zamakhsharī clearly shows the link between the three categories of precepts of which the Islamic code is made up, that is, (i) compulsory divine laws based on the fundamental teaching of the Qur'ān, (ii) practices derived from Prophetic tradition and (iii) rules of social and political morality also based on tradition. Meynard adds that Mouradja d'Ohsson followed this division in the first part of the religious code which he attributes to Islam.[32]

Occasionally Meynard is rather pedantic and finds difficulties of interpretation where there are none. For instance, having translated Maxim xii where the Muslim is enjoined to give assistance, pay *zakāt* until his death and is informed that charity is first among virtues, he proceeds to link it with *Sūra* 107 of the Qur'ān. Instead of simply saying that this *sūra* is known under the titles of *Mā'ūn* and *Ara'ayta*, he speaks of a disputed title. After the translation of Maxim lxvi which shows that the man who acts prudently does not swerve from the right path, Meynard says that *ṣirāṭ* is used in the primitive sense of route without the special meaning ascribed to it by Qur'ānic legends. But he forgets to mention that the word *ṣirāṭ* has the meaning of path in the very first *sūra* of the Qur'ān. However, by his careful translation, generally judicious annotation and reproduction of Zamakhsharī's text, Meynard has succeeded in bringing to the attention of different readers the work of an important Arab writer. It is clear that there are some affinities of thought between Zamakhsharī and La Rochefoucauld when it is a question of chastising man's vanity, hypocrisy and insignificance. But it is also true that many of Zamakhsharī's *Maxims* have a distinctly Islamic flavour in that they focus on God and man's dependence on Him, and are often inspired by the Qur'ān and the *Ḥadīth* of the Prophet. Thus the reader of these maxims, perhaps to an even greater extent than the reader of the *Chrestomathie*, is given extensive exposure to the Qur'ān, directly or indirectly, and to the sources of Islamic law. Because they are generally short and sharp in tone, they have some impact on him, even if they lack the depth and variety of Sacy's fragments. Although they complement Sacy in drawing attention to the wisdom found in Islam's holy book, they also contradict him in some way, as none of the far-fetched images Sacy thought were typical of Oriental literature and found unacceptable to French taste abound in Zamakhsharī. It may even be argued that there is nothing in Islamic civilization and French scholarship which makes them mutually exclusive.

Notes

1. This school set up by Colbert in the seventeenth century for the training of young interpreters in Middle Eastern languages continued to function until the 1790s. Its problems, especially of training, are highlighted in two manuscripts by Venture de Paradis entitled *Mémoire pour les affaires étrangères sur les enfants de langue destinés à servir de drogmans dans les échelles de Turquie* and *Projet d'un plan d'éducation pour les enfants de langue que l'état fait élever à Paris*. See *Papiers de Venture de paradis*, in B.N., N.afr. 8988. Venture was interpreter in Arabic language in various Arab countries in the 1780's

2. By Oriental studies I simply mean scholarly studies of Arabic, Persian and Turkish without any of the pejorative connotations associated with Orientalism in the current controversy on the subject. See the chapter on 'The Question of Orientalism' by Bernard Lewis in *Islam and the West* (O.U.P., N. York), 1993.

3. *Tableau historique de l'éruditon française ou Rapport historique sur les progrès de l'histoire et de la littérature ancienne depuis 1789 et sur leur état actuel* (Paris, 1810).

4. *Rapport historique*, p. 8.

5. The abbé Toderini took a different view in *De la littérature des Turcs*. See below.

6. See Henri Dehérain, *Silvestre de Sacy - ses contemporains et ses disciples* (Paris, 1938), p. v.

7. Edward Said, *Orientalism* (London, 1978), p. 12.

8. Bernard Lewis, op. cit., p. 112.

9. Dehérain, op. cit., pp. vii-ix.

10. *Chrestomathie arabe ou Extraits de divers écrivains arabes tant en prose qu'en vers à l'usage des élèves de l'école spéciale des langues orientales vivantes* (Paris, 1806), pp. 5-6.

11. *De l'utilité de l'étude de la poésie arabe* (Paris, 1826), p. 6. This essay was published in the same year as the revised edition of the *Chrestomathie arabe.*

12. *Mélanges de littérature orientale* (Paris, 1833, 1861), p. 47.

13. See my book *Voltaire and English Literature* (Oxford, 1979).

14. Said, op. cit., p. 128.

15. In prayer, the movements consisting of standing, reciting verses of the Qur'ān, bending and prostrating twice are called *rak'a.*

16. In extract vii, reproduced from Ibn Khaldūn's *History*, in the 1826 edition, the real cause of their fall is attributed to the Barmakides controlling all the public revenue of Rashīd. Perhaps the most significant information given in the extract of the revised edition relates to Rashīd's grandfather, al-Manṣūr. The caliph encouraged Mālik ibn Anas (712-95) to compose the *al-Muwaṭṭa'*, the earliest surviving law book in Islam.

17. See Chapter 2, above.

18. Among the Companions, Sacy includes the first three caliphs, 'Ā'isha, Ṭalḥa and Zubayr. Oddly enough, the Caliph 'Alī is excluded.

19. 'Lands' here does not mean lands attached to a property, but lands independent of it. The Prophet had advised 'Umar to give his property in charity (as an endowment) with its land and trees. See al-Bukhārī, *Ṣaḥīḥ*, text and translation, Muḥammad Muhsin Khan (Madina, 1971), iv, 22.

20. At this point in the 1826 edition of the text, Ḥārith makes a reference to Ibn 'Abbās (619-87). This gives Sacy the opportunity to say that the great Traditionist of Islam was very famous for the sharpness of his mind, his sagacity and foresight.

21. See his commentary on *Sūra* 21: 104 in *Le Coran*, ed. cit., i, 1105.

22. This is extract xxviii of the 1826 edition of the *Chrestomathie*. Al-Ḥamadhānī was not included in the 1806 edition. Sacy's technique of adding new names is reminiscent of Voltaire's in later editions of the *Lettres philosophiques.*

23. Seven schools of Qur'ānic 'reading', current in the first three centuries of the *hijra*, are recognized in Islam: they do not affect doctrine, but are concerned with the order and details of *sūras*. Ḥamza (d. 772) belonged to the school of Kufa.

24. Judgement Day is to last a thousand years according to *Sūra* 32: 5 and fifty thousand years according to *Sūra* 70: 4. These figures are, of course, not meant to be taken literally.

25. Said, op. cit., p. 139.

26. For example, for those interested in the poetry of the *Jāhiliyya* (the time of ignorance), that is, in the period preceding the times of Muḥammad, Sacy gave excerpts from the poem of Schanfari (Schanfara in the 1826 edition) known as *Lāmi'at al-'Arab* and one from Nābigha Dubyānī, which he says is sometimes joined to the *Mu'allaqāt*, the 'suspended poems' written by Labīd, Imru'l Qays and others before Islam.

27. W.M. de Slane, *Les Prolégomènes d'Ibn Khaldoun*, 3 vols. (Paris, 1863). Slane had also translated parts of Ibn Khaldūn's *History* dealing with the Maghrib as *Histoire des berbères et des dynasties musulmanes de L'Afrique Septentrionale*, 4 vols. (Paris, 1852).

28. See the article on ʿAntar in the *Encyclopaedia of Islam* (2nd edition) and Denise Brahimi, *Arabes des Lumières et Bédouins romantiques* (Paris, 1982), pp. 156-176.

29. He had been preceded by Gustav Weil who gave a German translation of Zamakhsharī's *Maxims*, published in Stuttgart in 1836. With A.J.B. Pavet de Courteille, Barbier de Meynard had also translated al-Masʿūdī's *Murūj al-Dhahab* as *Les prairies d'or*, published by Société Asiatique (Paris, 1971).

30. See the commentary of Si Hamza Boubakeur on this verse in *Le Coran*, ed. cit., ii, 1929.

31. See Chapter 4, below.

32. Ignace Mouradja D'Ohsson, *Tableau général de l'empire ottoman* (Paris, 1787), 3 vols. The work of the Armenian-born writer who served Sweden as a diplomat is often quoted by writers, including Meynard, in the nineteenth century.

CHAPTER 4

The representation of women in Islam
Some Muslim views of women

It is essential to provide an accurate yardstick by which Western representation of Muslim women may be measured. It is surely right that the reader should have some awareness of Muslim thinking on the question and it would be natural to view the role of women against a background in which Qur'ān and *ḥadīth* play the significant part, as these two texts lay down rules of conduct for men and women. As mentioned in Chapter 1, the Qur'ān had become available to European readers, especially from the seventeenth century onwards, in translations such as those of Du Ryer, Sale, Savary and Kazimirsky. *Ḥadīth* such as Al-Bukhārī's *Ṣaḥīḥ* was also available and was being increasingly used by authors including Savary, Murray and Desvergers. Bukhārī's *Ṣaḥīḥ* was in fact edited in Arabic by L. Krehl under the title *Le Recueil des Traditions mahométanes* (Leiden, 1862-68). Krehl edited the first three volumes and the fourth was completed by Th. W. Juynboll in 1908. A close reading of the *Ṣaḥīḥ* in previous centuries, as in modern times, could well provide interesting perspectives on woman's status. Although *ḥadīth* is primarily about the words and deeds of the Prophet Muḥammad, it also reveals some insights into the mentality of men and women of his and later times. As we all know, *ḥadīth* complements the Qur'ān and it often elucidates points which are not clear in the Qur'ān. However, more weight should perhaps be given to the latter because of its divine nature, there being no disagreement among Muslims about the text itself. There is, of course, divergence of views about the interpretation of certain verses. In the case of *ḥadīth* literature opinions differ as to whether some sayings, attributed to the Prophet, should be included in a canonical collection.

There is a Tradition in Bukhārī, where the Prophet is reported as having said: 'A number of accomplished men exist, but among women one can quote only four: 'Āsiya, wife of Pharaoh, Maryam, daughter of 'Imrān, Khadīja, daughter of Khuwailid and Fāṭima, daughter of Muḥammad' (cf. *Ṣaḥīḥ*, 5, pp. 74, 75, 103). This Tradition gained wide currency in the eighteenth and nineteenth centuries. It was popularized by French and English writers such as Savary, Desvergers and Murray who came across it in Abu'l Fidā''s biography of the Prophet (see above). The message of this Tradition is not in harmony with that of the Qur'ān. In *Sūra* 66: 10-12, for instance, the teaching is that God sets forth as an example to unbelievers the wives of Noah and Lūṭ, who were false to their husbands. By contrast, the believers are strengthened by the examples of the wife of Pharaoh, who asked God to save her from her husband and his misdeeds, and the mother of Jesus, who testified to the truth of the words of her Lord. Certain women may even receive inspiration from God. Such was the case of the mother of Moses, whom God asked to suckle her child and to throw him into the river if she feared for him (*Sūra* 28: 7). The difference between Moses's mother and especially chosen Prophets, for example, is that the latter had received a *risāla*, that is, a divine communication which had to be transmitted to mankind. If we are to believe Wadud-Muhsin, there would be likelihood of failure if women, who are given little regard in most societies, were selected to deliver the message. She sees here a strategy of effectiveness, not a statement of divine preference (p. 65).

The Qur'ān does not stress cases of wicked or outstanding women, as these do not form the majority, but is primarily concerned with the generality of women. The notable exception here is in *Sūra* 33: 30-34, where the wives of the Prophet are specifically addressed. Elsewhere the Qur'ān proclaims the absolute moral and spiritual equality of all women with men. To earn the future reward of the Hereafter which, according to *Sūra* 87: 17, is better and more enduring than this world, men and women need to have practised on earth charity, fasting, chastity and truthfulness and also shown patience and piety. As *Sūra* 33: 35 clearly states 'For Muslim men and women, for believing men and women, for devout men and women, for true men and women, for men and women who are patient and constant, for men and women who humble themselves, for men and women who give in charity, for men and women who fast (and deny themselves), for men and women who guard their chastity, and for men and women who engage much in God's praise, for them has God prepared forgiveness and a great reward.' The Qur'ān does not discriminate against women, who have the same status as men. For according to *Sūra* 40: 40, 'he that works a righteous deed – whether man or woman – and is a believer – such will enter the Garden (of Bliss)'. The same message is repeated in *Sūra* 4: 124. The Qur'ān teaches not only that women enter paradise as a reward for their good actions, but that husbands and wives enter together. *Sūra* 43: 70-71, addressing married couples specifically, states that there will be in paradise all that the souls could desire, all that the eyes could delight in. It should be mentioned that in Islam it is a canonical duty, laid down in *Sūra* 24: 32, for men and women who are single to be joined together in matrimony. What distinguishes people from one another is not a matter of gender: it is rather a question of *taqwā*, that is, piety. Indeed, *Sūra* 49: 13, which is addressed to mankind, proclaims that the most honoured person in the sight of

God is he who is the most pious. The sight of God is the greatest blessing bestowed on the virtuous believer in paradise.

It is not to be concluded from the above remarks that the affairs of this world, inferior as it is to the Hereafter, are neglected in the Qur'ān. On the contrary, it often brings us down to earth in its concern with practical matters. One of these important matters affects the material conditions of women. It has long been recognized that Islam was among the first religions to give women the right of owning property. A spirit of justice ensures that the man who leaves a widow assigns to her a legacy and provision for a year and a shelter in his home. However, the Islamic law on the rights of a widow to the inheritance of her husband, based on *Sūra* 2: 240 and governed by the provision of *Sūra* 4: 12, appears to treat males more favourably. It appears to give women a quarter of the succession of husbands who died childless and one eighth if they left children, after the payment of legacies and debts, whereas the men inherit half of the property of women who die childless and a quarter if they have children, again after payment of legacies and debts. Verse 176 supplements the rule of inheritance to the estate of a deceased person who has left as heir neither a descendant nor an ascendant. Again, the male heir has twice the inheritance of a female heir. On the question of inheritance *ḥadīth* seems to follow the Qur'ān closely.[1] It is generally but not always true that the male takes a share double that of a female in his own category. The proportion for the female of half the proportion for the male is only one of many proportional combinations possible. For instance, if there is only one female child her share of the inheritance is half (*Sūra* 4: 11). What happens to the other half? According to someone who was not strictly a Muslim, although well-disposed towards Islam, Edward Lane, it was paid into the public treasury.[2] The preference given to men in such matters is due to the fact that they are *qawwāmūn*, that is, support women from their wealth (*Sūra* 4: 34). This line clarifies the meaning of *Sūra* 2: 228, which is about men having 'a degree (of advantage) over them', that is, women. The *daraja* men have over women is that they can also initiate divorce against their wives without arbitration, whereas women may obtain divorce only on the intervention of a judge. But the situation of women who have independent means and are not being supported by men does not seem to be discussed in the Qur'ān. In Muslim societies one often hears of men's encroachments on women's financial and other rights, but such infringements have no Qur'ānic sanction.

Despite appearances there is no misogynist trend in the Qur'ān.[3] Prejudices against women are rather to be found in later Islamic history. Shaykh Yūsuf Qaraḍāwī, who opposes those who want to prevent women from holding public office, argues that in its attack on Islam the West uses the words and deeds of contemporary extremists.[4] This may be true to some extent, but the misogynist prejudice, evident from certain reports, appears to have older foundations.

Perceptions of Muslim women in French and English literature – Women's souls and Paradise

To see God one had to enter Paradise and to enter Paradise one had to have a soul. As we have seen above, Islamic teaching is clear that women have souls and that those of them who have been virtuous and have performed what is required by God will join men of similar quality in Paradise and see God. However, totally unnecessary doubts about women's position were expressed by Suyūṭī whose male chauvinism is apparent from his autobiography. Yet his problem is not whether women will enter Paradise, but when women will see God in it. The problem for Western writers was different – whether Muslim women had souls and whether they went to Paradise at all.

It seems to have preoccupied them from the seventeenth century onwards. Indeed Antoine Adam pointed out in his critical edition of Montesquieu's epistolary novel, the *Lettres persanes* (1721) that seventeenth-century authors were worried about the true doctrine of the Muslims on the fate of women in the afterlife. So much so that the French version of Reland's *De religione mohammedica* (1705), produced by D. Durand in 1721, devoted the eighteenth 'Eclaircissement' to the subject whether women would be saved according to Muslims. There was nothing to worry about: a careful look at a translation of the Qur'ān should have removed any doubt European writers may have had. They were interested in the question for two main reasons – the status, spiritual and otherwise, of Muslim women and their moral behaviour. If the latter could be represented as having no souls and being therefore excluded from Paradise then their licentiousness would cause no surprise. Even a writer like Clot Bey, who is fairly well-disposed to Islam and is not particularly concerned with the question of women's souls and their presence or absence from paradise, claims in the *Aperçu général sur l'Egypte* that Muslim women are forced to remain virtuous up to the time of their marriage but become less scrupulous once they are married (see Chapter 5, below). In a sweeping generalisation he declares that in the East women's honesty never rests on solid principles of morality and that fear alone restrains them. According to him Egyptian women must be closely watched as they are much inclined to voluptuousness (p. 335). The denigration of women by utterances such as those of Clot Bey can only add significance to the question who is admitted to Paradise. European writers might wonder why Muslims are so preoccupied with Paradise when it seems so remote from everyday life. To many Muslims, however, it was and continues to be almost a living reality which is attainable. It is certainly at the heart of their aspirations.

In the article 'Gennah' of his influential *Bibliothèque orientale* (1697), d'Herbelot describes Suyūṭī as the author of a book apparently reflecting a popular Muslim belief, in wide circulation among the French, that women will not enter Paradise. No such book by Suyūṭī exists. The mistake does not come from him, but from d'Herbelot who also misunderstands a *ḥadīth* of the Prophet in which he reassured an old woman by telling her that all old women would become young on entering Paradise.[5] Voltaire understood the *ḥadīth* well. Inspired by George Sale in the 'Preliminary Discourse' to his translation of the Qur'ān in 1734, he wittily refutes the idea of women's exclusion in the text 'De l'Alcoran et de Mahomet' in 1748. He does not find it likely that such a clever man as Muḥammad would wish to be on bad terms with that half of mankind which leads the other half!

Indeed various attempts were made by Western writers in the eighteenth and nineteenth centuries to be fair to Islamic teaching on the question of women's souls and women's presence in Paradise. These were not altogether successful. In a letter to the abbé Conti dated 29 May 1717, Lady Mary Wortley Montagu, wife of the British Ambassador to the Porte, is critical of 'our vulgar notion' that Muslims do not think women have souls. To her this is a mistake and she attributes to Muslims the idea that women 'are not of so elevated a kind and therefore must not hope to be admitted into the paradise appointed for the men who are to be entertained by celestial beautys'. She says that there is a place of happiness 'destined for souls of the inferior order where all good women are to be in eternal bliss'.[6] What she says has nothing to do with Islamic teaching on the subject. There is no mention of inferior and superior souls in Islam. In another letter dated February 1718 to the same person, an apparently genuine letter written in French and translated into English in 1719, she tells him that it is certainly untrue, though a popular idea, that Muḥammad excludes women from all participation in a future happy life. Muḥammad, she argues, was 'trop galant homme' and liked the fair sex too much to treat it in such a barbarous way (p. 375). On the contrary, he promises a very nice paradise to women, even if it is one separated from their husbands. She believes that the majority of Muslim women would not be less happy on that account and that the separation will not make their paradise less pleasant. To enjoy future happiness they did not have to be useless on earth: they should spend their time making little Muslims as far as possible. Then comes an extraordinary remark: virgins who die virgins and widows who do not remarry will die in a punishable sin and will be excluded from paradise. All this is surprising coming from a person who is not hostile to Islam. Her remarks are not at all true to its spirit.

The idea of a separate paradise for women may have been inspired by Jean Chardin whose travel book on Persia, the *Voyages en Perse*, was often used by Montesquieu in the *Lettres persanes*: it enjoyed an enormous reputation long afterwards. In it Chardin refers *inter alia* to the tradition of the exclusion of women from paradise, but he argues that it is only in the sense of their being separated from the men. According to him the men will have in paradise celestial women more beautiful than women from earth will be at the Resurrection. As to resurrected women they will pass through a place of delight and, like the blessed men in their own place, will enjoy all types of voluptuousness.[7] Both Chardin and Lady Mary Montagu may be referring to a separate paradise for women, but the paradise constructed by the male writer is certainly more sensual than that of the woman writer.

In the *Lettres persanes* Montesquieu even surpasses Chardin in his description of a woman's sensual paradise. There is no doubt that readers felt the impact of Montesquieu who has enjoyed such a reputation in European thought ever since and who also propagated many myths about Islam. Several times he insisted on the idea that Muslim women do not have souls and do not enter paradise. In letter 24 the Persian character Rica is made to declare that women are inferior to men and that 'our prophets tell us that they will not enter paradise'.[8] However, the wittiest technique of showing the exclusion of women from paradise is used in letter 125 where the action takes place in India. After Rica has mentioned the difficulty of describing the pleasures of paradise in all religions he narrates the story of a Hindu woman who had just lost her husband but is refused permission by the Muslim governor of the town to burn herself, as her female relatives had done before. A young Hindu priest supports her wish, arguing that she would find, in the hereafter, her husband with whom she would start a second marriage. Thereupon the woman, who hated her late husband, said she gave up the idea of burning herself and informed the governor that she would convert to Islam! The implication is clear: there is no hereafter for Muslim women.

Less witty but more sensual is Letter 141 which is highly significant for the perspectives it opens on European male sexual fantasy regarding Muslim women. One of the harem companions of Zulema, the author of the Persian tale narrated by Rica, asks her whether she believed this ancient tradition of Muslim doctors that paradise was only intended for men. She confirmed that it was a common belief and that everything had been done to degrade women and that the Jews of Persia maintained that women had no souls. She believed that such offensive views originated in men's pride: men do not realise that on Judgement Day God will not distinguish between His creatures and that access to paradise is gained only through virtue. At this point of the narrative Montesquieu seems to be voicing authentic Islamic teaching with its emphasis on *taqwā*, piety. The tone soon changes. Zulema holds out the promise that in the hereafter

God will match the reward of virtuous men who will be in a paradise full of celestial and ravishing beauties. Their female counterparts will be in a 'lieu de délices' where they will be intoxicated by a torrent of delights with divine men who will be submissive to them. Not content with this Zulema tells the story of Anais who was murdered by her cruel husband. But after death she went to the 'séjour de délices' promised to virtuous women. At first it was a green meadow with bright flowers surrounded by streams, the waters of which were purer than crystal, leading to copses and magnificent gardens where the only sound was the humming of birds. There is nothing in this description of paradise to which Muslims could object since the Qur'ān abounds in descriptions of *jannat* where the blessed live for ever in gardens surrounded by streams. But in the letter the women's senses are then set ablaze by the dance of divine men, the pleasures increasing all the time. Anais is taken naked into a splendid bed where two beautiful men received her: her intoxication went beyond her desires. That was how in his male sexual fantasy Montesquieu drew a picture of woman triumphant while it was men who were locked up in harems!

Voltaire produced a mixture of serious and flippant techniques to refute the myth about women's exclusion from paradise. In chapter VII of the *Essai sur les moeurs* (1756), he maintains seriously that the myth is groundless raillery such as all nations use against others, pointing to vision of God as the supreme beatitude. In *Femmes, soyez soumises à vos maris* (1767), however, the tone is bantering. Voltaire invents a woman who indignantly asks an abbé whether it was true that Muḥammad had so much contempt for her sex that he claimed women were not worthy of entering paradise. The abbé comforts her by saying that what was said of Islam was not a bit true and that people have been deceived by ignorant and wicked monks. Women will go to paradise like men and no doubt love-making would take place there but it would be different from earthly love-making! Voltaire uses the article 'Alcoran ou plutôt le Koran', published in the *Questions sur l'Encyclopédie* in 1770, to refute writers such as Montesquieu by pointing out how false was the idea that women owned no property in this world and that in the next they would have no place in Paradise. Despite his efforts and those of Reland and Sale before him the myth about women's celestial exclusion persisted throughout the eighteenth century. The witty techniques at the service of exclusion prevailed over those of inclusion. Volney claimed in the *Voyage en Egypte et en Syrie* (1787) that Muḥammad did not do women the honour of treating them as a part of mankind in 'his' Qur'ān and did not mention them in connexion with the reward of the afterlife.

Could the nineteenth century show some evolution in attitudes? The tone was certainly more sober, judging by what the Romantic poet Byron wrote. His criticism of Muslims, however, sounds harsh in the epistle 'To Miss E (lizabeth) P (igot)', dated 9 October 1806. His lines run like this:

> Eliza! What fools the Mussulman sect,
> Who to woman deny the soul's future existence,
> Could they see thee, Eliza! they'd own their defect,
> And this doctrine would meet a general resistance.
>
> Had their Prophet possess'd half an atom of sense,
> He ne'er would have woman from Paradise driven,
> Instead of his Houris a flimsy pretence,
> With woman alone, he had peopled his Heaven.

In the third stanza he claims that Muḥammad deprived women's bodies of spirit.[9] Byron's poem *The Giaour* of May 1813 refers to the Islamic 'creed' of the soullessness of women in these terms:

Oh! who young Leila's glance could read
And keep that portion of his creed
Which saith that woman is but dust,
A soulless toy for tyrant's lust?

Byron, however, corrects himself in his note by saying that the idea is 'a vulgar error', very much in the manner of Lady Mary Montagu some hundred years before. One does not know how he worked out that the Qur'ān 'allots at least a third of paradise to well-behaved women; but by far the greater number of Mussulmans interpret of their own way, and exclude their moieties from heaven'.[10] There is, however, some progress in his thought on the subject in *The Bride of Abydos,* written in December 1813. It describes Zuleika thus:

And oft her koran conned apart;
And oft in youthful reverie
She dream'd what Paradise might be
Where woman's parted soul shall go
Her Prophet had disdain'd to show
(lines 103-107).

Woman has at last been given a soul by Byron, but she does not know its destination. Contrary to what Mohammed Sharafuddin states, Byron shows no commitment to accuracy here.[11]

In the *Essai sur les moeurs des habitants modernes de l'Egypte* (1822) Chabrol de Volvic, who had accompanied Napoleon in the expedition to Egypt in 1798, thought that Muḥammad did not go to the lengths of 'Umar in contributing to the moral degradation of women. However, his religious system was against the fair sex. To strengthen the monstrous edifice of his so-called paradise, he had to exclude women from it (p. 407). Some pages later while describing Islamic accounts of what happens on the Day of Judgement, Chabrol, like

Byron, has a footnote in which he points out that the exclusion of women is an error. In the chapter on 'Laws and Religion' of the *Manners and customs of the modern Egyptians* (1836) Lane tries to set the record straight by stating that exclusion of women is contrary to the Islamic faith, although many Christians have asserted that Muslims believe women have no souls. As he points out, in several places in the Qur'ān, Paradise is promised to all true believers, whether males or females. But he then spoils it by narrating fantastic stories about countless servants and wives available to men in Paradise, implying that the stories have a Qur'ānic origin when this is not the case at all.

Nerval was more consistent than Chabrol and Lane. In the first chapter of Appendix 1 of his *Voyage en Orient* (1851) he suggests that the European claim that Muslims do not believe in the souls of women should be abandoned. An important aspect of Nerval's discourse is to be found in the suggestion that the Prophet prays to God to open Paradise to the true believers, including their wives, who practised virtue. Perhaps the most significant service to Islam performed by Nerval was that he actually quotes the Qur'ān, *Sūra* 43: 70, about husbands and wives entering Paradise together, although he does not give the precise reference. In the light of this and other texts which he says might be quoted, Nerval wonders about the origin of the common prejudice. He traces it back to Sale who has been misinterpreted while quoting the *ḥadīth* about the old woman becoming young on admission to Paradise. Nerval quotes it correctly. In the section entitled 'Inconvénients du célibat', the fourth item in the chapter on 'Les femmes du Caire', Soliman-Aga speaks in favour of segregation on the ground that it ensures peace between men and women. It suffices for the men back home at night to find well-dressed women with smiling faces and dancers to make them think of a paradise peopled by pure and untainted beauties who alone are worthy of being the wives of true believers. Nerval sees there not so much contempt for women as the survival of a platonic idea whereby pure love rises above perishable objects, the loved women being merely the symbol of perfect love which exists permanently in heaven. He thinks that such ideas are responsible for the myth that Orientals denied women a soul. Nerval points out that, on the contrary, truly pious women live in the hope of finding their ideal achieved in heaven. He seems to have an acute perception of the psyche of Muslim men and women, to whom Paradise means so much. He insists that women saints are known in Islamic religious history and that the Prophet's daughter is queen of this female paradise.[12] Although Nerval may provoke some scepticism in the reader with his conception of platonic love in the Islamic paradise, the information he gives on Fatima is accurate. In the eyes of the Shīʿites, Fāṭima represents 'the embodiment of all that is divine in womanhood'. Later Sunnī literature, under the influence of Shīʿite traditions, but without going to the same lengths, has progressively enhanced the status of Fāṭima. The Sunnīs do not reject the *ḥadīth* in which she is declared to be 'queen of the women of paradise next to Maryam, daughter of ʿImrān'.[13]

The contribution of Richard Burton to the debate is worth noting. In the *Personal Narrative of a pilgrimage* he suggests that certain 'Fathers of the Church' did not believe that women have souls and that Muslims never went so far. He is rather ambiguous here because one would not know from him how far Muslims went. But in chapter 3 of Appendix I entitled 'Ḥajj, or Pilgrimage', he reproduces what he calls a compendium of Shāfiʿī pilgrim rites translated from a treatise by 'a learned doctor whose work is generally read in Egypt and in the countries adjoining' (ii, 281). In it the pilgrim is recommended to visit the Qubā mosque, where he should pray for himself and for 'his brethren of the Muslimin, and the Muslimat, the Muminin and the Muminat' (p. 293). This gives Burton the opportunity to explain that 'these second words are the feminines of the first; they prove that the Moslem is not above praying for what Europe supposed he did not believe in, namely, the souls of women'. One would have wished Burton to make his point by direct quotation from the Qur'ān instead of using this roundabout way. But he was nearer the mark than Pierre Loti who in *Aziyadé* (1879) makes his heroine say that she was not sure that according to the Qur'ān women had souls like men (p. 26) or, for that matter, Pauline Kra who, as late as 1970, was proclaiming *inter alia* the existence of a Mohammedan tradition that women will not enter paradise.[14]

Women inside the harem

The above sections were primarily concerned with Islamic teaching on the status of women in general and with some Muslim perspectives derived from the early centuries of Islam while at the same time they stressed Western approaches to the question of women in Paradise. The reader was frequently taken to the rarefied atmosphere of Heaven, from which he needs to come down to earth, preferably in a soft landing. He should now take the opportunity to look at the role of women in specific Muslim countries in the eighteenth and nineteenth centuries so that he may see to what extent practice is in harmony with theory. Although life in the harem affected only a small proportion of the Muslim population – upper and middle class society and dependents – this did not matter to many Western writers because they were fascinated by the harem from the eighteenth century onwards. That was partly because it was then inaccessible, especially to men, and thus came to acquire the flavour of the forbidden fruit. The vivid imagination of male writers supplied what reality denied them.

The harem, which was either a section or the whole of a private house occupied by women, was perceived by many Western writers, male and female, if not as the essence of Islam, at least as its most distinctive feature.

There was a chance that women writers would produce more sober accounts of harems since they had direct access to them. By virtue of her position Lady Mary Montagu was able to visit ladies of high position in Turkey. In a letter from Adrianople to Lady Mar dated 18 April 1717 she describes how she was entertained to dinner by the Grand Vizier's lady. She was met at the door by the latter's black eunuch who helped her out of her coach with great respect through several rooms where finely-dressed female slaves were in attendance. She noticed little magnificence, the hostess claiming that she had little time or money to spend on superfluities: the money she had was spent on charity and both her husband's time and her own was given to devotion. As a mark of hospitality the hostess was keen to serve her every course. The visit concluded with coffee and perfumes 'which is a high mark of respect' and the slaves played dance music. At the suggestion of her Greek lady interpreter Lady Mary visited the Kahya's lady. Here everything was on a grander scale. Lady Mary was met by two black eunuchs who led her through a gallery where she saw young girls dressed in fine light damasks brocaded with silver. On a sofa covered with fine Persian carpets sat Fatima, the lady of the house, dressed in a caftan of gold brocade, her arms adorned with bracelets of diamonds, leaning on cushions of embroidered satin. At her feet were two young girls almost covered with jewels. Lady Mary was speechless with admiration as soft tunes were played and some of the girls danced. The air was perfumed with amber and other rich scents. After this magnificent display of Oriental opulence the guest was so charmed that she thought she had been 'in Mahomet's paradise' (i, 352). How accurate is all this? Lady

Mary's description creates the impression of imagined, not real splendour. Another letter dated 10 March 1718 to Lady Mar and describing a visit to Sultāna Hafise, favourite of Muṣṭafā II, makes the picture of the harem only slightly more realistic. According to Lady Mary, Hafise was ordered to leave the harem immediately after his death and get married. Her supplication to the reigning Sultān (Ahmet III) was of no avail. She chose Abu Bekir Effendi, the Minister for Foreign Affairs, but she apparently never allowed him to visit her, passing her time mourning 'with a constancy very little known in Christendom, especially in a widow of twenty one' (p. 381). Although she had no black eunuchs her husband was obliged to respect her as a former Queen and not enquire into what was done in her apartment. She entertained lavishly with fifty dishes of meat: the knives were of gold and the table cloths and napkins were of embroidered silk and gold. She too had many young slaves and complimented her guest with perfumes. Aware that what she was describing sounded extravagant Lady Mary commented that travellers such as herself are laughed at as fabulous and Romantic if they say anything new. She added that she had been to a harem where the winter apartment was panelled with inlaid work of mother of pearl, ivory of different colours and olive wood.

The images of the fictitious harem projected by Montesquieu in the *Lettres persanes* and which fired the imagination of European readers long afterwards are mostly negative and they vary according to the character that writes the letter. Thus the hero Usbek who is not an omniscient narrator, gives a fragmentary view of it. He believes it is the abode of innocence (letter 26). But to the first eunuch who confesses that he has never known a peaceful day in it, it is an awful prison (letter 9). It is clear from letter 3, written by Zachi to Usbek, that the harem is a place where the female characters are preoccupied with the most trivial things and where the master is judge in a beauty competition where all his wives take part. Zachi's main achievement was to triumph over her rivals. In letter 7 from Fatmé to Usbek, Fatmé admits that although she was born free she is a slave because of the violence of her passions. Her natural disposition necessitates that she be locked up. She is among the most sensual of women, her veins burn with desire and she would give up the whole world for a kiss from Usbek. Most of the women are so unhappy that one of their aims is to trick the eunuchs who guard over them. It is clear that discipline soon breaks down in the harem where unauthorised men manage to gain entry. Usbek suspects Zélis of infidelity, but as Solim tells him in letter 159, Roxane proved to be a greater culprit. In the last letter of the novel Roxane who has turned an awful prison into a 'lieu de délices et de plaisir' breaks the news of her infidelity to Usbek who mistook violent hatred for violent love. Letter 141 is striking not only because of the sensual descriptions of a fictitious paradise but also because of the *coup d'état* operated by the false Ibrahim. He gets rid of all eunuchs, keeps open house, allows the women to remove their veils and to mix freely with men. The message the *Lettres persanes* is trying to convey is that no harem is needed in Islamic society.

As it happens in French thought of the eighteenth and nineteenth centuries, one writer often contradicts another. Although in much of the *Voyage en Orient* Nerval relies less on first-hand experience and more on his imagination and what he has read he attempts to refute Montesquieu. In section VIII entitled 'Les Mystères du harem' of the chapter 'Le harem', following his visit to the harem of a palace in Cairo, he argues that the delights of the harem, an all-powerful husband or master, charming women getting together to make the happiness of one man are an illusion one must be rid of and that religion or custom tempers this notion which has deceived so many Europeans (p. 206). He sees the harem as a sort of convent (though not in the manner of the blind Usbek) where an austere rule prevails and where the main function of the women is to bring up children, to spend time on embroidery and to direct slaves in housework. He is not unaware of the tales circulating in cafés about the adventures of lovers disguised as women in order to gain access to the harem. To him, however, these tales belong more to Arab imagination than Muslim manners. His reading of Muslim psychology is that the Muslim is not given to adultery and would find it revolting to share a woman with another. Nerval was also critical of the notion of harems where women had never seen men. In the first chapter of Appendix I on the condition of Muslim women, he added a passage relating to this topic in the *Revue des deux mondes, La Silhouette,* and the *Scènes de la vie orientale* that all travellers had come across women of the harems in the streets of Constantinople, although they were in carriages and not on foot.

Montesquieu's male sexual fantasy is absent from *The Natural History of Aleppo* by Alexander Russell, who was a resident physician in Aleppo in the 1740s. He was held in high esteem by the Pasha and, despite what Lane claims, Russell studied Arabic during his stay in Aleppo and he spoke it very well. He has a chapter of his book entitled 'The Turkish harem at Aleppo' where he uses his professional position and direct experience of the harem to make shrewd observations on what he sees inside it. The clear impression to emerge is that the harem is well regulated. In charge of all matters is an officer called 'Harem Khiafy' with one or two boys under him who have access to the apartments and are employed by the ladies in carrying messages or doing petty services. The boys are generally black slaves, but not eunuchs and their master is sometimes an eunuch, but more frequently a white slave or servant of advanced age. No male servants ever approach the door of the harem unless the master is present. All men, including doctors, and women who have business with the ladies must apply to him for admittance. Medical people – European or non-European – have access at all times when their attendance is required, but they are led to the patient's room when a slave loudly proclaims their approach. Even the grandee himself cannot enter the harem unannounced. This is to allow the ladies to appear veiled before him. Veils are removed only when women enter the apartment of their hostess. The grandee's presence may impose silence on the younger ladies but not on the elderly matrons who report to him news of the town circulated by female pedlars and Bedouin women who speak freely to men. But Russell knew of no illicit admission of strangers into the harem and he claims that he hardly heard about any case of adultery during the twenty years of his stay. Instead of the lavish entertainment described by Lady Mary, Russell mentions only the dispensing of coffee and tobacco for much of the time, sherbet and perfumes being reserved for particular occasions.

Unlike the women of the *Lettres persanes* those of a real Aleppo harem are not idle. They superintend domestic affairs, care of children (non-existent in Montesquieu), needle and embroidery work. Children were rarely sent to public schools after the age of nine and teachers would be employed to come to the harem. They are taught to read and write Arabic which they forget quickly. Russell quotes an exception – the case of a daughter of the Grand vizier, who had made surprising progress in Arabic literature: he was shown a very beautifully written manuscript from her.[15] He notes that in winter evenings while men were engaged in the outer apartment the ladies listened to a reading of Arabian tales. He came across a manuscript of the *Arabian Nights* which contained only two hundred and eight nights and he had a copy made and circulated to other harems. He was assured by some of the *'ulamā'* whom the women had induced to be of the audience that the latter were unaware of the existence of the book. But young women, unlike the older ones, did not strike him as being very pious. He bases this observation on the fact that during his mid-day visits he did not have to wait until prayers were over and he found so few who had performed their ablutions. Younger women fast but are less punctual at prayer.

Sophie Poole, sister of Edward Lane, provides one of the female accounts of life in a harem in nineteenth-century Egypt. In *The English woman in Egypt* (1844) she claims that her brother's account, though valuable, is derived only from other men and is imperfect and that he desired her to make up for its deficiency by her own observation and by what she could learn from the women themselves. She explains that contrary to popular belief in England the master of a house is not always the lord and that he may be excluded for days from his own harem when his wife is receiving visitors. She manages to strip the harem of the glamour it enjoyed in the eighteenth century with her down-to-earth description of daily activities: ladies of the highest distinction cook and make sherbet. Moreover, the Pasha's daughter in whose presence the ladies in attendance never raise their eyes herself supervises the washing and polishing of the marble pavements in her palaces. She deplores the fact that few women could read and write in Arabic (although there were exceptions) and that in general they were merely instructed in handiwork, but admits that their embroidery was extremely beautiful, 'superior to any fancy work practised in England' (p. 28). On her visit to the Pasha's harem she saw many black female slaves and some eunuchs dressed in gay Eastern costume forming a curious contrast and most picturesque background to the ladies and white slaves accompanying her. The Oriental aspect of the reception was further stressed with the information that a joint of meat was eaten without knife or fork. Like Russell in

Aleppo, she was impressed by the order and discipline observed in the harems of the great and wealthy and, according to her, the harem was well secured from illicit visitors.

For an alternative, albeit biased, view of the harem one may refer to Harriet Martineau's *Eastern life. Present and Past* (1848). As the royal harem in Cairo was not accessible she visited that of a gentleman of high rank. Although she was given the traditional cup of coffee, sherbet and pipes she had been unwise not to take an interpreter with her. As a result she had to endure monotonous hours of conversation by sign language. It is not surprising that she came to the most negative conclusions about harem life in Egypt. She saw no trace of mind in most of the women occupants except in a 'homely one-eyed old lady: all the young ones were dull, soulless and brutish' (p. 155). In her extreme judgement, 'Egypt was the most atrocious example of this atrocious system' (p. 157). She actually refers to Montesquieu on polygamy and must have been inspired by him in her story of eunuchs spying for their masters when used as guards of the harem. It is clear that she had been reading other writers' narratives as she states that it was not unusual for eunuchs to 'whip ladies away from a window'. She talks of cases of eunuchs forming close attachments with girls, which she could not possibly have learnt from one visit. Even when she visited a harem in Damascus in the company of a pleasant interpreter she only noticed that three half sisters were being shared by two husbands in the same house. Lady Duff Gordon qualified Martineau's attack on harems as 'outrageous' because of the implication, in her view, that they were brothels.[16]

Few accounts of harem life, however, can match that of Emmeline Lott who had been a governess to Ibrāhīm, son of Khedive Ismāʿīl. As the title of her book suggests, *Harem life in Egypt and Constantinople* (1865) is entirely devoted to harems.[17] Unlike other women writers whose information is based on fleeting visits she actually resided in three harems and her observations are firmly grounded in reality and apart from Ismail historical figures such as the Ottoman Sultān ʿAbdul ʿAzīz (1861-76) and the *Vali* of Egypt, Saʿīd (1854-63), appear in the background. Lott actually visited the harem of Saʿīd's widow who, in her view, was one of the few handsome women she had seen in any of the harems. The latter, her head covered with a dark silk handkerchief and wearing large diamond rings on her fingers, received her well. After a tour of inspection of all her apartments she concluded that all rooms were meagrely furnished. Indeed this was her impression of most of the rooms of other harems.[18] Such is her desire to destroy myths about the harem that she ends up by being unfair to Thomas Moore whom she quotes several times. When describing the harem situated on the banks of the Nile, opposite Ghezira, and the ladies of the harem, the Pasha's concubines, she says that she failed to notice the slightest trace of loveliness in them. According to her, Moore had painted them in glowing colours in his narrative verse text, *Lalla Rookh* (1817). In the section 'The Fire-Worshippers' the character Hinda who has been brought up in cloistered seclusion earns the following tribute:

> Oh what a pure and sacred thing
> Is Beauty, curtain'd from the sight
> Of the gross world, illumining
> One only mansion with her light!

Lott quotes these lines, but misunderstands the purpose of Moore who was trying to convey the loveliness of an idealised Romantic heroine and not to describe the ordinary women of a harem. Lott saw the latter had 'countenances pale as ashes, exceedingly disagreeable, flat and globular figures' (i. 75). They looked like old hags, some of them having been *iqbāls*, favourites, of Ibrāhīm (rather Ismāʿīl) Pasha. The black slaves were 'disgusting-looking negresses with flat misshapen noses, wide mouths and orange-coloured nails which made them look repulsive' (p. 215). They spent their time rolling about divans and mattresses. As she then had no Arabic or Turkish she could not understand their chatter and that led to her negative view of harem-life 'that myth-like Elysium of fertile imagination of both Western and Eastern poets' (p. 216).

The most famous of these Western poets not specifically referred to by Lott, though she may have had him in mind, was probably Byron, whose heroine Zuleika is idealised in *The Bride of Abydos*. In her father's eyes she has the beauty of the houris of the Islamic paradise. Giaffir says in Canto I:

> I hear Zuleika's voice,
> Like Houris hymn it meets mine ear'.

Elsewhere in the poem one learns that she was 'the light of love, the purity of grace' and that

> 'Zuleika, mute and motionless,
> Stood like that statue of distress,
> ... a younger Niobe'.

Byron may have inspired Victor Hugo for some of the imagery he uses in poems such as *Le voile* of the anthology 'Les Orientales'.[19]

Lott's attack on Moore and Byron is not gender-inspired, however, as she is equally critical of Lady Montagu who, in her opinion, had not the slightest opportunity to study the daily life of odalisques and had not been allowed to penetrate beyond the reception halls of the harem. So she sets about to remedy the situation with a detailed report on the life of female slaves and concubines. Discipline appears fairly strict in the harem with a Lady Superintendent of slaves in charge.

Lott noticed numerous slaves of Arab origin 'whose condition approximates to that of domestic servants in Europe' (p. 69). They could not leave the harem without permission, but they were often allowed to go out shopping, unaccompanied by eunuchs. They are often sent to schools and some of them can read Arabic and Turkish, but none can write. Lott gives no precision about these schools. The slaves generally remain celibate, although they are sometimes freed and given away in marriage. They thrive on *bakhshish* which is distributed on special occasions. The black slaves, on the other hand, who were from Nubia and Ethiopia mainly, were employed in mean and laborious duties of the household. Except for the nurses who waited upon the Pasha's family these slaves were not emancipated. Yet the slaves of various origins, dressed in different coloured muslins and wearing handkerchiefs on their heads, had hands and ears profusely ornamented and had gold watches suspended from their necks by massive gold chains (p. 76). Lott becomes more uncharitable later as she regrets that such immense wealth consisting of diamonds, amethysts, topazes and sapphires should 'sparkle on tawny and ebony skins of slaves, many of whom were repulsive in their looks and whose habits and appearance in general were totally repugnant to European feelings' (p. 261).

On the occasion of their visit to the palace of Sultān 'Abdul 'Azīz at the village of Babec near Constantinople Lott accompanied the party including Ismā'īl's mother and wife when they called on the *Vālide Sultāna*, the Sultān's mother. She noticed that the domestic life of the odalisques there began at four in the morning when the ladies of the Sultān's harem said their prayers 'which they did every two hours during the day (all of them being fanatics or most religiously inclined)' (ii, 213). At five all the inmates were up and at six the Grand Eunuch said prayers to the ladies of all three harems and touched the centre of their foreheads with his finger. At ten in the evening, the Grand Eunuch 'who appeared to have taken upon himself the office of *Muftī* since our arrival at Bebek shouted forth the call to prayer' (p. 224). His power extends over all women – princesses, ladies of the harem and slaves – and he reads the Qur'ān to forty eunuchs in accordance with his daily custom (p. 284). So, the novelty of Lott's discourse lies in the fact that the harem is not the place commonly associated with voluptuousness but one where people pray regularly and read the Qur'ān. But other aspects of harem life spoil the picture, as the occupants did not spend all their time praying or reading the Qur'ān.

Apparently, eunuchs are adept at strangulation and stories of their exploits or those of their predecessors are common (p. 217). Slaves who broke anything by accident were severely punished in Egypt. One who broke a china vase was seared on her arms with a red-hot iron. Lott says that all slaves had burnt arms and all black slaves were marked with three scars on their faces, the vice-regal brand being three marks which distinguished them from those of private individuals, marked with two. His Highness behaved indiscreetly when Lott saw a female figure (one of his favourite slaves) enveloped in a large veil who went to spend the night in the guest chamber in the pavilion gardens, preceded by two eunuchs beating muffled drums. She also noticed that eunuchs had been bribed to let in soldiers who mounted guard at the outside gates of the harem. The sight of black female slaves of the vice-regal harem rambling at night with eunuchs and other muffled figures made her doubt the infirmity of the eunuchs. Lott's perception of harem life may have been partly distorted by the inappropriate treatment meted out to her on arrival when she was hardly given any furniture in her room.

Social life in the harem in Cairo and Constantinople is given some attention. The princesses spent some of their time cutting out pantaloons and dressing gowns which they gave to a German needle-woman to make up. They had nothing to do with kitchens where only men were employed. In the evening they entertained themselves by playing dominoes. Each princess employs a slave in arranging cigarette-paper, another in preparing tobacco, a third in making cigarettes which another one hands out on a silver tray. Lott preferred the ladies of the Sulṭān's harem in Constantinople, finding them 'much more civilised than those of the Viceroy's' (ii, 223). That may have been because they reminded her of European ladies of olden times. In the evening they would sing songs to their own accompaniment on castanets. Some would sit quietly in a group, plying at their distaffs and spindles, industriously employed in doing useful needle work and in repairing their own garments. Others played at cards, but all smoked and sipped coffee from cups of gold encrusted with diamonds. The author could not help concluding, however, that life in the harems was frightfully monotonous and that it produced melancholy while lethargic stupor clouded the mind in an atmosphere redolent of smells of tobacco and powerful narcotics. Lott was not particularly interested in the politics of the harem although on the occasion of her visit to the harem in the citadel of Cairo, the residence of Ismā'īl's mother, she briefly referred to politics. She felt uncomfortable in the presence of the Valide Princess on the ground that she meddled in weighty matters of state, that is, relations between the Sultān and the Viceroy.

Politics were of greater interest to Lucy Garnett, author of *The Women of Turkey and their Folk-lore* (1890-91). She showed how important was the role played by the women of the harem in Turkish history. She traces this role back to the end of the sixteenth and to the first half of the seventeenth century. In the nineteenth century she quotes the example of the nurse of Sulṭān 'Abdul 'Azīz who exerted considerable influence in the appointment and dismissal of the governor general and other important officials. Garnett's special interest, however, was the organization of the harem and much valuable information may be obtained from her in this connexion. It may have been common knowledge that the Sulṭān's household was composed entirely of women of slave origin, but what she shows particularly well is how discipline was exercised when such a large number of women – about one thousand, she claims – were brought under one roof. She points out that the harem had a constitution of its own, its customary laws, its high dignitaries, its intermediate and lower ranks, the *Vālide Sulṭāna* heading this feminine court, all members of which were required to take an oath of obedience to her by the new Sultān. To each of these women, excepting the *gueuzdes* 'those on whom the Sultān has cast an eye' (p. 386), is assigned a *dā'ira* – an allowance in money, a separate suite of apartments and a train of female slaves and eunuchs.

To a certain extent *The Women of Turkey* complements *Harem life in Egypt* with regard to the position of slaves. From the former one learns that slaves are bought for the Palace when very young so that they may be the better trained for the positions they are intended to occupy later. Thus 'negresses and others who give no promise of future beauty are placed under *kalfas* (ladies of the household) who bring them up as cooks, house-maids, bath-servants and laundry women' (p. 387). The 'finer specimens' who are destined for less laborious offices and may be called to fill 'higher positions' are taught elegance of deportment, dancing, singing and music and are initiated into all the 'graceful formalities of Oriental etiquette'. They are also taught Islamic religion and prayers while those who are meant to perform the duties of secretaries are taught to read fluently and write elegantly. It seems that their education may have been better than that of the Sultān's daughters, qualified by Garnett as 'desultory' (p. 392). The 'higher position' referred to above includes getting married to the Sultān. For though wives and favourites of the Sultān are generally chosen from among select beauties presented by the *Vālide Sulṭāna* and private individuals every slave in the palace may aspire to that dignity. Garnett quotes the case of the mother of Sulṭān ʿAbdul ʿAzīz who belonged to the lower ranks of the haremlik and that of Besmi who was born a slave but was later emancipated and married Sulṭān ʿAbdul Majīd I (1839-61). The other interesting example mentioned by Garnett is that if a *gueuzde* is not favourd by the Sulṭān she may be given a trousseau and a furnished apartment and in the case of an *iqbāl* she may be put on the civil list for a pension and she may be given in marriage to a chamberlain of the palace. The author actually met such a person who had been married by Sulṭān ʿAbdul ʿAzīz to his chief barber, apparently an important official at the Palace.

Women outside the harem

The great majority of Muslim women, that is, those belonging to the lower middle, peasant and urban lower classes lived outside the harem. A study of the role played by these women brings one closer to everyday reality. Moreover, empirical observations on the material conditions of women are to be regarded as complementary to the more theoretical discourses of the first section. The blending of such components may produce a more complete picture of Muslim women. As many accounts are available of social conditions prevailing in Egypt, this section will focus on Egyptian women.[20] The emphasis on the latter is also justified because of the impact of Egypt on other Arabo-Muslim nations, its importance past and present and its substantial population, numbering more than three million at the beginning of the nineteenth century and eleven million by the end. Many of the reform movements originating there later found an echo elsewhere in the Arab world.

Yet a writer like Savary whose contribution to the diffusion of knowledge about the Qur'ān and the Prophet is not negligible may create a misleading impression of the situation of women in Egypt. In his *Lettres sur l'Egypte* (1788) he waxes lyrical about the *almahs*, that is singing girls, who are credited with having received a better education than other women, with a good voice, mastery of language and poetical rules and without whom no celebration is complete. They are often invited to perform in harems and it is true that they are employed at weddings when they entertain the bride and her party at the baths.[21] According to Savary the ordinary people too have their *almahs*, but they lack the elegance, graces and knowledge of the other *almahs*. Cairo is full of them and he was struck by their lewd gestures and postures. When it comes to women outside this special category Savary claims that they have no role to play in public affairs. They are allowed to go to the baths once a week and to visit relatives and friends. They are not forbidden to cry on the tombs of the dead and Savary says that he often saw women on the outskirts of Cairo singing funeral hymns around tombs which they had covered with fragrant plants.[22] He sums up the lives of ordinary Egyptian women thus: bringing up their children, looking after their homes and living alone in the midst of their families (p. 150). However, he did notice women engaged in rice cultivation near Rosetta. In certain ways affinities seem to exist between Savary and Chabrol. In his book on Egypt the latter thought that the main occupation of the lower classes was to cook for their husbands and to fetch water which they carry skilfully in jugs on their heads (see Chapter 5, below). Their happiness consists in doing nothing and squatting on mats on the floor. This indolence which he finds typical of the Orient is more forgivable in Egypt because of the excessive heat. Where Savary simply noted women weeping at tombs Chabrol speaks of professional women mourners employed by the mosque and who wail loudly.

Chabrol's remarks on polygamy in Egypt may appear surprising. Whereas the general view is that it is practised by the wealthy Chabrol says that people of higher rank mostly have one wife, the desire to have children or to form a distinguished alliance being, according to him, the only factors which induce them to have a second wife. He finds polygamy more current among the lower classes.[23] He claims that they abuse the ease of repudiating their wives because it costs them only a modest dowry and that in their gross brutality they consider women unworthy of esteem. The novel information he provides on women of these classes is that apart from looking after their household they are also seen in the countryside sharing the work of their husbands in the fields or at least helping to make it less painful. Although they are forced to engage continually in outside work they still wear a *burqa*, a veil formed of muslin, worn on the nose and the mouth, especially when they see a man. Even more important is the information that the silk and cotton factories of Mahalla al-Kubra in lower Egypt employed between eight hundred and one thousand workers of both sexes.

In the chapter on 'Domestic Life' of the *Manners and customs of the modern Egyptians* Lane claims that for a bachelor who has become familiar with male Muslim society in Cairo it is not too difficult to obtain, directly and indirectly, correct and ample information on the condition and habits of the women. Apparently, many husbands of the middle and upper classes freely talk of affairs of the harem with one who shares their outlook and speaks Arabic. Lane's view is that in Egypt women are generally under less restraint than in any other country of the Ottoman empire. He noticed fairly frequently women of the lower classes flirting and jesting with men in public, while women of the middle and upper classes confined to harems do not consider themselves severely oppressed. He quotes the case of a divorced woman who refused to return to her husband and took him to court, although she lost her case before the judge. As to the women of the lower classes Lane thought they led active lives, even if they were condemned to greater drudgery than the men. Their main occupations included spinning cotton, linen, or woollen yarn at home and making fuel composed of the dung of cattle. Lane's conclusion was that the women were in a state of greater subjection to their husbands than was the case among the upper classes and they were rarely allowed to eat with their husbands. Some women in the towns were shopkeepers, selling bread and vegetables and thus contributed as much as their husbands, or even more than the latter, to the support of their families.

The artist and archaeologist E. Prisse d'Avennes (1807-79) who frequented the Parisian literary circle of Maxime du Camp, Arsène Houssaye and Théophile Gautier and became the founder of the review *Miroir de l'Orient* in 1852 had earlier left his impressions of modern Egypt in a manuscript.[24] The section entitled 'Moeurs et coutumes des Egyptiens au XIXe siècle' of the manuscript falls short of the reader's expectations. Despite the resemblance the title of his study has with those of Chabrol and Lane he contributes less than these writers to the Western perception of the role of Egyptian women. The beginning, however, is promising. He aims to correct a common European error consisting in believing that Oriental women are completely unaware of public affairs by pointing out that in every page of Ottoman history one finds women who intervene and are involved in the most important events. However, he gives the impression that all women in Egypt live in harems, although he rightly suggests that one can know something of their lives only from European and Levantine women who frequent them. This devotee of Montesquieu believes that the Egyptian woman is devoid of power and consideration and is treated like a slave by a man whom she flatters as one flatters one's prison guard and whom she hates because he treats her like a piece of furniture. Apart from embroidery, song and dance she has nothing to brighten up her life which is restricted within the family circle. Prisse d'Avennes could have culled such information from any author. In his desire to improve on stereotyped images of Muslim women he says that Muḥammad ʿAlī, the *wālī* of Egypt, often gives those who displease him to his mamlukes or beys who consider this favour as a mark of honour leading to success. He merely hints at the existence of prostitution in Egypt.

It is worth mentioning that prostitution was known in the times of ignorance and continued in the Middle East after the arrival of Islam which, like other religions, has not managed to eradicate it. Although prostitutes formed a small section of Egyptian women, who cannot be assessed on the basis of an unrepresentative class, like the women of the harem, they attracted an attention among European writers that appears out of proportion to their numbers. In the *Aperçu général* Clot Bey points out that prostitutes in Egypt had formed a corporation with rules and payed to the public treasury a considerable annual tax, but that the government of Muḥammad ʿAlī had given up on the tax and abolished prostitution.[25] He further tries to explain their existence by the loose morals prevailing in Egypt and by the fact that they were recruited from divorced women. The rise in prostitution may, however, have been caused by the disruption to family life resulting from Muḥammad ʿAlī's conscription policy and by the threat of starvation to their children faced by women who could not have the support of their absent husbands.[26]

As Victor Schoelcher, a critic of Muḥammad ʿAlī, explained in *L'Egypte en 1845* (1846), the reason behind the *wālī*'s abandoning this shameful tax and prohibiting the dance and trade of the courtesans was public outcry.[27] He mentions prostitutes being deported to Esneh, to the south of Luxor, and he queries the policy of dumping the prostitutes of Cairo and Alexandria there. According to him, driving away the prostitutes from the cities and spreading them in the provinces and villages of middle Egypt and the Nile delta is to infest ten places to save one. Besides, in the village of Kafr-Saya in the delta, the *almahs* were exercising their double function of dancers and courtesans, despite the laws of the Viceroy against prostitution. One result was that Esneh had become a disorderly place where all travellers stopped. The most famous of them perhaps was Flaubert who met Kuchuk Hanem there. He gives graphic and lurid details of his sexual encounters with Kuchuk and other prostitutes in his letters, one of which was to his friend Louis Bouilhet, dated 1 December 1849, and in his *Notes de Voyage* recording his travels to Egypt in the same period. Not surprisingly, Flaubert is included among nineteenth-century writers known to have suffered from a sexually transmitted disease. This did not prevent him from using part of the *Voyage* to give expression to his sexual fantasy later in major novels such as *Salammbo* (1862) and *La Tentation de saint Antoine* (1874).

Venereal disease was spread by the huge army Muḥammad ʿAlī had created in the 1820s and which later numbered between 250-300,000 men. Allowing women to join their husbands in military camps also created health problems. It then became clear that women health practitioners were needed to control the prostitutes of Cairo and other cities. So a School of Midwifery was created in 1832 in the School of Medicine, founded by Dr. Clot Bey in 1827 and attached to the hospital in Abu Zabal, north of Cairo. Schoelcher could not help expressing his admiration for the School of Midwifery which, to him, was a first in the history of Islam, since Muslim women were being employed in an important role. However, Khaled Famy sees the function of the School simply as a means of maintaining the health of soldiers threatened by syphilitic prostitutes and not the promotion of women's education. He mentions the employment of *ḥakīmas* in health clinics and police stations to check the virginity of young women. He sees this and the fact that they were not allowed to leave the School until they had found husbands from among the Egyptian doctors as a form of encroachment by the state on women's lives. He also stresses the low status of women doctors, enforced by an order of 1879. Whatever be the reasons for the opening of a School of Midwifery there is no doubt that it was an innovation in the world of Islam.[28]

In their modest ways Chabrol, Lane and Schoelcher contribute towards a more realistic perception of the position of women in Egypt. They are joined by Lady Duff Gordon who, in *Letters from Egypt (1862-1869)*, challenges the notion of Muslim women's utter subordination to men. She bears testimony to the outspokenness of Arab women: apparently when Sulṭān 'Abdul 'Azīz was due to visit Cairo Ismā'īl Pasha ordered all women of the lower orders to keep indoors for fear that they might 'shout out their grievances' (p. 73). She argued that women could and did, without blame, sue their husbands in law for the full payment of debt. Nothing, however, can match the outstanding contribution of Judith Tucker in her book *Women in nineteenth-century Egypt*. Using the registers of the *sharia* courts, those of the *Maḥkama Bāb al-'Alī* in Cairo and those of the *Maḥkama* in Mansūrah, an agricultural region in the Nile delta, she transforms our perception of women's social and economic role in nineteenth-century Egypt. She shows how all women – peasants and urban lower class included – used the courts to defend their interests against individual men and the state. While the upper classes rarely appeared in court, the peasants and lower class urban women appeared personally before the *qāḍī* in connexion with buying and selling property, defending inheritance rights, pursuing thieves, debtors and seeking familial support and divorce (p. 14).

It is not surprising that Muḥammad ʿAlī's military conscription deprived villages of men and that the women left behind assumed new roles in subsistence farming which became their responsibility (p. 42). In the absence of men women now became guardians of children in villages (p. 57). As a result of the *wālī*'s economic policies the lives of lower class and rural Egyptian women had been profoundly altered. Those formerly employed in textile cottage crafts, for example, were now employed in cotton and linen factories and the new industry of tarbush, that is, red cloth skull-caps, at Fuwwa, used exclusively female labour (p. 87). The number of women employed there was probably small, as was the case in the sugar and tobacco factories and cotton-processing plants set up by Muḥammad ʿAlī.[29] In towns many pedlars were women who sold bread, fruit, vegetables and dairy products: they were little affected by the change in the organization of agriculture and industry while the wealthier women traders supplied goods to the secluded women of the upper classes. A smaller group of wealthier and, presumably better educated, women were employed as tax farmers and administrators of *waqf* property (pp. 93-95). The remarkable fact is that despite the action of Oriental despots such as Muḥammad ʿAlī the *sharīʿa* courts still operated and often gave redress to women. After his death some aspects of his policy were reversed by ʿAbbās I (1849-54), but reinstated by Saʿīd subsequently. Although his attempts to industrialize failed, the new policies favoured merchants engaged in trade with Europe.[30]

It is never an easy matter to protect Muslim women from prejudices against them. As we go back in time it was even more difficult to do so. In nineteenth-century Egypt, as elsewhere in the world of Islam, they had to face prejudices that had accumulated over centuries. The attack against them was on two fronts. In the first place they had to contend with their male countrymen who had inherited the misogynist traits of some of the earlier Muslims. The latter had contributed to thwart the rather generous provisions of the Qur'ān and the Prophet himself for women. This situation produces a certain sense of despair among some modern writers who look back with nostalgic regret on *jāhiliyya* times when women, they think, were better off or enjoyed more freedom than under Islam.[31] It is a debatable point. If women appeared more active on the battlefront in the early days of Islam and even later, they do not make one forget the case of Hind, Abū Sufyān's wife, who chewed the liver of Ḥamza, the Prophet's uncle, at the battle of Uḥud. War atrocities did not, of course, last as long as contempt for women in peaceful times. As a sign of this contempt one may recall how some early Muslims used animal imagery against women – a device one has come to associate with the European polemical tradition of the seventeenth and eighteenth centuries against opponents.

In the second place Muslim women suffered from the myths European writers had been circulating about them from the seventeenth century onwards. One of these – the notion of soulless Muslim women – seems to have initially rested on a genuine misunderstanding of Islamic teaching. But it subsequently developed into European chauvinism at the expense of Muslim women. Soullessness was a proof of inferiority. Matters were not helped by the closer contact a few Egyptian women of ill-repute had with travellers who had gone East to seek sexual encounters.[32] Back home the travellers relived their experiences in titillating accounts which purported to give a true picture of Muslim women. To them it was natural that the soulless Muslim women would display loose morals since there was no Hereafter where they would be accountable. To be fair to travellers they were not the only ones to be using prostitutes. Moreover, awareness of the prejudices and practices of some Muslims might help temper indignation against the West. A demonstrable awareness might have been useful to Mohja Kahf who, in her book *Western representations of the Muslim woman* (1999), sought as a Muslim woman to deflect the debilitating impact upon her of such dominant representations through 'a strategy of wayward reading of texts' (p. 9). It is a pity that the book contains no Muslim views of women in the introduction to her survey.

There was some progress in the perception of Muslim women in the nineteenth century. That was partly because the harem had become more accessible, especially to European women who, despite some racial overtone in Lott's account, helped to strip it of the sensuality and chaos with which it had been tainted by Montesquieu in the eighteenth century and of the illusions of Romantic poets in the nineteenth century. Although it housed but a small percentage of Muslim women it had become symbolic of the exotic and 'otherness'. Therefore learning from women writers that the harem was fairly well disciplined and a place sparsely furnished where people actually prayed might be something of an anti-climax – a small price to pay for an injection of reality into a world where harem women no longer appear mysterious. Above all, the major contribution of the nineteenth century is the light it throws on the small progress made by Muslim women towards independence, social and economic. Gone is their helplessness, even in countries where Oriental despots are in evidence. The removal of a feeling of helplessness is only a small step in the right direction. For further progress to take place much remains to be done in various fields.

Notes

1. See al-Bukhārī on the book of *farā'iḍ* (inheritance) in *Ṣaḥīḥ*, vol. 8, pp. 470-502.

2. See *Account of Egypt*, Bodleian MS. Eng. misc. d. 34, fol. 132 vo.

3. See A.W. Boudhiba, *La sexualité en Islam* (Paris, 1975), p. 21.

4. Y. Qaraḍāwī, *Fatāwā Mu'āṣira* (1993), vol. 2, p. 373, quoted in A.Z. Yamani's paper, p. 15.

5. See Mary Hossain, 'Women and Paradise', *Journal of European Studies* (1989), vol. 19, pp. 293-310.

6. See *The Complete Letters of Lady Wortley Montagu*, ed. R. Halsband (Oxford, 1965), vol. 1, p. 362

7. *Voyages en Perse* (Rouen, 1723), vol. 7, p. 59.

8. *Lettres persanes*, ed. P. Vernière (Paris, 1960), p. 57.

9. *The Complete Poetical Works*, ed J.J. McGann (Oxford, 1980), vol. 1, p. 144.

10. *The Complete Poetical Works*, vol. 3, p. 419.

11. *Islam and Romantic Orientalism* (London, 1994), p. 221. There is no distinction in Islam between the soul of women and that of men.

12. These include Umm Ḥarām, a martyr who died in the seventh century and later Nafīsa, reputed to know the Qur'ān and commentaries by heart and whose shrine is near the mosque of Ibn Ṭūlūn in Cairo. See Margaret Smith, *Rabia. The life and work of Rabia and other women mystics in Islam.*

13. See the article on Fāṭima by H. Lammens in *The Shorter Encyclopaedia of Islam* (Leiden, 1974). The much longer article by L. Veccia Vaglieri in the new edition does not shed any more light on this particular point. The doubt expressed by M. Ṭāhā Ḥusain about Fāṭima in the Islamic paradise is unjustified, although his reservation on Nerval's example to illustrate ideal aspiration in Islam is justified. See his *Présence de l'Islam dans la littérature romantique en France* (Cairo, 1955), p. 355.

14. In *Religion in Montesquieu's Lettres persanes, Studies on Voltaire* (Geneva, 1970), vol. 72, p. 117.

15. In the section 'Les nuits du Ramazan' of the *Voyage* Nerval claims that women of the harem in Constantinople are learned and that every lady belonging to the Sultān's household receives an excellent education in poetry, music, painting, history and geography. Apparently, many of them are poets whose poetry circulates at Pera.

16. *Letters from Egypt (1862-1869)* (London, 1969), p. 121.

17. Her two-volume work, published in London, was dedicated to Khedive Ismā'īl.

18. Lady Duff Gordon, on the other hand, admired the harem she visited in Alexandria with its antique enamelled tiles covering the panels of

the walls, divided by carved woods, all very old and rather dilapidated but superb.

19. See Mohja Kahf, *Western representations of the Muslim woman* (Austin, 1999), p. 160.

20. In *The women of Turkey*, Lucy Garnett makes some interesting points about Kurdish women whom she describes as 'nominally Moslems' (p. 121). They do not veil themselves very strictly when abroad: their blue checked sheet and screen of black horse hair is seldom pulled down, except by ladies of high rank who wish to pass through the streets incognito, while women of the lower classes go about with faces uncovered. Male visitors are freely received by the assembled family and in the domestic circle women are treated as equals by men. Equally significant is that women of nomadic tribes take a lively interest in the social and political affairs of the tribe and that the Kurds leave to women the business of settling accounts with tax-farmers.

21. See Lane, chapter 6 of *Manners and customs.*

22. In *Une année dans le Sahel* (1879), p. 239, Eugène Fromentin claims that once a week, on Fridays, under the pretext of honouring the dead, the women of Algiers flock to the cemetery. It is simply a meeting place for pleasure-seeking women, a few of whom have been authorized to go out by their husbands. The trip is enlivened by conversation and laughter and the women sit near the tombs where they indulge in eating. They get rid of their veil which they hang on cactus plants when no indiscreet eyes are watching. The only indiscreet eyes were those of Fromentin himself. He later mentions a court proceeding involving a woman who was asking for a divorce, behind the iron bars of a window, invisible under her veil (p. 256).

23. In *Women in nineteenth-century Egypt* (Cambridge, 1985), Judith Tucker shows that according to the Mansūrah records of 1800-1820 polygamy was not widespread among peasant families in that period (p. 53).

24. See Bibliothèque Nationale de France, N. a. fr. 20424, fols. 2-20.

25. Judith Tucker points out that by the 1860s the state was permitting and profiting from prostitution (p. 153).

26. See Khalid Fahmy's article 'Women, Medicine and Power in nineteenth-century Egypt' in *Remaking Women. Feminism and modernity in the Middle East,* ed. Lila Abu-Lughod (Princeton, 1998), p. 42.

27. In the section 'Le harem' of the *Voyage*, Nerval explains that the *'ulamā'* complained without having any success for a long time and that it was only when pious Muslims of Cairo offered to pay the tax being levied on the prostitutes by the government that these women were exiled to Esneh, in upper Egypt.

28. For a detailed account of education in nineteenth-century Egypt, see Heyworth-Dunne's *Introduction to the history of education in modern Egypt.*

29. See Leila Ahmed, p. 132.

30. See Hourani's *A History of the Arab peoples*, pp. 275-276.

31. See Margaret Smith, p. 141 and Leila Ahmed, p. 42. According to 'Urwa b. Az-Zubair, 'Ā'isha said there were four types of marriage during the *Jāhiliyya*, but only one was a proper marriage. It is a kind of euphemism to describe the other three as marriages as they involve some abominable practices. See *Ṣaḥīḥ*, vol. 7, pp. 44-45.

32. Sexual encounters were also sought by European women in the Middle East. Isabelle Eberhartd found in Algeria a place where she could indulge her sexual passions. Sometimes British women such as Jane Digby and Emily Keene fell in love with Muslim men in the Middle East and decided to marry them and settle there, while Gertrude Bell was initially drawn there after failed love affairs. See Derek Hopwood, *Sexual encounters in the Middle East* (Reading, 1999), p. 109 and pp. 226-228.

CHAPTER 5

Travellers to the World of Islam

European perceptions of Islam were derived from a variety of writings, the most popular writing being perhaps that of travellers to the Middle East. The popularity of these writings was due to the fact that travellers' accounts were accessible to the ordinary reader whose interest in Islam may have been stimulated by earlier fictitious works such as Giovanni Paolo Marana's *L'espion du Grand Seigneur* 1684, 1686, its continuation in English as *Letters Writ by a Turkish Spy* in 1687, both based on manuscripts in the original Italian, Antoine Galland's translation of the *Arabian Nights* between 1704 and 1717, and Montesquieu's *Lettres persanes*, 1721. Fiction and other types of writings coming from the pen of the two masters of the French Enlightenment – Voltaire and Diderot – kept alive the interest in Islam in the period that stretches from the 1740s to the 1770s. The late eighteenth century also produced stimulating popular literature on the world of Islam, the most influential books being Mouradga D'Ohsson's *Tableau général de l'empire ottoman,* 1787 and Volney's *Voyage en Egypte et en Syrie*, 1787. To these must be added the *Della letteratura turchesca* by the abbé G.B. Toderini (1728-99), first published in Venice in 1787, then translated by the abbé de Cournand into French in 1789 and by Hansleutner into German in 1790.

In a sense, Volney's *Voyage* marks the culmination of more than two centuries of travel writing on the Middle East. How to explain this European fascination with the region? It was nourished not only by literature of the imagination but it also had a more solid foundation based on reality – the diplomatic relations between the European powers and two rival Muslim empires: Ottoman and Persian. Ottoman envoys from the Porte had been sent to France as early as 1533, including Sulaymān Āghā in 1669, and at the level of ambassadors in the eighteenth century. Following the repulse of the Ottomans from Vienna by a coalition of Christian forces in 1683 and the resulting peace, travel to the Ottoman Empire and interest in Sunnī Islam naturally increased. Relations between European countries and Persia were late in developing. Ground was made up during the reign of Shāh ʿAbbās I (1587-1618) of the Safavid dynasty of Persia (1502-1722). Abbas allowed European missionaries and traders to settle in the main centres of the Empire, the Persians being then perceived as the most tolerant of Islamic communities. After the foundation of the new French East India Company in 1664, many French trade missions went to Persia. As a result of their country's foreign policy towards Persia the number of French travellers to it increased. These were joined by other Europeans. Travellers to both the Ottoman and Persian Empires were generally appreciative of the architecture of the mosques and interested in the religious practices they observed and, in the case of Shīʿite Persia, the spectacular celebrations of Muḥarram in the streets. Some were simply curious about the beautiful gardens, the designs of the streets and the public baths. Travel to the Middle East had thus become a long-established tradition by the early decades of the nineteenth century.

Travellers' narratives of the following years dealing with the Ottoman Empire, the Holy Land and neighbouring provinces, Egypt and Arabia, cemented this tradition. They had perhaps become even more important because they reached a wider public with little knowledge of Middle Eastern languages who were yet keen to know something of the pillars of Islam, its legal provision, its moral teaching, its educational system, its holy places and its architecture. It should be pointed out that these themes are not neatly arranged by travellers for the benefit of readers and that the information is only gradually revealed to them. Moreover, the importance of travellers should not be exaggerated. In his stimulating chapter 'The Western Image and Western Studies of Islam', Maxime Rodinson, after acknowledging our debt to specialists who 'transmitted the findings of the history of religions, of historical linguistics and of physical anthropology in the popularized form of a boundless magnification of the power of religion, language, and race' included travellers among the group of people to whom the problems of actual contemporary life in Middle Eastern countries had been left for practical observation.[1] The suggestion that all travellers contributed in some practical way to this study of the contemporary Middle East and living Islam needs to be qualified, as it is only partly true.

While accepting that the manners of living cities are more worthy of observation than the remnants of dead cities, Gérard de Nerval, for example, complains to Théophile Gautier at the end of August 1843 that he has already lost the more beautiful half of the universe and that soon he will know of no place in which he can find refuge for his dreams.[2] He deeply misses the Egypt of his imagination: Egypt imagined is obviously better than Egypt experienced and remembered. Nerval unashamedly proclaims the superiority of a reconstructed East to the actual East.

Nerval is not the only writer to declare his preference for an imagined Orient. Before him Lamartine had, in his *Voyage en Orient* (1835), expressed similar feelings, even if there was an evolution in his mental state later. As he set out on his journey on 8 October 1832 and sees the plains of Canaan, he seems to regret that up to that point travel had preoccupied his eyes and his mind. He would have preferred a voyage of the heart and soul.[3] But things change. Often during his travel in Judaea and Palestine, poetic impressions became merged with souvenirs and the journey became a prayer. In other words, an imaginary Orient was taking shape in Lamartine's mind. This does not mean that Lamartine saw nothing of the Orient as it existed in the first part of the nineteenth century. He did meet real people going about their business and leaving him with factual impressions of the Middle East and Islam. But it would be more appropriate to note that with Lamartine, as with others, the imaginary world co-exists with the real world so that there are limits to the practical nature of their observations. In the case of Chateaubriand, it is not so much the imagination as the history of previous centuries that often eclipses the present.

His *Itinéraire de Paris à Jerusalem* (1811) cannot be said to inaugurate the tradition of travel to the Middle East in the nineteenth century. However, such was its impact and such was the stature of its author and that of the author of the *Voyage en Orient* that these books led a critic to draw some hasty conclusions. One was that the tradition of travel to the Orient, abandoned since Chateaubriand, was revived with a new vigour between the 1830s and 1840s. The fact is that it had never been abandoned, either shortly before or after him.[4] Throughout the century European travellers continued to visit the Ottoman Empire, Persia or Iran, the Holy Land, Syria, Lebanon, the Arabian peninsula and North Africa, especially Egypt. Inspired by love of the exotic, they also had anthropological, commercial, economic and political objectives. Whereas in the seventeenth and eighteenth centuries, the Arabian peninsula had received scant attention from travellers, excepting Carsten Niebuhr, in the *Description de L'Arabie (1773)*, now they went to the Yemen[5] and other parts of Arabia, even if J.L. Burckhardt and R. Burton found safety in disguise when they visited the holy cities of Makka and Madina. Apart from the Ottoman Empire, what fascinated travellers most was Egypt.[6] After the golden age of travel to Persia earlier,[7] Egypt's turn came. Cairo, its capital, had always attracted interest for various reasons. To Nerval it became the city of the *Arabian Nights,* although Baghdad was that city. All the stories of the *Nights* passed through his head from the moment of his arrival in Egypt. On one occasion Nerval follows some women in a street of Cairo crossed by rich bazaars. Imagining that he is reliving the adventure of the young friend of Bedreddin (in *Night* 133), he wishes he could see the women's faces behind their veils in exchange for the price of his rich garments (*Oeuvres,* ii. 121). Egypt, however, was not merely the land of dreams where European travellers could indulge their fantasies. Its invasion by Napoleon in 1798 was no dream but an event of historical significance. The Institut created by the Emperor there in August 1798 was not only an agency for French domination but it also fostered the academic study of modern Egypt in various fields, culminating in the publication in twenty-three volumes between 1809 and 1828 of the *Description de l'Egypte.* On a more modest scale was the cultural contribution made by the Société Egyptienne, that is, the Association littéraire d'Egypte, the library founded by Dr. Abbott.[8] For his part Jean François Champollion had led a scientific expedition to Egypt in 1828, making a major advance in the study of inscriptions and hieroglyphs and subsequently creating a school of Egyptologists. If the study of ancient Egypt by Champollion did not bring with it any immediate advantage to that of modern Egypt and Islam, at least it served to maintain the interest of the general public in that part of the world of Islam.[9] So a reader curious about Egypt had at least three choices: ancient Egypt, the Egypt of dreams and Islamic Egypt of the nineteenth century.

The Ottoman Empire

It should be pointed out that the Middle East is too vast a region to facilitate discussion of every country forming part of it. One needs to be selective. We may perhaps begin with the Ottoman Empire, considered moribund by Europeans but not yet dead. Many writers referred to 'Turk' and 'Turkey': these terms, not used by the Ottomans themselves, are often unavoidable. What new insights could the reader expect to find in Toderini's *De la littérature des Turcs*? Here it is worth mentioning that despite its title the book deals not only with Turkish literature, but also with other aspects of Islamic civilization. The author's remarks on the 'Turks', especially at the beginning, are always placed in a wider context which brings Islam to light and always stress the Arabs' contribution to Turkish cultural achievement. Toderini has some affinity with d'Ohsson in that the Italian and the Armenian-born writer who served Sweden as a diplomat focus more attention on the Turks than other peoples of the Middle East. He made a deep impact on subsequent writers discussing Turkey, as they often quoted him (see below). Like d'Ohsson,[10] Toderini was well placed to give readers his impressions of the Ottomans and Islam. He was attached to Gazzoni, the Venetian ambassador whom he accompanied to Constantinople in 1781, staying there until 1786. In the preface to his work Toderini states that he visited Turkish academies and kept on friendly terms with Ottoman scholars, frequented their libraries and got hold of many manuscript catalogues and reports which he had translated. On a more delicate and controversial point, he claims to have appealed to the *muftī*, that is a scholar known for his learning and his ability to rule on disputed questions by the exercise of independent judgement, for a *fatwā* (a decision given in cases of law and conscience by an expert in the *sharīʿa*). Such a claim gives the impression that Toderini's views on Islam are always based on direct experience. Although this is often the case, he also has recourse to textual sources at other times.

As a philosophy teacher Toderini could be expected to show some interest in Islamic theology. Among the various questions on dogma, liturgy and moral teaching he chooses to focus on the dispute that plagued Islam in the ninth century – the question of the uncreated Qur'ān, which gave rise to fierce controversies before it was accepted by Sunnī Islam in about 849. Toderini was perhaps too ambitious in wishing to tackle a complex theological issue which had baffled previous European writers.[11] He has some understanding of the significance of this question for Muslims when he states that much of the authority of the Qur'ān seemed to them to be taken away if it is deemed to be created since no man has ever been able to make two verses which equalled its elegance and eloquence. However, like many other Westerners, he does not fully realize that to the Sunnī Muslim, the Qur'ān is the book of God, His speech and is part of His essence. It is therefore uncreated: if it were created, it would be like other creations of God and it could lose some of its significance and perish.

Greater awareness of legal issues in Islam is shown by Toderini who thinks that *fiqh*, styled Turkish jurisprudence by him, is one of the most learned and brilliant studies of the Muslims (i. 23). He adds that it is considered sacred and canonical, coming from the Prophet as head and founder of religion, inspired by a divine light. Muslims would express themselves differently, looking on Muḥammad not as founder, but as reformer of Islam. Toderini is on firmer ground with the remark that when the Qur'ān, the *Sunna* and the theologians are silent on a point of law, it is fixed by the *Qānūn-nāmeh* or royal legislation associated with Mehmet II and Suleyman (1520-66). However, he seems to exaggerate the power of the prince. For he makes many statutes, except in matters of faith, depend on the will of the sovereign who can dispose of the property, the person, the liberty and the life of his subjects. To defend his point of view he maintains that sometimes the *muftī* through fear or adulation modifies his *fatwā* to satisfy the prince's will and that many *muftīs* who have delivered their judgement in accordance with the law have been deposed by the latter. Toderini then alters his stand, acknowledging that the *'ulamā'* (the body of informed Muslim religious scholars) may be sent into exile, but that their goods cannot be confiscated and that they cannot be put to death. He seems to contradict himself with the statement that the right of property is respected by the sultan for his Turkish subjects and other subject nations. He draws attention to the imperial document given to the patriarch of the Armenians in Constantinople in 1782. In it the sultan stipulates that the gardens, vineyards and other property belonging to the churches should be protected. Toderini categorically maintains that Rycaut and Montesquieu strayed from the truth, particularly Montesquieu when he claims that the sultan is master and heir of the property of his subjects. In his view, it is using a false proof to show Oriental despotism (see below).

Toderini denounces the law of talion of Muslims, because he believes it condones crying injustice. Leaning on L. Marracci, translator and commentator of the Qur'ān, he states that the master can kill his slave, that the Muslim free-born or slave can kill a non-Muslim without incurring the death penalty. Now the Qur'ānic law, which even today is applied in countries such as Saudi Arabia, is different. For *Sūra* 2: 178 provides: 'O believers! It is prescribed to you (to apply) the law of the talion in case of murder: a free man for a free man, a slave for a slave, a woman for a woman.' This law of the talion marks some progress on the *tha'r* or blind vengeance which puts all the clan of the victim under the obligation to exact vengeance on the murderer or any member of his clan, leading to lengthy and often bloody feuds. The Qur'ānic verse adds that with the agreement of the victim's family compensation is acceptable.

The emphasis is, as to be expected, on the culture of the Turks. Right at the start, Toderini tries to dispose of a popular prejudice which he says is deeply rooted in the minds of many European scholars who firmly believe and even write that Muḥammad, fearing that the practice of science might harm his doctrine, strictly forbade all types of study and made the ignorance of his followers the basis of his religion. Toderini was probably thinking not so much of scholars as of other Europeans. For scholars of his century and later times made a significant contribution to the diffusion of knowledge about Islam. To destroy the popular prejudice, the abbé quotes words which the Prophet is reported as having said: 'Seek knowledge be it from the furtherest boundaries of China.' He also expresses his strong admiration for the phrase engraved on the door of the library of Mehmet II at Constantinople: 'Study of the sciences is a divine commandment for the true believers'. The conclusion he draws on the Prophet's teaching is fair: the latter had never preached ignorance. He then devotes a whole chapter to the studies of the Turks with regard to religion, noting how the Qur'ān, being the foundation of religion and the civil laws of Muslims, became the first object of their study. He was struck by the countless *tafāsīr*, that is Qur'ānic commentaries, in the library of the Hagia Sofia, of which he had a catalogue in his manuscripts, and in other libraries of Constantinople. He knew of the existence of many *tafāsīr* by cultured Turks in the library of Sulṭān

'Abdul Ḥamīd (1725-89). He also saw professors of *tafsīr* teaching in the mosques: while entering the Sulemaniya in Constantinople he noted some poor students who were listening to the lesson in religious silence.

It is refreshing to note the ways in which Toderini stresses the achievement of the Turkish people, especially in various cultural fields not directly linked to religion. The quantity and quality of books in Arabic, Arabic translations of Greek originals which the Turks possess, the honour and considerable advantage which accrue to the Ottomans from their cultivation of literature strongly impressed him. Toderini claims he knows no nation that is keener on the sciences and more devoted to study. The Voltaire of the *Lettres philosophiques* (1734) would very much have liked to hear that there is no nation where knowledge is given greater consideration and where the most dazzling and lucrative jobs are given to scholars. On the other hand, if every educated Turk knows Arabic and Persian, he cannot profit from the new Enlightenment from Europe because of the pride which he feels for his literature and because of the Muslim superstition which makes him scorn all forms of education coming to him from countries foreign to his religion. Thus he would consider it a kind of opprobrium to learn European languages, styled 'languages of the infidels' (I. 7). Toderini, however, notes some evolution among the Turks of his day. He knows two who read and write Italian and he quotes the case of a young Turk who kept on asking him for logarithmic tables. Toderini's real aim in *De la littérature des Turcs* is to refute Tott[12] who claimed the Turks had produced no literature and also Savary[13] who was mistaken about Turkish literature, although it had fallen from its first glory over the past sixty years. He points out that with the help of so many books of eloquence that the Turks read with care it is not surprising that there are many good writers among them. As far as prose is concerned, all the scholars agree to give first place to the *muftī* Choja Suddedin, who had been translated into Italian by Bratuto.

The end of volume 1 and volumes 2 and 3 highlight the literary achievement of the Turks. Poetry is at the forefront, for the Turks having before them the excellent models of poetry existing among the Arabs and Persians and 'naturally inclined to cultivate poetry could not help having good poets' (I. 190). Toderini quotes 'Abdul Luftī who speaks of three hundred poets from Morad (Amurath I, 1319-89) to the time of Suleyman I. In *Zubdatul Ash'ār (Flower of poetry)* nine Turkish poets appear among a selection of five hundred and forty other poets, the most famous poets being Baki Effendi and Kahiri Misri. To uphold his point of view, Toderini has recourse to Demetrius Cantemir.[14] But he also has his own sources. For example, he points out from among his manuscripts a notebook consisting of light Turkish plays which were appreciated by the educated people. At Constantinople, he notes the existence of a famous academy of poetry which gives writers academic names distinguishing them on the basis of their talent and the good verses they have written. He also quotes 'Abduallāh Manreeset who told him that under Muṣṭafā III (1757-73) poets often formed assemblies and held academic sessions.

Volume ii of *De la littérature des Turcs* gives pride of place to the academies and libraries of Constantinople. The author is particularly interested in four academies, the first of which dates from before 1453. He recognizes that the academies of Constantinople never had the same lustre as those of the Arabs and Persians, but they are no less significant, being regulated by wise laws and composed of learned teachers, endowed with rich foundations and capable of accommodating and feeding in separate colleges a large number of students. Toderini's remarks are certainly exaggerated, for these academies are made to surpass all those of European nations. It would appear that before the capture of Constantinople the Ottoman princes showed their generosity in founding, amidst wars, many academies of literature and religion where *mudarris*, *qāḍīs, muftīs* and *'ulamā'* were trained. Toderini mentions the foundation of an academy at Bursa by Orcan in 1335, which became famous for its practice of the liberal arts. Apparently, its teachers drew a large number of students from Persia and Arabia.

Among the sultans who distinguished themselves by their interest in the arts, Toderini singles out Mehmet II, using d'Herbelot, but also notes obtained in 1784. He also mentions the academy of Sultan Selim I (1512-20), which had strong collections in Arabic, Persian and Turkish to which Ottoman and European writers do justice. He then refers to thirteen public libraries in Constantinople, hoping that specialists in Oriental languages might be encouraged to draw up a catalogue of all the manuscripts in Turkish libraries, for this was the only way of enriching by a new fund of knowledge the literature and sciences of Europe (ii. 30). He pays particular attention to the library of the Topkapi Palace about which travellers and scholars have spoken but locked in their closets and relying on reports 'éloignés de la vérité'.[15] From a catalogue copied in forty days by a page of the harem, the reader learns that this library contains books on religion, the sciences, history, moral philosophy and politics. As for Mehmet II who was skilled in science and literature, he neither burnt nor destroyed any of the libraries of the Greek emperors. Moreover, he enriched Ottoman literature with books from Europe which he had translated into Turkish.

The moral philosophy of the Turks appealed to Toderini very much. He obviously had the élite of the people in mind.[16] The teaching derived from books seems to him to confirm the practice of their everyday life. For the Turkish nobility, the pages, the courtiers and harem officials are brought up with a politeness of manners superior to the urbanity and civility of other nations. The great are the first to salute their inferiors. Toderini shows that in all libraries, there is a separate and numerous section on books of moral philosophy. He thinks that in this field the Turkish contribution is strengthened by sentences and precepts derived from the Qur'ān. However, he minimizes their Qur'ānic inspiration by suggesting that they have been transcribed from the Old and New Testament. He says that the Turks also rely on the fables of Pilpai, translated into Turkish prose by Ali Celebi for Sultan Suleyman because of their lessons in moral philosophy. Toderini may have even borrowed a fine trait from Mehemet Effendi, Turkish ambassador to France in 1720 and one of the jewels in the crown of Turkish moral philosophy. He mentions the *Feranameh,* dedicated to one of the sons of Amurath III (1574-95) by Navali, his teacher. In his view this book is written in the same taste as the books written by Aristotle for Alexander. In this field, then, Toderini's efforts may have strengthened those of Barbier de Meynard when he later translated Zamakhsharī (see above).

In his survey of Turkish civilization, Toderini did not overlook the Turks' interest in the sciences. Indeed chapter 8 which deals with physics and natural history is one of the most interesting chapters in the book. The reader learns there that the study of physics is open to all Muslims in the academies of Constantinople. Toderini affirms that it is necessary to the Turkish *'ulamā'* and that one needs to know logic and physics before embarking on Islamic theology. How the world of Islam would be enlightened if what Toderini says were always true! The abbé believes that Muslims had the advantage over Europeans because in the midst of so many translations from Greek into Arabic, two were close to Aristotle's philosophy, al-Fārābī and Avicenna while Latin translations of Arab works were spoilt by the commentaries of the abbé Andres (1, 106).

Apart from Euclid's *Optics,* translated into Arabic by Nasireddin, the Turks have that of Alhazen, that is, the Arab Ibn al-Haytham (965-1039). Toderini appreciates Alhazen's *Optics,* the *Kitāb al-Manāẓir,* published in 1572, because 'it has a useful and witty discussion of astronomical refractions' (1, iii). One learns that in book 7, chapter 4 of Alhazen, is a fine theory for the use of spectacles. But as Toderini points out, spectacles were invented by Europeans two centuries later, by Savino Armati, towards 1250. He maintains that the famous passage of Roger Bacon who made some look upon him as the inventor of spectacles and telescopes is precisely the one taken from book 7 of Alhazen. Indeed, the *Kitāb al-Manāẓir* has influenced not only scientists like Roger Bacon and Peckham, but has left traces in the optical works of Kepler and Newton. Thus, two centuries earlier, Toderini had anticipated to some extent the position taken by the historian of Islamic science, Ziauddin Sardar. The latter thought that the history of science should be remade, as it casts doubt on the intellectual integrity of the West.[17] It is clear, however, that Toderini's perspective on Turkey relates more to the past than to his own times.

This does not necessarily mean that Toderini is unaware of weaknesses in the scientific performance of Islamic countries such as Turkey in the late eighteenth century. In his view the particular weakness lies in Turkish medicine. It is not that the Turks underrate medicine – all the public libraries are full of medical works. Although operation on the human body is supposed to be forbidden in Islam, Turkish medicine has recourse to it. In fact, Constantinople is a vast metropolis full of Turkish, Jewish, Greek, Arab and Christian doctors. The exchange of medical information combined with a rich supply of good books from all countries and in all languages should have provided medicine in Constantinople with the enlightenment of European academies. Yet nothing of the kind happens: contemporary Turkish medicine languishes. Toderini attributes the weakness to the Turkish government. He points out that Muṣṭafā III who liked science and was interested in medical studies wanted to remedy the situation, but all his plans died with him. As an example of Turkish weakness in medicine, he says that in his days few Turks used inoculation, since the common people would consider it contrary to destiny and religion.

Nevertheless, in volume iii Toderini has praise for the Ottomans, 'the only ones among Muslims to have introduced a national printing press for the advancement of study and science' (iii, 15). Indeed, the first Ottoman press was created in 1726 in the reign of Sultan Ahmet III. Toderini takes the opportunity to mention Turkish and European books published after that. He is thus to be placed in the line of European writers from Galland to d'Ohsson about whose sympathy for the Turks there can be no doubt. Of course, he does not approve the behaviour of the Turks when he observes that the mosaics in the Hagia Sofia have been spoilt by them. He even claims that they desecrated all churches which they converted into mosques.[18] His great merit, however, lies in his attempt to destroy the myth that Islam preaches ignorance by loudly proclaiming the great efforts made by its representatives in the Ottoman Empire to promote literature and science. His attempt is commendable, even if he often forgets contemporary Turkey to delve into the past. But as happens with many other writers, the sympathy he shows for the Turkish people does not go further by encompassing their religion. For that one has to wait until Lamartine.

There is a familiar note in the account of Turkey given in the early nineteenth century by Thomas Thornton, who spent some fifteen years in Constantinople and the Turkish provinces, fourteen of these at the British factory in Constantinople. The title of his book, *The Present State of Turkey* (1809), is reminiscent of earlier works on the subject such as P. Rycaut's *The present state of the Ottoman Empire* (1668). However, although the two themes that preoccupy him – the culture of the Turks and Turkish despotism – have been discussed by previous writers like Montesquieu and Toderini, he shows some refinement in tackling these questions. In order to get to grips with his subject, Thornton sets it in its broader historical context which often involves reference to other Muslims such as the Arabs. He dismisses the theory that the alleged ferocity of the Turks can be attributed to Islam, which he says has been much misrepresented since Muḥammad not only allowed but advised his followers both male and female to apply themselves to learning, its acquisition being a religious duty. This leads him to stress the cultural achievement of the early Abbasid caliphs and to omit mentioning the destruction caused by Tamerlane so as to concentrate on him as patron of Ḥāfiẓ and promoter of the fine arts. He defends Mehmet II against the charge of being cruel, perfidious and iconoclastic, preferring to see him as a man of piety, learning and with a knowledge of modern languages and an interest in science. The conqueror of Constantinople did in fact establish a great complex of schools which trained the high imperial officials as did Suleyman the Magnificent whose reign Thornton describes as the Augustan age of Turkish literature.

Thornton draws attention to the natural consequence of the love of learning which distinguished many of the Arab caliphs. They showed a desire to diffuse and perpetuate knowledge by multiplying copies of works of their most esteemed authors and depositing their collections in public libraries which they endowed with funds for the salary of librarians and maintenance of buildings. As he points out, the example of these princes was imitated by the Ottoman sultans and several viziers, a *madrasa* (college) and *kitāb-khāne* (library) being considered as appendages necessary to a *jāmiʿ* (mosque).

After paying due homage to d'Ohsson and Toderini for information on the cataloguing of books in Constantinople libraries, Thornton refutes the suggestion that the Turks are illiterate. On the contrary, the *'ulamā'* undergo a long and laborious course of study. The studies in *madrasas* are conducted with order and method and these include grammar, logic, rhetoric, theology, Qur'ān and *tafsīr*, philosophy and jurisprudence. [19] More than Toderini perhaps, Thornton understands too well the nature of Turkish backwardness in science. He is scathing about the fact that contemporary Turks know nothing of telescopes, microscopes, electrical machines and have not kept up to date with the discoveries of the last centuries in navigation, geography, agriculture, chemistry and other sciences. What they do in these disciplines is based on antiquated routine.

Despite his strictures, Thornton is really well disposed towards the Turks. In literature, for example, he is against applying the principles of European literary criticism to judge the Turks. He points out that in European poetry imagery is sparingly used whereas the 'Asiaticks are impelled at pleasure by the capricious wantonness of luxuriant imagination to form the most heterogeneous combinations' (p. 49). Everyone who knows Milton will not share this view of uncontrolled imagination being uniquely Oriental. Thornton's fairmindedness, however, cannot be questioned. The criteria he lays down are exacting. He states that knowledge of an Oriental language is not enough to judge Oriental poetry. The critic should not only be aware that all sources of poetical imagery are so different from those of European nations, but should have instructed himself in the natural history of Asia, modes of living of Asians, their civil and religious institutions and the chief events of their history. Thornton also admires the passionate fondness of the Turks for history. Without quoting any name, he pays homage to Ottoman historians who have compiled their works from the authentic records of their own nation, however different in style from European productions, and for their fidelity and impartiality. What he particularly admires in them is their aim of being useful to their fellow citizens rather than gaining the favour of their princes by flattery and misrepresentation, for they expose and censure the vices of sultans and rash counsels of ministers.

The Present state of Turkey offers some interesting observations on Turkish despotism. Thornton sees its basis in the fact that legislative and executive powers are vested in one person, unlike James Porter who sees its basis in the absence of law and contract. He also takes issue with Montesquieu in the *Esprit des lois* (book v, chapter 12) because the latter defines Turkish despotism not as it is observed in human society, but by comparison drawn from the abuse of power over brutes or inanimate matter. He challenges the notion that because the Turkish government is despotic by nature and in theory therefore people should conclude that all its possible atrocities really exist in practice. He even considers the power of the Ottoman sultans over their subjects to be as legitimate as that of every other sovereign in the world. He argues that Turkey is free from despotism because in a despotic state the law can be nothing but the will of the master and because universal fear of the monarch is essential to its existence, whereas the sultan is bound by paramount religious law and the army exerts a power which the sultan himself is constrained to fear. Thornton shares some affinity with Anquetil-Duperron who had shown that a code of written laws binding both prince and subjects existed in Turkey and India as did individual rights of ownership.[20] Thornton, however, insists that though in theory the sultan was the proprietor of all immovable wealth in the empire, except funds destined for religious purposes, he was restrained both by law and custom in the exercise of this right over the property of his subjects, which was not immediately employed in the service of the government and that only in default of natural heirs did such property lapse to the crown.[21] He challenges Porter who had maintained that the power and dignity of the *ʿulamāʾ* was perpetual and hereditary.[22] His point is that power and dignity are hereditary not in individuals but in the order and that the *ʿulamāʾ* now hold office only for a year. He finds in the *ʿulamāʾ* checks and balances to the arbitrary power of the sovereign while the law authorizes the sultan to banish the *ʿulamāʾ*, but not kill them. However, Thornton has to admit that if Islam teaches the reciprocal duties to be observed by the prince and his subjects, it cannot enforce a just administration of government.

The Holy Land and neighbouring countries

Even if Chateaubriand was not the first traveller to the Middle East in the nineteenth century, a study of travellers' impressions of the area cannot ignore the part played by the future diplomat and French Minister of foreign affairs in the shaping of the Western image of Islam. Chateaubriand himself claimed in the preface written for the edition of his Complete Works that soon after publication the *Itinéraire* served as guide to a number of travellers because of its exact descriptions and that it became a topographical sketch. While a chronological treatment of travellers' accounts might be helpful in determining whether any evolution took place in the century with regard to a better understanding of Islam, Chateaubriand makes such an arrangement impracticable. For he is often referred to by other travellers and later writers. Lamartine, in particular, invites comparison with him not only because they both visited some of the same regions of the Middle East, but also because the Romantic poet often challenges his predecessor's account, referring to him now explicitly, as when he refutes Chateaubriand's idea that Tasso's *Jerusalem delivered* was inspired by the geography of Jerusalem, now implicitly, in polemical fashion.[23]

In the preface to the first edition, Chateaubriand gives the reader some interesting information about his aims in the *Itinéraire*: the latter is to look upon it not so much as a journey as memoirs covering a year in his life.[24] He further explains that a traveller is a type of historian, his duty being to describe faithfully what he has seen or heard; he should neither invent nor omit anything (ii. 702). Above all he must not keep quiet about the truth or distort it. We shall soon see to what extent he practises what he preaches. Chateaubriand himself admits in the prefaces to the editions of *Les Martyrs* (1809) that he went to the Orient merely to visit the location where he had placed the action of his Christian prose epic. Despite this admission, Chateaubriand's interest in Islam and the Muslims was far from being superficial. After all, his impressions of the religion and its followers were based on a visit to a number of Middle Eastern countries. It seems that Lamartine in the 'Avertissement' to the *Voyage en Orient* wished to cast doubt on his predecessor's achievement in the *Itinéraire* by suggesting that Chateaubriand really wrote a poem on the Orient. The suggestion can be only partly true: not everything in the *Itinéraire* relies on poetic imagination. Lamartine, however, may be nearer the mark with the statement that Chateaubriand went to Jerusalem as a pilgrim, the Bible, the Gospel and the Crusades in his hand. If that is so his image of the Muslims could hardly avoid being distorted.

Before even reaching Jerusalem, that is, on his way via Greece as he heads towards Lakonia, Chateaubriand provides the reader with actual glimpses of the Muslim at prayer. He notices the janissary who said his prayer, washed his elbows, his face and hands and turned towards the east as if to call for light. He has obviously misunderstood the order of proceedings. One does not require a knowledge of Islamic doctrine to realize that ablutions have been made to follow instead of preceding prayer and that the Muslim is not performing a poetic gesture but simply turning in the direction of Makka. A few pages later (pp. 807-808), Chateaubriand appears to appreciate the piety of the Turk who says a prayer over the head of a child, but the appreciation of the moving and respectable piety is nullified by the afterthought device 'même dans les religions les plus funestes' which follows. In Egypt Chateaubriand's failure to understand Islamic prayer becomes glaring. As he travels from Rosetta to Cairo by boat he notices Turkish traders who got off, prayed on their heels, with faces turned towards Makka and in the middle of the fields they made 'des espèces de culbutes religieuses'. Chateaubriand does not take kindly to the prostrations accompanying prayers which have been reduced to the level of mechanical gestures made without any sense of the spiritual.

Muslims are a people without faith, as he describes them after a visit to the Church of the Nativity in Bethlehem (p. 990). Contrast does not operate in favour of their religion: as he comes out of the grotto where he finds the wealth, arts and religion of civilized nations, he says that he is transported amidst Arab hovels and half-naked savages. Whenever Islam is set against Christianity in the *Itinéraire* an objective approach is difficult to achieve. It would appear that Chateaubriand has eyes not to see. His stay in Constantinople, earlier on, weighed on him so much that he did not look at any of its beautiful mosques (p. 944). The reason may be that he believes the Turks know absolutely nothing of architecture, since they only made Greek and Arab buildings look ugly by imposing on them massive domes and Chinese pavilions (1086). However, in the *Journal de Jérusalem* he conceded that the mosques of Jerusalem which had been built not by Turks but by Arabs were fairly elegant (1730, n. 2).

Indeed, Chateaubriand's visit to Jerusalem enabled him to make some positive remarks on Islamic cultural achievements. Chateaubriand at first gives greater credit to the Arabs in the field of architecture. However, he erroneously attributes the creation of all Arab monuments to the time of the capture of Jerusalem by ʿUmar ibn al-Khaṭṭāb, the second Caliph, in 638. Pointing out how the Arabs, following the Caliph's banner, seized Egypt and Spain where they filled Granada and Cordoa with marvellous palaces, he traces back to the reign of ʿUmar the origins of Arab architecture of which the Alhambra is the masterpiece, as the Parthenon is the apotheosis of Greek architecture. The comparison between Arab architecture in Spain with Greek architecture appears like a compliment. But the compliment is modified as the aim is really to show that even in architecture the Arabs are lacking in originality. As they did not know the Greeks they could not borrow anything from them. However, these 'peuples vagabonds, conquérants, voyageurs' did manage to imitate the ancient Egyptians: the minaret of an Arab mosque imitates the Egyptian obelisk, while the columns are a replica of the pillars in the temples of Thebes and Memphis. On the other hand, all architecture, even Gothic architecture, is Egyptian in origin. Chateaubriand fails to mention any other association between Arabs and Greeks, in particular the Arabs' enormous contribution in the transmission, through translation, of Greek science and philosophy from the ninth century onwards.

One feels that Chateaubriand is more at ease describing monuments of the past, be it Arab monuments, than reacting to the nineteenth-century world of Islam. He gives a commendable account of the history of the Dome of the Rock in Jerusalem (although, like many other people, he mistakenly designates it as the mosque of ʿUmar). This building was begun by the fifth Umayyad Caliph ʿAbd al-Malik (685-705) in 687 and completed in 691 on the site of the abandoned

Temple of Solomon. Chateaubriand was not given the opportunity of visiting the interior of the Dome. Even if he had been given the opportunity, he would not probably have grasped the significance of the Qur'ānic inscriptions around the interior. These proclaim the greatness of God, declare that 'God and His angels bless the Prophet', and call upon Christians to recognize Jesus as an apostle of God, His word and spirit, but not His son'.[25] The Dome is not a mosque but a shrine erected above the sacred rock (*ṣakhra*) and similar to other domes scattered over the Muslim *ḥaram* (sacred place). It was viewed as 'a symbolic act of placing Islam in the lineage of Abraham and dissociating it from Judaism and Christianity.[26] According to a *ḥadīth* the Prophet Muḥammad is reported as having left his footprint on a detached piece of marble on the south-west of the rock on the night of his ascension to heaven on his horse al-Burāq after having prayed with Abraham, Moses and Jesus on the ruins of the Temple of Solomon.[27] The Qur'ān, however, is more concise about this episode: it glorifies 'God who made His servant (Muḥammad) travel by night from the Holy Mosque (the Ka'ba) to the furthest mosque (the Temple of Solomon in Jerusalem) whose precincts We did bless' (from *Sūra* 17: 1).

Chateaubriand regretted that ambassador Deshayes de Courmenin had declined the offer of the Turks to visit the inside of the Dome. So any description by a non-Muslim could take place only from the outside. What Chateaubriand says about the inside is, as he willingly admits, mere speculation. The outside is fairly accurately described as an octagonal building. The Dome is covered outside with lead, Qur'ānic passages being inscribed in interwoven characters to form a frieze around the building. As Chateaubriand says, 'Umar on visiting the Rock which was covered with debris on the site of the Temple began to clear off the rubble and the Rock soon came into sight (p. 1080). The traditions agree that ʿUmar had a Muslim place of worship erected on the deserted Temple. Chateaubriand adds that it became as sacred as the mosques of Makka and Madina. He also mentions the extensions made by ʿAbd al-Malik and the embellishments due to Caliph El Louid (that is, al-Walīd I (705-15) who covered it with a golden cupola. He is mistaken in attributing the cupola to Walīd I as an existing Kufic inscription shows it was ʿAbd al-Malik who erected the 'Qubbat al-ṣakhra'. But his point about Muslims considering the *ṣakhra* as sacred as the mosques of Makka and Madina is valid. It is remarkable that a writer who so often misrepresents what is significant to Muslims manages somehow to convey the centrality of Jerusalem in Islam. In this connection, there is a tradition recorded by the traditionist al-Zuhrī, according to which Muḥammad classed Makka, Madina and Jerusalem as places of pilgrimage of specoal value.[28]

It seems, however, that Chateaubriand exaggerated the importance of ʿUmar in Islamic history. Not only does he trace the beginnings of all architecture back to him, but he also twice makes him the founder of the Umayyad dynasty (pp. 1079, 1083). In fact, this dynasty was founded by Muʿāwiya ibn Abī Sufyān, who usurped power after Caliph ʿAlī's assassination, transferred the capital of Islam from Madina to Damascus and turned the Caliphate into an hereditary institution. When he does not exaggerate, Chateaubriand sometimes invents. Thus he describes a meeting with an Armenian patriarch whom he calls Arsenios. Apparently, this Arsenios did not exist and the formal reception which Chateaubriand claims to have had with the patriarch was nothing more than an interview with a person of lesser importance about whom there is no mention in the records. The real patriarch was then Theodore III (1799-1819).[29]

From Chateaubriand's point of view, it did not matter too much that Arsenios was mere fiction, for he served a convenient purpose, which was to have another person show contempt for the Turks. Arsenios thus complemented the numerous attempts of Chateaubriand himself to belittle them. On his way to Constantinople, Chateaubriand climbs a mountainous region which would be full of oak, pine and other trees had the Turks not destroyed everything: they are a true plague (p. 934). At Galata he sees a silent crowd which always seems to escape the attention of a master. As he passes from a bazaar to a cemetery, he cannot help thinking that the Turks simply exist to buy, sell and die (p. 942). The oversimplification used to describe the life of a Turk produces the inevitable conclusion that they are not really a people, but a herd led by an imām to be slaughtered by a janissary. Yet when they have power their main tendency is to betray greed, threaten members of religious orders with beating, imprisonment and death.[30] Now, the Turks are found not only in Turkey, but also in Palestine. For instance, the sumptuous meal to which Chateaubriand is treated in Jaffa by the priest in charge of the hospice is followed by a litany of the sufferings endured by the priests, including a daily snub and the payment of exorbitant sums. Extortion and greed are *leitmotiv* in the *Itinéraire*. The curate of Jaffa warned him against visiting the Aga, because in Jerusalem Chateaubriand would be charged a huge sum of money if he wished to be escorted: he would never be able to satisfy the people's greed and enter the holy site without the risk of being torn to pieces. The curate gave Chateaubriand countless examples which clearly proved to him the corruption, love of money and anarchy prevailing there. When he entered the Church of the Holy Sepulchre, the Turk who had been informed of his visit opened the doors, but Chateaubriand had once more to pay 'à Mahomet le droit d'adorer Jésus Christ' (p. 1069).

The belittling of Turks wherever they are and other Muslims is often achieved by means of animal imagery. The Turks of

Constantinople are attracted by their masters as birds are fascinated by snakes (p. 942). On the coast of Caesarea, Chateaubriand spots a wandering Arab who, like a vulture, follows with an avid eye the boat sailing through the horizon and lies in wait for the remains of the shipwrecked traveller. At Jericho, he attends festivities held on the occasion of an Arab wedding. These included devouring a roast lamb with one's bare hands (p. 1011). His enjoyment at discovering among the descendants of Ismael (the Arabs) memories of Abraham and Jacob leads him to describe Arabs he met in Judaea, Egypt and Barbary. When they start talking he notices their dazzling white teeth which are like those of jackals and snow leopards. The Arabs of Bethlehem may well enjoy listening to tales, sipping coffee around a fire on the shores of the Dead Sea, but they are another type of savages, differing from those of North America in their delicate customs. It is not at first easy to establish where lies Chateaubriand's preference. The Arabs have a good start: one feels, says Chateaubriand, that they were born in that Orient where originated all the arts, the sciences and religions. There is a kind of hierarchy among their tribes: masters, servants and domestic animals. The North American savages, on the other hand, lead solitary lives, wearing bear skins, wielding arrows, never having tamed the horse to hunt deer. Like cannibals, they eat flesh and drink blood at their banquets and they leave no historical records glorifying their past.[31] In the case of the North American savage everything points to one who has not yet attained civilization; in that of the Arab, every thing points to a man who knew it, but lapsed into the wild state. So in the end, the American savage has the upper hand over the Arab whose story is thus one of progressive degradation.

The excursion into ethnology occupies only a small part of the *Itinéraire*: the crusade against Islam takes much greater space. If he is willing to acknowledge the tolerance of the

Caliph 'Umar who allowed Christians free exercise of their faith, Chateaubriand is more interested in setting the scene for a vigorous defence of the Crusades by referring to the persecution of Christians in Jerusalem by the Fatimid Caliph al-Ḥākim more than three centuries later. The Fatimids were still reigning in 1076 when the Crusades appeared on the frontiers of Palestine. At this point Chateaubriand rejects the negative view of the Crusades offered by Enlightenment writers, suggesting that the Christians were not the aggressors. Throwing all chronological perspective overboard, he wonders why if the subjects of 'Umar (d. 644) can invade Sicily, Spain, even France where Charles Martel defeated them (732), those of Philip I (1052-1108) cannot go around Asia to take revenge on 'Umar's descendants right up to Jerusalem. It is as if Islamic history stopped completely with 'Umar. In his view the perception of the Crusades simply as a movement for the liberation of a tomb in Palestine is too narrow, when the issues at stake were far wider. Who should triumph in the world, a religion enemy of civilization, favouring ignorance, despotism, slavery, that is, Islam, or a religion which has revived among the moderns the genius of learned antiquity and abolished slavery?

The revival of learned antiquity, as everyone knows, owes much to the Arabs. But to the nineteenth-century champion of the Crusades, the latter were acting to save the world from an inundation of new barbarians. Part of the rhetoric relies on stereotyped views of Islam and the tendency to polarize: the spirit of Islam (mahométisme) is persecution and conquest, while the Gospel only preaches tolerance and peace. This is very much in the tradition of earlier Christian apologists such as Grotius and Pascal. An exact calculation of the period – seven hundred and sixty-four years – during which Christians put up with all the evils inflicted by the Saracens is followed by a series of rhetorical questions justifying the cause of the holy wars and stigmatizing a religion which enjoys ill-treating people and despising literature and the arts. While pointing out how the Crusades weakened the Muslim hordes in Central Asia, preventing Europe from being a prey to the Turks and Arabs, Chateaubriand admits that they saved it from its own revolutions.

The rhetorical questions give way to a rambling history of the Crusades interspersed with incidents from the Old Testament regarding David and Bathsheba. Then Chateaubriand comes back to modern Jerusalem, though he does not stay there for long. His account is punctuated with remarks disparaging Oriental nations who are made to almost welcome invaders in their countries. Why? That is because they are servile: accustomed to follow the fate of a master, they have no laws which bind them to principles of order and political moderation. Guided by the sword, they know nothing about liberty; property they have none and force is their God. When conquerors take long to appear, these nations are like leaderless soldiers, citizens without a law-giver and a family without its head (p. 1069).

The real aim of Chateaubriand lies elsewhere: it is to paint a grim picture of the sufferings of Christians in the Holy Land throughout the ages. He makes much of the expenses incurred by pilgrims entering it, going to the length of reproducing in Italian (which he says is understood by every one) a breakdown of expenses drawn up by a Father at the convent of Saint Saviour. The proofs he adduces to make his point about the persecution of Christian priests are extracts, in the wrong order, from Deshayes's *Voyage du Levant* (1624) and Père Roger's *Description de la terre sainte* (1664). He says he could produce whole volumes about similar testimonies recorded in travels to Palestine, but prefers to quote from a register from the archives of the convent. What he does not tell his reader is that this archival material dates from centuries before, from 414 to 609 A.H., that is, from about 1039 to 1249 A.D. Such lapses in chronology appear to have escaped his notice: what matters to him is that these writings show the poor Fathers, custodians of Christ's tomb, simply taken up with defending themselves on a daily basis, throughout centuries, from all types of insults and tyrannical acts.

It is clear that Chateaubriand did not succeed in the aims he set out to achieve in the preface to the first edition of the *Itinéraire*. What undermines his objectives is his lack of balance, his seeing everything in black and white – Christianity being good and Islam being evil. He covered not a year in his life but centuries of history, especially of Christian history, while trying to resurrect the past. He gives too much attention to this past which he wants his reader to perceive as superior to the present, the past belonging to non-Islamic civilization, the present to an inferior civilization. He records not so much what he has seen as what he has read: this, for example, accounts for his extensive quotations from Tasso's *Jerusalem delivered* and from European travellers. Such literary reminiscenses detract to some extent from the value of his narrative. Yet a rather significant achievement of the *Itinéraire* lies in the recognition, be it limited, of the centrality of Jerusalem to Islam.

Curiously enough, Lamartine who in many ways is so different from Chateaubriand, bears a strange resemblance to the latter in the sentiments he echoes in 1832 when he is near the ruins of Baalbek in Lebanon. He would like the Christians of the West to wear the mantle of protectors and future liberators in their attitude towards the Christians of the East who, he says, are drowned in the 'mahométisme' that surrounds them, threatens them and often persecutes them (ii. 21). He sees the latter as Europe's allies, thinking it is high time to launch a European colony in the heart of Asia, to bring modern civilization to the birthplace of ancient civilization and to rebuild a new empire on the ruins of the crumbling Ottoman Empire. Nothing is easier than to increase the population which has been decimated by Islam through its atrocious administration. The reproach against Islam is that it is guilty not of brutal ferocity, but of criminal carelessness, of a fatalism which does not itself destroy but allows everything around it to perish. Lamartine tries to give a balanced verdict on it: he sees its main drawback in its passive resignation, its excessive reliance on God who does not act on behalf of man, as the latter is meant to act on his own behalf. Instead of God being the spectator and judge of human action, Islam has assumed the divine role of spectator.

What Lamartine is denouncing is not really the religion of Islam, but rather the indolence of the Turks whom he calls 'mahométisme'. For Islam read Turks. The confusion is partly due to Lamartine's inability to grasp the position of Islam on fatalism. Throughout the *Voyage en Orient* he loudly proclaims that it teaches fatalism, being unaware that the complexity and refinement of Islamic destiny hardly resembles the caricatured image of fatalism projected in popular writings, including his own. But he recognizes the merit of Islam which he deems to be a very philosophical religion that requires only two major duties of man: prayer and charity, the two highest principles of any religion. These principles are the source of Islamic tolerance – a tolerance which other religions have excluded from their dogma. He believes that in this respect Islam has made more progress towards religious perfection than other religions which insult and ignore it. Islam is moral, patient, resigned by nature, qualities which foster integration in countries occupied by Muslims, who should be enlightened, not exterminated. Moreover, it is used to living in peace and harmony with Christian communities which it has allowed to act freely in its holy cities like Damascus and Jerusalem.

These positive images of Islam are marred by European obsession with colonial designs. Like Leibniz and Chateaubriand before, Lamartine believes that a European adventurer with five to six thousand soldiers from Europe could easily conquer Asia, from Smyrna to Basra and from Cairo to Baghdad, using the Maronites of Lebanon in support. The desert Arabs too would be helpful since they can be won over by gold – their god – and they can be pushed back further into the desert, to be drawn into civilization gradually. Lamartine's plans for the Middle East are more fully developed in the 'Résumé politique' tagged on to the end of the *Voyage*. He has no doubts about the need for France and Europe to expand and their mission is to fill in the void soon to be left by the crumbling Ottoman Empire which would pave the way to anarchy, disorganized barbarism and lands without peoples and without guides and masters. One need neither hasten the fall of the Ottoman Empire nor prop up a lifeless phantom. What needs to be done is to agree to share the spoils, under Europe's patronage, so that the human race may prosper and flourish and civilization spread in the former Empire. Action is best taken under the aegis of a Congress which groups together European powers with territories bordering on the Ottoman Empire or having interests in the Mediterranean. These powers may take, under the title of protectorate, part of the Empire which would have been assigned to them by the Congress. Lamartine's vision seems to have been prophetic. Most of his dreams were fulfilled by the time of the first world war and thereafter. The Sykes-Picot Agreement of May 1916 divided the Arab provinces of the Ottoman Empire into zones of permanent influence. The Treaty of Versailles (1919) stipulated that these countries could be recognized as independent, provided they accepted a 'mandate' from European powers which would give them assistance and advice.[32]

Fortunately, Lamartine's imperialist agenda occupies only a small section of the *Voyage*. It is clear that for him the fault lies not with the religion but with the weakness prevailing in the world of Islam. Even when he is asking the European powers not to aid barbarism and Islam against civilization, reason and the more advanced religions oppressed by them, the object of his disparagement still remains the Osmanlis whose inertia has created deserts everywhere and allowed the Barbary states to become independent and to forget their common cultural and religious heritage. Colonial sentiments should not be allowed to obliterate the originality Lamartine reveals in his attitude to Islam as a religion. Whereas other Europeans – past and present – often show sympathy and a liking for Muslims of various origins but are sceptical about their religion, Lamartine generally appears well disposed towards Islam, even if he does not fully grasp its teaching. His sympathy for the religion enables him to stress what he perceives as its distinctive contribution to civilization – tolerance. He may well have achieved more than the modest objectives he sets out in the 'Avertissement' to the *Voyage* and at the beginning of the text. In the former, he claims that he gave little thought towards presenting a complete and faithful description of the countries he passed through, impressions of places, peoples and customs, because he thinks the *Correspondance d'Orient* of Michaud and Poujoulat gives the most complete, varied and attractive account of the Orient. He states in the latter that he had always dreamt of a voyage to the East as a great act of his inner life.

Lamartine is not content with stressing the principle of tolerance advocated in Islam. On a number of occasions he takes delight in showing its practical application. He visited the convent of the Latin Fathers of Nazareth who, he thought, held the ceremonies of their religion with as much liberty, security and publicity as they might in the streets of Rome.

With Chateaubriand evidently in mind he says that Muslims have been much denigrated, despite the fact that religious tolerance and respect are deeply stamped in their manners. Muslims are so religious themselves and set so much store by the exercise of their own religion that the religion of others is the last thing they would attack. They may not like the symbols of Christianity, but their scorn is really reserved for those who do not pray to God in any language. Lamartine noted the marks of deference and respect that the inhabitants of Nazareth, including the Turks, gave to the Fathers who were honoured not less than a bishop in the streets of a Catholic town.

As he leaves Nazareth on 20 October 1832, Lamartine dismisses the romanesque and false picture of Holy Land convents drawn by travellers. This includes the idea that monks leave the delights of civilization in the West to risk their lives or lead a life of hardship and martyrdom among the persecutors of their faith – the blaspheming Turks and Arabs – on the very spot where the mysteries of their religion hallowed the earth. He thinks the idea is grand, but has no basis in reality. For there is neither persecution nor martyrdom; around these convents a Christian community is at the service of its monks. The Turks do not worry them in the least; on the contrary, they protect them. They are the most tolerant people on earth, who understand best prayer in any language or form. They only hate atheism which they consider degrading to human intelligence. These convents are, moreover, protected by Christian powers, represented by their consuls and any complaint made by the Superiors is transmitted to the consul who writes to the Pacha and justice is done immediately. The monks Lamartine saw struck him as being very happy and well respected.

When he reached Jerusalem on the 29 October, five or six Turks who were keeping watch over the Church of the Holy

Sepulchre saluted his party gracefully and ordered one of the attendants to accompany them in all parts of the Church. His description of the Church is preceded by reflexions that challenge the stereotyped idea of persecution from the Turks. Holders of the sacred monument of the Christians, they preserve it and maintain an order and a silent reverence which Christian communities fighting over it fail to maintain. Without the Turks the sepulchre would have passed to the warring factions of Greeks and Catholics in turn and would have been made inaccessible to the enemies of the victorious communion.[33] This so-called brutal intolerance with which ignorant people charge them is really tolerance and respect for what others adore. Wherever the Muslim sees the idea of God in the thought of his brothers, he shows respect. Muslims are the only tolerant people. Lamartine concludes by challenging Christians to ask themselves what they would do if they acquired Makka and Madina through the fortunes of war.

However, he does contradict himself on the question of Muslim tolerance on two occasions. That may be because there is no attempt on his part to hide the blots on the landscape of the world of Islam. These mainly take the form of fanaticism. In Beirut, for example, Lamartine entertains the reader with the story of his cook Aboulias, a Christian Arab from Aleppo (i, 218-220). Before this, Aboulias had a Muslim Arab as trading partner but a quarrel broke out between the two on the sharing of profits they had made in their trade. The Muslim associate engineered an ambush against Aboulias in which witnesses in the pay of the former heard the Christian blaspheme the Prophet, a mortal sin for an 'infidel'. Aboulias was condemned to be hanged: sentence was carried out, but Aboulias survived because of a broken rope. He was later caught and led to the Pacha who, says Lamartine, in accordance with a Qur'ānic text favouring the accused, gave him the alternative of being hanged a second time or converting to Islam. Aboulias chose the second alternative; after a while he escaped from Aleppo and became a Christian again. Lamartine is rather vague about the Qur'ānic text. Perhaps he had in mind *Sūra* 5: 33-34, which prescribes the punishment against those who wage war upon God and the Prophet: this includes execution or exile from their country, unless they repent. There is no mention of conversion for a Christian found guilty of blaspheming.

On the outskirts of Damascus, Lamartine and his party have to wear Oriental dress so as not to be recognized as Europeans. That is because the behaviour of the fanatical inhabitants of Damascus and the neighbourhood warrant such a precaution. Their Armenian guide had to wear a black turban like the other Christians of Damascus. The Muslims of Damascus are unique among Orientals in their religious hatred and their horror of European costume. Unique too is their refusal to accept consuls or agents of Christian powers: a long time was to pass before the provisions of the Vienna Convention of the 1960s relating to the establishment of consular posts abroad came into force. Yet a M. Baudin who wears Arab dress and passes as an Armenian trader acts as consular agent of France and the rest of Europe. His house, like those of other Christians, is a hovel outside, but a delicious palace inside. Again, Lamartine attributes this state of affairs to the tyranny of the fanatical population which forces these poor Europeans to hide their wealth under appearances of poverty. He distinguishes between the common people, known for their fanaticism, and the agas of Damascus, two of whom, friends of Baudin, received him courteously.

In Constantinople Lamartine visits the slave market. Before he actually describes the slaves he sees, he ponders on the length of time it has taken man to regard slavery as a crime. The market is the place where the lives, bodies, souls and liberty of others are sold as one sells an ox or a horse. When a Turk is dissatisfied with a female slave, he sends her to the market but with no real intention of selling her: the purpose of such a gesture is simply to humiliate and chastise her. Yet even such a scene of desolation is tempered by acts of generosity. Lamartine witnessed two or three acts of mercy which Christian charity would envy. On seeing Turks buying old slaves who had been thrown out of their masters' homes because of their age and infirmity, he wondered how these could be useful. He was informed that many Muslims had out of charity bought old, infirm slaves of both sexes from the market in order to feed them in their homes.

Lamartine makes many genuine attempts at doctrinal *rapprochement* between Islam and Christianity. Unlike previous Christian apologists, Lamartine does not compare Islam with Christianity in order to elevate the latter at the expense of the former. In Greece he sees on the face of a Turk that calm resignation and serenity which the doctrine of predestination is supposed to give Muslims as that of Providence gives to true Christians. He finds in both religions worship of the divine will. He goes to the extent of proclaiming that Qur'ānic teachings are those of Christianity altered but not distorted, Islam being full of virtues and Muslims being the people of prayer. This leads him to project oversimplified images of Islam and Muslims. If the Turks do not create, they do not destroy anything either: they let nature act freely. Apparently, they only need trees, greenery, fountains, silence and mosques. They are thus only one step ahead of the noble savage of Rousseau. When roused from their apathy, they run on their horses and fly fearlessly to death for their Prophet and their God. So Lamartine shows little progress from writers such as Diderot in his evaluation of the notion of destiny among Muslims. He believes the dogma of fatalism has turned them into the bravest nation and even if life in this world is pleasant Muslims need only make a slight effort to reach the hereafter which promises beauty, calm and love. The inference is that Muslims have little interest in the affairs of this world. Their religion is that of heroes, but resignation links it to Christianity. In discussions with the governor of Jaffa later, Lamartine reassures him that though born a Christian he too worshipped Allah's sovereign will and that the words fatalism used by Muslims and providence by Christians express the same thought. What he does not realize is that the Qur'ān is firmly set against popular fatalism, with its excuses for evading duties imposed by divine law. Though it vigorously opposes fatalism, it contains frequent expression to the truly religious sense of dependence on God for protection from evil.

If in the parallel between Islam and Christianity, especially on the question of tolerance,[34] Lamartine shows objectivity, rarely uses Islam for polemical purposes and marks some progress in European thought, he seems to continue the tradition of regarding Islam as a form of deism. At first he enlists the support of the governor of Jerusalem who not only stigmatizes his co-religionists for blocking the entry of Christians to the Dome of the Rock, but utters words of which Voltaire's character Zadig would have been proud. For the governor believes all men are brothers, although they adore, each in his own language, the common Father who makes His sun shine on the worshippers of all prophets and knows everything (I. 201). The reflexions he makes on Islam at the monastery of Antoura in Lebanon are even more unambiguously deist. Lamartine feels it is unthinkable that Muslims could be converted since their religion is a practical deism with the same moral teaching in principle as Christianity, but without the dogma of the divinity of man. Islamic teaching rests on a belief in divine inspiration, proclaimed by a wiser man and more favoured by divine emanation than the rest of mankind. Lamartine claims to have seen a large number of deeply religious Turks and Arabs who accepted in their religion only its rational and human elements. According to him Islam is a practical and contemplative theism.

Lamartine's contribution towards illuminating other aspects of Islam through his travels to nineteenth-century Middle East might have been greater if he had refrained from delving into past history. In this respect he resembles Chateaubriand, though his rapid excursion into Ottoman history, from Mehmet II to Selim III and Maḥmūd II, is not as extensive as Chateaubriand's history of the Crusades. Under the cypress trees in Constantinople, he reconstructs the tragedies of Ottoman sultans such as Selim III, mentioning atrocities committed during the capture of Constantinople, but highlighting the tolerance of Mehmet II. Through his friendship with the Piedmontese officer Calosso employed by Maḥmūd II as military adviser under the name of Rustem Bey, he had access to the inner court of the harem in Constantinople where he insists that nobody had entered since Lady Mary Wortley Montagu, that is, since 1717-18. But little of note comes out of his visit to this mysterious place and nothing is said about women in the harem in his account.

Egypt

Here it must be said that the *Observations on the manners and customs of the Egyptians* (1800) of John Antes, who resided in Cairo and its vicinity for some twelve years, delivers less than its title promises. Apart from making the valid point that many travellers, knowing no Arabic, therefore hire a Greek or Armenian as interpreter, partly guess the nature of things, make assertions that are often quoted and copied by others for the whole next century, he says that he sees no filth in the streets of Cairo and believes that the plague only rages among people of the lower classes. That is because they are superstitious and take no quarantine precautions.

Much more significant was the Comte de Chabrol's *Essai sur les moeurs des habitants modernes de l'Egypte* (1822), published in volume 2 of the collective work of the Napoleonic expedition, the *Description de l'Egypte*. Chabrol de Volvic offers some interesting, if unfavourable, perspectives on the people of Egypt and Muslims in general. He was particularly keen to show the contrast between the mores of the Egyptians and those of the French. In trying to account for the astonishing passivity of the former he adduces the following factors: a climate that never changes, a belief in fatalism which he takes care to attribute to the masses of the people only and exposure to the caprices of oppressive tyrants. New dangers arise daily and lack of foresight becomes for the Egyptians, as for Orientals in general, a kind of shelter against violence. The Egyptians can walk to their death in silence and such is the apathy of the urban inhabitants, compared with the French, that they could be taken for stupid men. This outward apathy in gesture, speech and action masks a fiery imagination, heightens their sensations and renders them capable of performing the boldest acts. Despite their nonchalance, their powers of concentration and remembrance attain the highest point. Chabrol recreates a stereotyped image of Oriental languor: the Egyptian is buried amid perfume, incense, music, songs, pleasures of the harem, although he likes to tell or listen to stories. He claims that the Egyptian is weighed down by the absence of laws, excepting religious dogma which is a barrier to intellectual progress. Here again the influence of Volney is felt. But Chabrol commends the restraint shown by Egyptians of most classes, except the masses, in practising a polygamy allowed by the law. It is clear that he wishes to establish a distinction between the various classes of Egyptian society.

Chabrol is scathing about the practice of education in Egypt. In schools children learn nothing else apart from passages of the Qur'ān which they recite in a loud voice. When they chant and swing the upper part of their bodies, the constant movement combined with the jarring sounds of voices turn Arab schools into a rather strange spectacle for Europeans. Schools, which are numerous in towns, are rare in villages and they are not maintained by public funds. Indeed, the generosity of individuals makes up for the indifference of the government. He found that even the teaching of the Azhar mosque in Cairo was inadequate: the teachers taught little more than the Qur'ān and the traditions of the first disciples. It is odd that Chabrol does not mention the traditions of the Prophet. While he acknowledges the merit of the Abbasid caliphs in having works of Greek philosophy translated into Arabic, he also points out that these translations no longer exist in Egypt. Though he recognizes the achievement of the Egyptians in poetry, grammar and rhetoric, his criticism of their performance in the applied sciences is as strong as that of Thornton concerning Turkish education.

Rather surprisingly, the engineer Chabrol shows some acute perception of the religion of Islam as it is practised in Cairo. If there is little new in his remarks on circumcision and if Ramaḍān, the month of fasting, is made to lose much of its significance since it is turned into a carnival at night, Chabrol again insists on separating the masses from the rest of the population. The former spend their time enjoying themselves in the cafés where old men become public orators and tell marvellous stories, while the saner section of the community spend the night in useful conversation. This surely is an odd way of describing the activities pursued by pious Muslims who recite the special prayers of *tarāwīḥ* at night during Ramaḍān. Chabrol is completely unaware of *tarāwīḥ*. His interest lies elsewhere: it is the visual and the external that often strike him. As he watches the people at mosques, they appear a motley crowd of individuals engaged in practices and occupations that are not in keeping with the sanctity of the place. What baffles him is their incongruous activities: the devout praying, poor people destroying vermin, the idle sleeping and craftsmen plying their trade. He adds that these practices are not restricted to Egypt.[35]

Indeed many of the shrewd observations contained in the *Essai* apply not only to Egypt but to other countries of the world of Islam. Whereas other writers speak of the tolerance of Islam towards other faiths, Chabrol conveys to readers accustomed to hear of bloody conflicts following religious schisms his astonishment at the tolerance shown by the four *madhhab* (schools of law) of Sunnī Islam towards one another. None of them wants to proselytize, but he singles out the Ḥanafī Muslims for their tolerance. Though he shows no strong interest in theological speculation, he argues that a belief in the immortality of the soul is the foundation on which rests the faith of the Muslim who waits for the last Judgement. He also reflects some understanding of Muslims' attitude towards Jews and Christians who, according to the *'ulamā'*, were to be regarded as true believers before the mission of Muḥammad. When he states that the followers of Moses and Jesus are regarded as 'infidels' by Muslims after the arrival of Muḥammad who in the latter's view came to change laws made by previous prophets, he probably reflects popular Muslim views. The Qur'ān simply states that there is no salvation outside Islam.

The *Essai* reveals an impressive grasp of the nature of the functions of many officials in Islam. With Sunnī Islam in mind all the time, Chabrol points out that anyone who can read and pray can be an imam and that there is no hierarchy among imams who are simply attached to mosques. As he says, the descendants of the Prophet, the *sayyids* or *sharīfs*, were regarded with special respect and the sultan chose from one of their number a *naqīb al-ashraf*, 'a marshal of the nobility'. His office had much prestige in the empire. Chabrol is fairly accurate in his assessment of the office of *qāḍī* (judge) who has jurisdiction in civil and criminal matters. The *qāḍī*'s competence in penal matters, however, concerns certain acts forbidden by the Qur'ān such as unlawful sexual intercourse, theft and drinking wine. Chabrol also describes well the function of the *muftī* of Istanbul, the *shaykh al-Islām*, head of the *muftīs* appointed by the government to interpret the law, who acted as religious adviser of the sultan.[36]

Chabrol made a deep impact on Edward Lane whose work *Manners and Customs of the Modern Egyptians* (1836) is more often quoted today than Chabrol's work. Lane acknowledged his debt to Chabrol and to Alexander Russell, author of *The Natural history of Aleppo* (1754), revised by his brother Pat in 1794 (see Chapter 4, above). In the preface to *Modern Egyptians,* Lane spoke of the excellence of Russell's book, but claimed that it was rather an account of Turkish than of Arab manners and that both brothers were insufficiently acquainted with Arabic to 'scrutinize some of the most interesting subjects of inquiry'. Because Lane wanted to give a thorough account of Egyptian manners himself his approach was very conscientious: he started studying Arabic language and literature in London before going to Egypt in 1825. A year after his arrival he felt able to converse with the people he frequented with 'tolerable ease'. He integrated with local Muslims of various ranks by living as they lived, conforming with their general habits... abstaining from eating food forbidden by their religion and drinking wine and even from habits merely disagreeable to them such as the use of knives and forks. This apparently paid dividends, for he says in the third manuscript of *Description of Egypt* (1829-31) where he wrote a few chapters on modern Egyptians that he was treated with respect and affability by all nations among whom he confined himself almost exclusively, and that he assumed their dress.[37] He further added that his aim was not simply to be that of the ordinary tourist, enjoying sights such as pyramids and temples.

In the first version of the *Description* entitled *Draft of the Description of Egypt* he gives further evidence of his integration into Muslim society by describing how he was in the 'frequent habit of visiting mosques, where I prayed either by myself, or (on Friday) with the congregation, or reposed' (Bodleian, Mss. Eng. mis. d. 34, f. 76). For someone who, in the words of his great nephew, Lane-Poole, never changed his belief in the essential doctrines of Evangelical Christianity, Lane seems to have gone to extraordinary lengths in his wish to strengthen his Islamic background. If Lane-Poole is correct, then Lane was merely going through the motion of praying. His second visit to Cairo from 1833 to 1835 served to consolidate his studies in Arabic and his integration into Arab society where he was fully accepted by the poets and scholars of Cairo.[38] The hiring of two professors of Arabic and Islamic studies as his regular salaried tutors must have been helpful.

What has all this intense preparation and alteration in style of living produced? Lane's perception of Islam is certainly among the most interesting in the nineteenth century. Whatever may be the view of his critics,[39] it must be stressed that his observations, like Chabrol's, focus as much on Islam in general as on the modern Egyptians. That Lane is well disposed towards Islam is evident from the beginning. This, of course, does not prevent him from recognizing what he perceives as flaws in the Egyptian system. One such flaw is the fanatical intolerance with which he says the people of Egypt – he presumably means some Egyptians – formerly treated non-Muslims. He attributes the improved situation to Muḥammad 'Alī to whom European travellers should, in his view, be grateful. The other flaw relates to the shocking and widespread practices of bribery and suborning false witnesses which are condoned in Muslim courts of law. Lane really means the tribunal of the *qāḍī* of Cairo. And here the indictment is based on hearsay evidence, that of the *muftī* of Cairo, whose long stories Lane narrates with apparent relish.

Description of Egypt reveals how impressed he was, particularly on the first occasion, by the sight of Muslims engaged in their devotions. What struck him particularly was the attitude and solemn behaviour of the worshippers who even in a busy market-place appear 'wholly abstracted from the concerns of the world' (f. 6). Moreover, he finds the practice of praying in a public place (he probably means a *muṣallā*) so general in the East and attracts so little attention that all who do so cannot be charged with hypocrisy and motives of ostentation. Specifically Egyptian was the behaviour of the boatmen of the Nile who seldom neglected an opportunity to visit the tomb of a famous saint in the belief that such an act would be followed by a blessing. The boatmen often made votive offerings at the tomb and transmitted the custom to the *fallāḥīn*. If we are to believe Lane, when they speak of a deceased saint they frequently testify to a degree of respect for him not much inferior to that with which they regard a prophet and quite unauthorized by any precept of Islam.[40] Like Tassy, Lane distinguishes between what Islam teaches and how it is practised (see below). After mentioning that it was not safe (or at least at the time of his visit to Egypt) for an undisguised Christian to enter the mosques for fear of being robbed and ill-treated, he himself was able to visit the shrine of al-Ḥasan, grandson of the Prophet, close to the Azhar mosque, generally esteemed the most sacred mosque in Egypt. Lane reflects the popular belief that the head of al-Ḥusayn, Ḥasan's brother, was taken there after he had been killed at Karbala in Iraq. He is pleased with the handsome hall, the roof of which was supported by numerous marble columns while the pavement below which the head of the martyred Ḥusayn is supposed to be buried was covered with carpets. On his visit to the shrine he saw a lofty, square saloon, surmounted by a dome and over the spot where a sacred relic is buried is an oblong monument covered in green silk with an inscription around it. He says that every visitor walks round this enclosure reciting, though inaudibly, the *fātiḥa*, a ceremony also observed on visiting other tombs. Lane makes concessions to the ordinary reader, especially one brought up in the Catholic tradition who is familiar with descriptions of visits to shrines.

Yet in his desire for *rapprochement* with Islam, Lane twists the meaning of the Qur'ān. In the preface to *Modern Egyptians,* he says that on his first visit to Egypt he avowed his belief in the messiah, in accordance with the words of the Qur'ān, as the word of God infused in the womb of the Virgin Mary and a Spirit proceeding from Him (p. viii). The reference is clearly to *Sūra* 4: 171. Lane appears to be treading on dangerous grounds here. By referring to only part of the verse, he is certainly ambivalent. While both Christians and Muslims can subscribe to the belief described in Lane's selection from the Qur'ān, the full text of the verse clearly states that Jesus is only an apostle of God, that he is a spirit proceeding from God but not God and it firmly repudiates the idea of Trinity and calls on Christians not to exaggerate.

What stands out in *Description of Egypt* is the stress on Islam as a living experience. That is why the practice of Islam often appears at variance with its teaching. An observer such as Lane may find, on the one hand, the devout manner of the whole assembly and the 'exactly simultaneous changes in their attitudes of prayer' (f. 171) at the Azhar singularly striking, while lecturers address circles of attentive listeners or read commentaries on the Qur'ān. On the other hand, he may notice others eating and drinking or sleeping and sometimes men carrying bread and other food for sale. He may also see many houseless paupers pass the night there, although such customs are not altogether in accordance with the sanctity of the place but 'peculiarly illustrative of the simplicity of Oriental manners'. This dichotomy means that various patterns of behaviour are accommodated in the world of Islam and that Oriental manners are not to be judged strictly in accordance with Western criteria. However, faced with what Chabrol and others remarked on the same topic before, it is difficult to maintain the view that for the first time in Europe Islam and its culture were being presented by Lane as a lived experience.[41]

This in no way reduces the significance of *Modern Egyptians* itself. The *Description,* being simply a brief introduction to it, did not give Lane much scope to enlarge on the topic of Islamic beliefs. Chapter iii of *Modern Egyptians* entitled 'Religion and Laws' gives him this opportunity. Here Lane's indebtedness to Chabrol is immediately felt. But what Lane borrows he amply repays and he refines upon Chabrol. Whereas the latter merely says that the Sunnīs of the four schools tolerate one another, Lane stresses that they agree in deriving their code of religion from four sources: Qur'ān, traditions, concordance of the early disciples and analogy. To the belief in the immortality of the soul and future rewards in paradise and punishments in hell, Lane adds the belief in the balance in which good and evil works shall be weighed and in the bridge extending over the midst of hell 'finer than a hair and sharper than the edge of a sword' over which all must pass and from which the wicked shall fall into hell. He does not identify the source of this belief which is not based on the Qur'ān, although it is indeed held by Muslims. In the *Iḥyā' 'Ulūm al-Dīn* (iv:x) the great theologian al-Ghazālī has a section entitled 'the subtle bridge' which discusses this belief at some length.

Referring to imāms in Sunnī Islam, Lane emphasizes the difference between their condition and that of Christian priests.

As he says, they have no authority above other persons and do not enjoy any respect but what their reported piety or learning may obtain them. And it often happens that they earn their livelihood by other means than service of the mosque, as their salaries are very small. Some of them engage in trade, while others recite the Qur'ān for a fee in private homes. There is nothing fictitious in Lane's observations on the Sunni imams. Yet he is not averse to propagating myths about Muslims elsewhere. He makes the pleasures of paradise consist of the company of girls whose stature will be proportioned to that of men, that is, the height of a palm tree or about sixty feet. He attributes to Muslims the belief that man's first parents were of this height. One wonders where he obtained this information and that about the souls of martyrs residing until judgement day in green birds which eat of the fruits of paradise and drink of its rivers. In one sense we should not be too surprised. For in the preface to *Modern Egyptians* he had considered the fictitious *Arabian Nights* to be the embodiment of the manners and customs of the Arabs, including the Egyptians. This means that Galland's warning to readers in the preface to his translation of the *Nights* that the tales were clearly to be read as inventions had gone unheeded. Rather like De Tocqueville but also with a touch of Jansenism, Lane claims that according to Qur'ānic doctrine admission of Muslims to paradise does not depend on their merit, but purely on the mercy of God and on faith and that the felicity of each person will be proportioned to his good works. Qur'ānic teaching is rather different: faith in God should be combined with good works (see Chapter 1, above).

Lane has on the whole captured the true spirit of Muslim prayer which, as he says, is such an important duty that it is called the 'key of paradise'. He gives a detailed description of ablution which he simply calls a preparation to prayer without, like previous European writers, attributing any special virtue to it, that is, he does not say that ablution washes away one's sins. But he does mention the fact that most people rush through it, omitting almost all the prayers that should accompany it. He sees in the washing of the body an act of cleanliness, not a religious act, except on Fridays and on the occasion of the two main festivals of *'Īd al-Fiṭr* and *'Īd al-Aḍḥā*. He distinguishes between the compulsory and optional part of prayers. The reader unfamiliar with Muslim prayers is assisted by illustrations of postures. There is every justification for Lane to concentrate on Friday prayers as these are the main congregational prayers in Islam which most practising Muslims offer. His account is thorough and impressive. The utmost solemnity and decorum observed by Muslims while they are absorbed in the adoration of their creator, which Lane mentions, must apply particularly to the Friday prayers. Here Lane refers to the Qur'ān, *Sūra* 62: 9-10, to show that Muslims are required to abstain from worldly business only during prayer time. In practice some will stop working after prayers.[42] Lane gives the right order of proceedings: the imām's sermon is followed by '*farḍ*', that is, compulsory prayers consisting of two *rak'as*.[43] The sermon which he translates into English gives the flavour of a typical Friday *khuṭba* in which there is a skilful reconciliation of Sunnī and Shī'a Islam with blessings on the Prophets Abraham and Muḥammad and praise for the Rightly-Guided Caliphs and the family of 'Alī. Lane justifies this detailed account of Friday prayer in Egypt on the grounds that his countrymen generally have very imperfect and erroneous notions on the subject, many of them imagining that Muslims pray to their Prophet as well as to God. What Muslims do is to seek the intercession of Muḥammad and other persons.

It would thus appear that Lane tried very hard to be fair to Islam. His attitude to 'holy war' is further evidence of his desire to strike a just balance. After saying that war against the enemies of Islam, who have been the first aggressors, is enjoined as a sacred duty and he who loses his life in it is promised the rewards of martyrdom, he takes issue with some commentators, including Muslim commentators. The latter claim that Muslims are commanded to put to death all idolaters who refuse to embrace Islam, excepting women and children who are to be made slaves. But, as Lane argues, the precepts on which this assertion is founded relate to the pagan Arabs who had violated their oaths and long persevered in their hostility to Muḥammad and his followers. This gives him the opportunity to set the record straight by saying that he had been misled by popular opinion into representing the laws of 'holy war' as more severe than according to the letter and spirit of the Qur'ān and the Ḥanafī code. He acknowledges his debt to D. Urquhart, author of *The Spirit of the East* (1838), in revising his position on the subject and concludes that no precept exists in the Qur'ān which, taken in context, can justify unprovoked war.

Books on Egypt seem to have been given a further impetus by the publication of *Modern Egyptians.* Indeed it was the ambition of Eusèbe de Salles, first interpreter of the French army in Africa, a professor at the Ecole des Langues orientales and member of the Société Asiatique, to continue Lane's work. However, the *Pérégrinations en Orient* (1840) is at best but a pale reflection of *Modern Egyptians*. De Salles's strong linguistic and philological background acquired over a period of twenty years and his extensive travels in the Middle East were used to produce a work of anti-Islamic propaganda. Our modern crusader writes more like a Chateaubriand than a Sylvestre de Sacy. For he believes that Christianity has continued the work of the Crusades and sees with glee the expulsion of the barbarian or the 'infidel' (that is, the Muslim) as the final outcome of the wars which the French fought in Egypt, Greece and Algeria in the nineteenth century,

Bonaparte and Kleber being the modern equivalent of the Crusaders Baudouin and Godefroy. He too believes that the *Arabian Nights* constitutes the best preparation for the study of the manners of the Arabs, particularly the Egyptians. He sees no evolution in the history of the Arabs. Therefore to study the modern Middle East is to go back to the darkest period of the European middle ages, if not to more primitive times: the pastoral life of the modern Egyptians/Arabs, the behaviour of the wandering tribes with their hospitality, wars and brigandage are the same as those prevailing in Abraham's time. De Salles's greatest irony is at the expense of both the rich Egyptian whose harem must consist of a Circassian, an Abyssinian and a Negro slave and the masses who know only two words: Allah and money – the substitute for liberty, planning, welfare and knowledge.

The same year as the *Pérégrinations* saw the publication by Dr. Antoine-Barthelemy Clot (also known as Clot-Bey), founder of the School of Medicine of Cairo and Inspector General of medical services of Egypt, of his *Aperçu général sur l'Egypte*. Although it is a work of apologetics and propaganda dedicated to Muḥammad 'Alī, governor of Egypt (1805-48), it offers some valuable insights into Egypt in the period 1805-40. The background is set with a rapid history of Egypt from 640 to Bonaparte's expedition, viewed as the completion of the exalted ideal of Leibniz who had proposed to Louis XIV a plan to invade Egypt. Clot-Bey paid homage to the wise tolerance of Napoleon, the skilful respect he showed for the religion and manners of the conquered people who became more willing to have extensive contacts with Europe later. This French colonialist even believed that Egypt's regeneration would have been completed if French domination had lasted longer. Admirer of Muḥammad 'Alī whom he called a bold and enlightened innovator, he stressed the qualities of his hero, including the tolerance he showed towards the Greeks in Egypt while other Pashas persecuted Christians through fanaticism in other parts of the Ottoman Empire. Indeed Christians and Jews of all nations were welcome in Egypt. Clot-Bey referred to Muḥammad 'Alī's sending to Paris young Muslims 'destined to spread our enlightenment on the banks of the Nile' (p. 53). There is some exaggeration in Clot-Bey's statement. For when a group of students asked for Muḥammad 'Alī's permission to make a tour of France and acquire first-hand knowledge of French life he refused it. It was not so much enlightenment that was the aim of Muḥammad 'Alī in sending students to France as the acquiring of military, medical and engineering skills by them in order to further the interests of his military policy.[44] But the ideas of the great eighteenth-century French thinkers did filter through later in the professional schools created by the ruler of Egypt.

Like other writers, Clot-Bey too feels that people's conception of Islam is so inaccurate and false that a rapid sketch of it is justified without making an apology of a religion that is not his. His account is fairly well balanced, being particularly successful in showing the moral teaching of Islam with its emphasis on piety, the first of virtues. However, it does not exclude the inevitable legend. For instance, women pilgrims are not allowed to climb to the top of Mount 'Arafāt unless accompanied by their husbands, while those who are not married must take a husband under the circumstance. He admits that this temporary union is a pure formality and is easily dissolved after the pilgrimage.

Sometimes a comment on a general principle in Islam leads to a description of a particular situation in one country – Egypt. Thus in the section 'slavery in the East', Clot-Bey argues that the cruel thirst for gain which has created and maintained slavery among European colonials has given it such a repulsive mark that he hesitates to use the word slavery when talking of servitude in the East. Unlike Lamartine,

Clot-Bey maintains that among Orientals slavery is neither cruel nor degrading, the slave being not considered a material object. The European settler appreciates the Negro only for material benefits he may gain from him, forgetting his humanity. The Muslim, on the other hand, always sees a man in his slave. He treats him in such a way that one could describe Oriental slavery as a true adoption in a family. The main distinction between Oriental and Western slavery lies in the respect for human dignity. The slave can even aspire to a brilliant future. To make his point Clot-Bey gives as an example the militia of Mamluks who governed Egypt for so long (that is, until 1517): it was recruited among its own members. Coming back to his times, he says he found in the markets of Cairo Greek slaves who had been snatched from their country when it was about to regain its independence (p. 272). He subsequently found them occupying almost all the senior posts in the civil government and the army. Moreover, the Sulṭān only marries slaves, the same being true of the Viceroy of Egypt and his sons.

Clot-Bey has to admit that not everything was perfect in the Egypt of Muḥammad ʿAlī. While tolerance had reached such a point that Europeans could enter mosques without any danger in his day, the mosques themselves were crumbling to pieces (p. 230). Here he stresses the paradox of the situation obtaining in Egypt. There may be four hundred mosques in Cairo, but often travellers are struck by the state of dilapidation in which the mosques are to be found. They cannot reconcile this situation with the piety of Muslims and the respect with which they hold the buildings of their faith. It would appear that this reverence, taken to extreme lengths, is responsible for their neglected state. The Egyptians seem to be afraid to violate the sanctity of these monuments by repairing them. It is only when they threaten to crumble that people decide to rebuild them.

The homage to Muḥammad ʿAlī is continued by H. Gisquet in his book *L'Egypte, les Turcs et les Arabes* (1848). Not only does he confirm Clot-Bey's point about access to mosques being given to Christians under Muḥammad ʿAlī, but he also has warm praise for the latter's efforts in putting an end to the brutal persecution to which Christian religious establishments were allegedly subjected. His praise is supported by the information that the Lazarist fathers obtained a huge piece of land, free of charge, where they were planning to erect a building which would extend the activity of the Roman Catholic missionary order founded in 1625 by Saint Vincent de Paul. Muḥammad ʿAlī apparently also gave some funds for the repair of a church and encouraged the creation of a boarding school run by the Sisters of Charity. His behaviour was in marked contrast to that of other Muslims in Egypt. However, it is on the negative aspect of Egypt that Gisquet wishes to concentrate. The attention he devotes to burial in modern Egypt appears excessive. Wanting to outdo Volney for whom he has great admiration, he paints a depressing picture of the people of Alexandria who speak in a barbarous idiom, and whose guttural sounds imitate the croaking of frogs. They are covered in rags, lying on the ground in abject poverty, surrounded by garbage and devoured by vermin. If one were to believe him, this faithful and painful picture could apply to all the families of the *fallaḥīn* and to almost all the villages of Egypt. He concedes that the apparent poverty in Cairo may be a device used by families to protect themselves from the rapacity of officials. Oriental luxury such as the dazzling products of China and India one comes across in the *Nights* is hardly to be found in the bazaars of Cairo which are very disappointing in reality. Instead one may find some luxury in parts of the Jewish quarter.

The greater the expectations that are raised in dreams or through the imagination, the slighter the chance of their being fulfilled in actual life. The *Correspondance* of Nerval proves this point admirably. It is not that the modern Egyptians are not people 'd'une douceur admirable': they would be the best on earth, had it not been for their keenness for *bakhshish* (tips). They appear better than the half savages of Mount Carmel and the Lebanon.[45] Cairo, which he mistakenly takes to be the city of the *Nights,* is rather downgraded and dusty: the Cairo of Mamluk times was better than the Cairo he saw. Nerval does not think much of a café of the European quarter 'vulgairement nommé Mousky'. To it he prefers the Oriental cafés one finds in Paris and their 'trèfles, colonnettes, lambris de porcelaine, oeufs d'autruche suspendus' (*Oeuvres*, i, 893). He is convinced that he will recognize 'his' Cairo of old in Paris at a performance of Gautier's ballet *La Péri* where in the second act the scenery representing Cairo had been produced by Cambon. Here Nerval is referring to Charles-Antoine Cambon (1802-75), a French painter who was initially interested in watercolours, but later became associated with Philastre with whom he designed a considerable number of sets for operas, plays, and ballets. Better still, he has reconstructed Cairo beneath a crumbling mosque amid the dust and is sure of finding at the opera 'le Caire véritable, l'Egypte immaculée, l'Orient qui m'échappe' (*Oeuvres*, i, 897). From Constantinople he writes to his father (at the beginning of October 1843) to say that in the *Journal de Constantinople* he gave vent to his feeling of disillusionment with regard to Egypt. It is not simply Egypt but the whole of the Orient that is involved in his shattered dream. Yet reality is not far away. Among the ceremonies he witnessed in Cairo were the festivities marking the Prophet's birthday and the return of pilgrims from Makka. He was amazed by what he saw: fanatics were in a state of exaltation similar to that of the 'convulsionnaires'; they allowed the leader of the pilgrims who was on horseback to trample over them. They even claimed that they had sustained no injury in the process, although a Negro had to be rescued.[46] If Nerval could be criticized for giving free rein to his imagination, his account of Islam is sometimes based on actual experience.

By comparison Barthélemy Saint-Hilaire appears to have had his feet more frequently and more firmly on the ground. He was certainly better disposed than Gisquet towards the Egyptians. The aim of his *Lettres sur l'Egypte* (1856) was to popularize the efforts made by Egypt over half a century to 'civilize herself'. He felt that the Egyptians, of all Muslims, deserved the sympathy of Christian Europe. Unlike many other writers he did not think Egypt had to reject its Muslim faith, since Islam was not opposed to its progress. But what it had to change was its deplorable customs which had nothing to do with Islam. The land of the Pharaohs could save itself from torpor and poverty only by adopting European arts and industries and manners. In the patronising words of Saint-Hilaire, Egypt could not do anything by herself. This sounds like nothing more than a variation on the theme of the high achievement of Napoleon's expedition which, in Saint-Hilaire's view, sparked off the idea of reform on Egyptian soil. He has a solid grasp of the land reforms initiated by Muḥammad ʿAlī himself and continued by his successors. But he makes a controversial judgement about Islamic law when he says that it does not recognize individual property and that by making the state the sole owner of the land confers upon it the right of using it as it pleases. He claims that Muḥammad ʿAlī had, so to say, inherited the whole of Egypt with a few exceptions and that he had achieved his aim by indemnifying the rare owners who could prove their title. Among the exceptions Saint-Hilaire includes mosques which had acquired a long time before and still owned property held in trust for religious purposes as *waqf*. In fact these religious endowments together with tax farms had been confiscated by Muḥammad ʿAlī in his attempt to bring all agricultural land under his control so that he might extend the cultivation of cotton.[47] One has to agree with Saint-Hilaire that never before had such a major reform been made in the land ownership structure of a country since the French constituent assembly was set up. He further states that ʿAbbās I (1849-54) who succeeded his grandfather Muḥammad ʿAlī abolished the monopoly over the sale of cotton and other products. This may have happened in the later years of his reign when Muḥammad ʿAlī, under pressure from Europe, was compelled to give up his monopoly and turned Egypt into a supplier of raw materials and importer of finished goods at prices fixed on the world market. Saint-Hilaire mentions that Saʿīd (1854-63), ʿAbbās's successor, reversed previous policy, levied a tax which he himself and members of his family paid as owners of personal property. What really happened was that Muḥammad ʿAlī in his last years granted lands to members of his family and others who could bring them under cultivation and pay the land-tax, thus creating a new class of land owners.[48] As Saint-Hilaire points out, Said gave the *fellahs* the right of selling their products to whomsoever they pleased, provided they paid their taxes – a right they did not have under Muḥammad ʿAlī. He welcomed this development which turned *fallaḥīn* into landowners.

For other interesting perspectives on the Egypt of the period 1850-1860 drawn in a lighthearted, satirical vein, one may also turn to the novel *Le Fellah* (1869) by Edmond About. With Muḥammad ʿAlī now dead but still fondly remembered by some, About allows his hero, the *fellah* Ahmad, to be cynical about the policy of sending young Egyptians abroad in order to study European civilization. The hero, who is grateful to His Highness for sparing no effort for his education, narrates how he successively studied medicine, law, agriculture, chemistry and engineering. He then notes that for everyone who becomes a minister, engineer, admiral or prefect, two or three will at most become paid translators – he probably means petty clerks – in Cairo hotels! On the other hand, the image of Islam and the *fellah* is quite positive on the whole. Ahmad, who no longer believes in the refinement of Oriental manners, fasts, gives charity and is hospitable, thereby demonstrating typical Islamic qualities. He works harder than the European peasant and consumes much less. He even brags about there being more religion in the little finger of a Muslim than in the whole body of a Catholic. While he acknowledges the superiority of Christian Europe in science and technology, he claims that the humblest Muslims have the upper hand over Christians in their moral perfection. Rather jingoistically he suggests that Christian architects will never make any thing to equal al-Ḥasan's mosque or the tombs of the Caliphs while an old bazaar rug appeals much more to his imagination than the carpets coming from London and woven cloths in silk and gold show more originality than anything from Lyon. Ahmad betrays anti-European feelings at times. He claims that if some European is attacked by chance this is no sign of fanaticism, but simply the poor taking revenge on the rich. While there is equality among races in Egypt every European who lands there thinks he is master of the country. He introduces the laws of his own country, but he does not intend to respect them. Instead he uses them to violate Egyptian laws and the only authority he recognizes is that of his consul. Ahmad appears too articulate for a peasant: he probably reflects About's own views.

Arabia

In the nineteenth century Arabia does not enjoy any politico-economic importance derived from oil production. However, it is the birthplace of Muḥammad and the heart of Islam. A reader interested in gaining some insight into the observance of one of the pillars of Islam – pilgrimage – would naturally turn to travel accounts about the country. Nineteenth-century travellers have a distinct contribution to make in this field. This is not to imply that pilgrimage had never been reported upon before by a European. For it had been described, for example, in a book published in 1704 at Exeter by Joseph Pitts. The author of *A true and faithful account of the religion and manners of the Mohammedans*, who had been captured by Algerian corsairs, spent fifteen years in slavery. During this time he was forcibly converted to Islam and he made the pilgrimage to Makka. He may even have written the book according to printers' specifications.[49] In the circumstance one could not expect to have unbiased reporting on Islam from a writer who thought that it was 'a miscellany of popery, Judaism and the gentilism of the Arabs' (p. 13) and who frequently relied on another traveller, Thevenot.[50]

Could more be expected of the Swiss-born writer John Lewis Burckhardt on the subject of pilgrimage? He had visited the Middle East between 1809 and 1817, although it was not out of personal interest in the Arabs or their culture but simply in order to comply with the instructions of the African Association to which he had offered his services for the exploration of Africa. The Association merged with the Royal Geographical Society in 1831. Burckhardt showed little sympathy for Islam, claiming that the Qur'ān 'incited its followers to unceasing hatred and contempt of all those who profess a different creed' (*Travels in Arabia*, 1829, p. 206). This book, however, cannot be easily dismissed. In it Burckhardt is particularly harsh towards Chateaubriand who, in his view, had given a highly-coloured account of Palestine and its priesthood and had often totally misrepresented the facts. That he dressed like an Arab and wore a beard is not particularly significant. More significant perhaps is the fact that he sought to give a factual account of pilgrimage to Makka. He is fairly accurate in describing the principal duties incumbent on a pilgrim.

So a reader unfamiliar with the ceremonies of *ḥajj* learns that the pilgrim has to (1) wear the *iḥrām*, a white garment made of a single cloth, (2) be present on the 9th of the month of Dhu'l-Ḥijja at the sermon preached at Mount Arafat, some seven miles from Makka, (3) listen to a similar sermon at Muzdalifa, a place between Minā and 'Arafāt on the 10 of Dhu'l-Ḥijja, (4) on the 10th, 11th and 12th of Dhu'l-Ḥijja perform the symbolic act of throwing stones at the devil at the pillars of Minā, (5) sacrifice an animal if he has the means, (6) return to Makka and visit the Ka'ba. In connection with the last rite Burckhardt could have mentioned the *ṭawāf*, that is, the walk round the Ka'ba seven times, although he did mention it earlier (p. 75). At that point he had also mentioned the brisk walk, seven times, between the hills of Ṣafā and Marwa. Unlike Chateaubriand, Burckhardt does not make any of these acts of devotion appear mechanical: they are all accompanied by the appropriate prayers, but he does not give their actual wording.[51] Pointing out how the pagan Arabs used to extol their ancestors after returning from 'Arafāt, Burckhardt says that Muḥammad abolished the custom by a passage in the Qur'ān. He is rather vague about this and not strictly accurate. Without forbidding the practice, the Qur'ān, *Sūra* 2: 200, commands Muslims to invoke God with greater conviction. At the same time Burckhardt has an eye on the realities Muslims have to face on pilgrimage. In connexion with the wearing of the *iḥrām*, he observes that whether it is worn in summer or in winter it is equally inconvenient and prejudicial to health, particularly among northern Muslims who, accustomed to thick woollen clothes, are obliged to take them off for many days. But such apparently is the religious zeal of some that even if they arrive several months before the pilgrimage they vow on wearing the *iḥrām* not to throw it off till after completion of their travel to ʿArafāt and they remain for months covered only with this thin cloak. Such hardships and others often lead to premature deaths and Burckhardt noticed the corpses of pilgrims lying in the mosque before being quickly buried.

Like the Swiss traveller preceding him, Richard Burton preferred the anonymity of disguise when going on pilgrimage to Makka. As disguise was easy on account of the vast and varied multitudes present during pilgrimage, he felt it was prudent for the British Vice-Consul at Jeddah to prevent European travellers from going to Makka without it. In his book published in 1855-56 he follows Burckhardt in describing the same phases of pilgrimage and often relies on his account. But there are also significant differences between the two. It is primarily a question of mentality. In his first chapter Burton explains the reasons for his going on pilgrimage: he was thoroughly tired of 'progress' and of 'civilization', interested in Moslem inner life and 'longing to set foot on that mysterious spot which no vacation tourist has yet described'.[52] In the preface to the third edition, he argues that in the Muslim pilgrimage there is nothing so offensive to Christians.[53] In Appendix I (ii, 280) he even challenges some European writers who tried to represent the pilgrimage as a fair. He does not want to speculate whether the secular or the spiritual element originally prevailed but he concludes that the pilgrimage is essentially religious, accidentally an affair of commerce. Burton seeks *rapprochement* with Muslims because they venerate Abraham, the father of the faithful. His technique is to quote some honest men who hold that Islam, in its capital tenets, approaches much nearer to the faith of Jesus than do the Pauline and Athanasian modifications which have divided the Indo-European mind into Catholic and Roman, Greek and Russian, Lutheran and Anglican (i. xxiii). In view of his pronouncements, the reader is assured of a sympathetic understanding of the pilgrimage and the Arabs.

When he at last reached the Ka'ba in Makka, Burton felt deeply moved: of all the worshippers who clung weeping or who pressed their beating hearts to the stone 'none felt a deeper emotion than did the Ḥājī from the far north (ii, 161).[54] But he confesses that whereas Muslims showed the feeling of religious enthusiasm, he only felt the ecstasy of gratified pride. Unlike Burckhardt, Burton tries to penetrate into the inner feelings of Muslims who, for the first time, contemplate the Ka'ba with fear and awe. Whereas the former simply says that he recited all the necessary prayers which he repeated after his guide, Burton actually gives the words of the prayers he recites and these are by and large fairly accurate, especially when he symbolically stones the devil at the pillars in Minā. He chose to visit the Prophet's tomb at Madina first instead of starting his visit at Makka like most pilgrims. He takes great care to stress the difference between this visit, technically a 'ziyārat' which is only meritorious and the ḥajj to Makka which is a duty laid down by the Qur'ān. As he points out, *'ṭawāf'* or circumambulation like the one at the Ka'ba must never be performed at the Prophet's tomb nor should the tomb be visited in pilgrim's dress. He takes the opportunity to castigate some Indian Muslims who prostrated themselves before it. His guide asks him to repeat a long prayer after him at the tomb. Burton adds in a footnote that the visitor is allowed to shorten it, but on no account to say less than 'Peace be upon Thee, O Messenger of Allah'. In this long prayer one phrase is made to produce a slightly comic effect, as Burton writes: 'O Messenger of Allah, Intercession! Intercession! Intercession!' (i. 317). The ordinary Muslim pilgrim actually says: 'Peace be upon you, O intercessor of sins (before God)'.

The *Personal Narrative* does not always concentrate on pilgrimage. For Burton also takes the opportunity to give his impressions of the people and institutions of Madina and Makka. He does not particularly like the Madanī whose manners he finds graver and somewhat more pompous than those of any Arabs he met – a trait borrowed from the Turks, he thinks (ii. 17). Above all, he objects to their hypocrisy, their mouths being as full of religious salutations and 'hackneyed' quotations from the Qur'ān as of indecency and vile abuse: they preserve their reputation as the sons of a holy city by praying only in public. However, their redeeming trait appears to be generosity and manliness. Always trying to score a point against Burckhardt, Burton shows that the Madina of the 1850s still abounded in books despite the attacks of the Wahhābīs. Large collections of books were to be found in two *madrasas* near the Ḥaram, apart from extensive private collections and a large *waqf* or bequest of books presented to the mosque. Burton's conclusion was that Madina was not guilty of the charge of ignorance levelled at it by Burckhardt, although no facilities for the study of anything apart from the purely religious sciences existed. Many students therefore went to study in Cairo and Damascus (ii. 25). Although Burton's stay at Makka was short, he found the citizens more civilized but more vicious than those of Madina. He accounts for their dark skin by the fact that the Makkans were the offsprings of black slaves, the Sharīf being almost a Negro. However, the most unpleasant peculiarities of the Makkans were their pride and coarseness of language.

More interesting perhaps was Burton's perception of the Bedouins of the Hijaz. Before discussing the Bedouin he attempts a classification of the Arabs – a classification which at first appears to have some affinity with that found in ethnological studies of the century. Despite the admission that the Hymiaritic tribes which emigrated to the Hijaz mixed with races from the Yemen and with the Hebrews, he makes the surprising statement that the Badawī of the Hijaz preserves in purity the blood transmitted to him by his ancestors. He feels the need to remedy the deficiency in James Bruce, author of *Travels to discover the sources of the Nile* (1790), and Burckhardt by providing a physical description of the Bedouin and suggesting that deformity is checked by the Spartan restraint upon population and that no weakly infant can live through a Badawi life (ii. 83). He accounts for the preservation of national characteristics through systematic intermarriage. No genetic disorders apparently occur from the union of first cousins and Burton maintains that the theory of physiologists who prove degeneracy among the offspring of close cousins is faulty and based on insufficient facts. He obviously likes the free and simple manners of the Bedouins who are protected from affectation, awkwardness and embarrassment – the disease of civilization. The Bedouins may be ravenous and sanguinary, but they are not reckless and their best traits are determination, gentleness and generosity. They are not cowards, for the danger faced in raids and blood feuds, the continual uncertainty of existence, horsemanship and martial exercises, all instil courage in them. Like Lamartine, Burton admires the chivalry of the Bedouins whom he turns into children of ʿAntar (see Chapter 3, above). He particularly likes the chivalry which makes the society of the Bedouins so delightful to the traveller. The Bedouin is turned into a noble savage who also appreciates poetry and even if he has little religion, he has a sense of honour and boundless hospitality. Burton likens him to the North American Indian, but unlike Chateaubriand gives him the preference over the latter because of his kind treatment of women.

It seems then that by reading travellers' accounts of the Middle East readers not only became aware of some aspects of Islam peculiar to the individual countries being described but gained some insight into the more permanent features of the religion. However, if they wanted information on countries such as Algeria and Persia, they did not need to rely entirely on travellers. Diplomats and political figures like Gobineau and de Tocqueville could easily provide it (see Chapter 6, below). Still the perspective opened on the world of Islam by travellers proved refreshing. Toderini may even have surprised his readers with the demonstration that the Turks did have a culture to which the Arabs had contributed in some way. Granted that Chateaubriand and Lamartine had their own agenda in visiting the Middle East, their writings are still significant. They are to be assessed not by their ulterior motives but by the perspectives they provide on what really stands out in Islam. Thus the centrality of Jerusalem in Islam, well understood by Chateaubriand, will not appear like a twenty-first century fabrication. On the other hand, one should be a little wary of Lamartine's good intentions. For all the emphasis on tolerance in Islam a price has to be paid. Lamartine seeks to impose popular fatalism as well as a vague deism as the official teaching of Islam. However, one cannot fail to appreciate his attempts at *rapprochement.* The tendency to take refuge in the past or in dreams betrayed by Lamartine and Nerval is fortunately counterbalanced by the reality of nineteenth-century Egypt sketched by Clot-Bey, Saint-Hilaire and Lane.

Notes

1. In *The Legacy of Islam*, eds. J. Schacht and C.E. Bosworth (Oxford, 1974), pp. 49-50. He maintained his position when he enlarged on this paper in his book *La Fascination de l'Islam* (Paris, 1980), p. 86.

2. Nerval published a *Voyage en Orient* in 1851. This work is in volume ii of the *Oeuvres*, eds. A. Beguin and J. Richer (Paris, 1956). His *Correspondance* is in vol. i. See particularly I, 893.

3. *Souvenirs, impressions, pensées et paysages pendant un Voyage en Orient* (Paris, 1835), 4 vols. in 2; ii. 26.

4. Claudine Grossir, *L'Islam des Romantiques 1811-1840* (Paris, 1984), p. 109.

5. In *Voyage en Abyssinie précédé d'une excursion dans l'Arabie Heureuse* (Paris, 1838), pp. 43, 64, E. Combes and M. Tamisier paint a rather negative picture of the Yemenis: they challenge the notion of sobriety among Bedouins,

stressing their gluttony and lack of hospitality. Their aim was to show the superiority of Europeans to the ignorant Yemenis. Paul Emile Botta was more positive, stressing the hospitality of the imams, their religious tolerance and their well-regulated society and sedentary culture. See *Relation d'un Voyage dans L'Yemen* (Paris, 1841), pp. 21, 131 and 142-3.

6. Even today Egypt continues to fascinate. It is one of the rare countries of the Middle East that have prompted the setting up of a learned society at first devoted almost exclusively to the study of travel to it. This society was set up in 1997 following the annual meeting of the British Society For Middle Eastern Studies.

7. See Jeanne Chaybany, *Les Voyages en Perse et la pensée française au xviie siècle* (Tehran, 1971). Nineteenth-century studies of Persia include those of James Morier, *A Journey through Persia, Armenia and Asia Minor in the years 1808 and 1809* (London, 1812) and Amédée Jaubert, *Voyage en Armenie et en Perse* (Paris, 1821). While Morier is well disposed towards Persia, Jaubert, shows a fairly ambivalent attitude towards it, although he liked Fatḥ ʿAlī Shāh and his ministers. For some account of Persia, see below.

8. See J.M. Carré, *Voyageurs et écrivains français en Egypte* (Cairo, 1933), 2 vols., especially ii. 36.

9. Although he is known primarily for works such as *L'Egypte sous les Pharaons* (Paris 1814) and *Précis du système hiéroglyphique des anciens Egyptiens* (1824), he also published a work on modern Egypt, the *Lettres écrites d'Egypte et de Nubie* (1833) where he showed appreciation of the countless mosques of Cairo with their beautiful minarets, even praying in the mosque of Ibn Ṭūlūn. He claimed that thanks to the Fatimid and Ayyubid Caliphs, Cairo was a still a city of the *Nights*.

10. Writers such as Mouradja d'Ohsson and Volney have been discussed in my book *Images of Islam in eighteenth-century writings*.

11. For example, Marana, author of *The Turkish Spy*. See *Images of Islam*, p. 113.

12. The baron Francois de Tott, author of the *Mémoires sur les Turcs et les Tartares* (Paris, 1784).

13. C. Savary wrote a translation of the Qur'ān (1783) and the *Lettres sur l'Egypte* (1788).

14. The most well known of his works is the *Histoire de l'agrandissement et de la décadence de l'empire ottoman* (Paris, 1743), 2 vols.

15. Toderini has in mind J.A. Guer, author of the *Moeurs et usages des Turcs* (see Chapter 2, above). But his attack does not apply to Charles Pertuisier, attaché to the French embassy at the Porte, who wrote the *Promenades pittoresques dans Constantinople et sur les rives du Bosphore* (Paris, 1815), 3 vols. Pertuisier speaks of sixteen libraries put together by the Sulṭāns, the library of the Topkapi Palace being of the first rank. He says that

foreigners could have access to them, especially to the library of Sulṭān 'Abdul Ḥamīd (he means Maḥmūd II), I. 218-19. After paying homage to Toderini, Michaud mentions other libraries not visited by the latter. See *Correspondance,* iii. 42-50.

16. As did Pertuisier who drew a parallel between the Turks and the Chinese in this respect. He actually refers to Toderini, op. cit., I. 224.

17. See 'Can science come back to Islam?' *New Scientist* (23 October 1980), no. 1224, p. 213.

18. See Michaud, *Histoire des Croisades* (Paris, 1825), I. 221.

19. Cf. Pertuisier who gives a similar account of the teaching programme in *madrasas,* but provides further information on primary schools in Constantinople. He says that these are maintained by pious foundations, but the children of the élite are taught at home by private tutors (i. 237, 293). See also Michaud, *Correspondance,* iii. 100.

20. Anquetil-Duperron, *Législation orientale* (Amsterdam, 1778).

21. This is also the view of Pertuisier. cf. op. cit., ii. 367. The comte Andreossy, a former French Ambassador to London and Constantinople and a member of the Institut d'Egypte, maintains that the Ottoman Sulṭān does not impose an arbitrary despotism on the whole of his subjects, as is generally believed in Europe: limits are set by the Qur'ān and custom. The Sulṭān, says Andreossy, differs in this from the Emperor of Russia who is himself the source of power, but whose uncontrolled power has been recently modified by the senate. See *Constantinople et le Bosphore de Thrace pendant les années 1812-1814, 1826* (Paris, 1828), p. xx.

22. James Porter, *Observations on the religion, law, government and manners of the Turks* (London, 1768).

23. *Voyage en Orient,* ii. 216.

24. *Oeuvres romanesques et voyages,* ed. Maurice Regard (Paris, 1969), ii. 701.

25. From *Sūra* 3: 45, *Sūra* 19: 91-92.

26. See Albert Hourani, *A History of the Arab peoples* (London, 1991), p. 28. Kenneth Cragg notes that 'the calligraphy from the Qur'ān is based on passages incriminating Christology and the doctrine of the Trinity and underlying the role of Jesus as prophet and as an exemplary "Muslim"', *The Arab Christian* (London, 1992), p. 53. As he points out, one of the purposes of the Dome was to outshine in splendour the Church of the Resurrection nearby.

27. See the commentary of Si Hamza Boubakeur on *Sūra* 17 in *Le Coran,* ed. cit., I. 923.

28. See the articles Al-Quds and Qubbat al-Ṣakhra in the *Shorter Encyclopaedia of Islam,* eds. H.A.R. Gibb and J.H. Kramers, Leiden, 1974. The significance of Jerusalem for Muslims is stressed in *Sūra* 17: 1 and in Traditions of the Prophet, one of which is: 'Whoever wants to see a part of Paradise

let him look at Bayt al-Maqdis' (Jerusalem). Jerusalem was the first place towards which Muslims turned in prayer for sixteen months. There is also an abundant Islamic literature extolling the *faḍā'il* (excellences) of Jerusalem. Two papers by Kenneth Cragg and Marwan Abu Khalaf at the conference 'The centrality of Jerusalem in Islam', S.O.A.S., 22 August 1998, developed this theme.

29. See G. Der-Sahagian, *Chateaubriand en Orient* (Fribourg, 1914), p. 291 and Chateaubriand, ed. cit., ii. 1729, n. 2.

30. In Jerusalem Chateaubriand says he came across 'Abduallāh who displayed sordid avarice like most Muslims (p. 1120). Yet a few pages later he cannot help acknowledging that a certain Abu-Gosh refused to accept money for a lamb the latter had roasted for him (p. 1128).

31. There is a parallel between them and the Arab butcher of Jerusalem who after the slaughter of a lamb gives the impression of having slaughtered a man because of his ferocious looks and his bloodstained hands (p. 1125).

32. See Hourani, *A History of the Arab peoples*, p. 318.

33. In his entry of 18 November, 1832, after a visit to the monastery of Antoura in Lebanon, Lamartine speaks of the existence of irreconcilable hatred between diverse Christian communions more than between Turks and Christians.

34. J.M. Tancoigne, one of the *Jeunes de Langues* at Constantinople, says that in Smyrna the Greeks have, like the Armenians, a metropolitan archbishop and many beautiful churches where the Turks allow them to celebrate their religious rites in peace. See *Voyage à Smyrne* (Paris, 1817), p. 38

35. Michaud, *Correspondance d'Orient*, vi. 150, noted some people praying in Azhar mosque while pedlars sold their wares: his conclusion was that travellers could think that they were now in a sacred place, now in a café or bazaar. M. Gilsenan quotes Tomas Gerholm, author of *Market, Mosque and Mafrag* (Stockholm, 1977) who finds the Friday mosque in Yemen to be a kind of extension of the market. Gilsenan himself sees the market as an extension of the mosque. See *Recognizing Islam* (London, 1990), pp. 176, 177.

36. See Hourani, op. cit., pp. 224-25.

37. British Library, Add. Mss., 34080, f. 184. This manuscript was edited for the first time by J. Thompson, Cairo, 2000. The second version, with unnumbered fols., is in Sackler Library, Oxford, Griffith Institute Archives, Lane mss. 6. 1.

38. See Leila Ahmed, *Edward W. Lane* (London, 1978), pp. 36-37.

39. For example, Edward Said, in *Orientalism*, p. 167.

40. In the chapter 'Religion and Laws' of *Manners and Customs of the Modern Egyptians*, p. 111, Lane points out how the peasantry of Egypt have retained the customs of their Bedouin ancestors, transgressing the limits assigned by the Qur'ān in case of blood revenge.

41. Leila Ahmed, op. cit., pp. 117-19.

42. In Tunis, for example, Friday prayers at the Zaytuna, the 9th-century mosque of the city, are said later than elsewhere (at 3 p.m.) to allow Civil Servants to attend. Presumably they do not return to work afterwards.

43. Non-Muslims are sometimes confused about the correct order. Cf. A. Hourani, *History*, p. 48.

44. J. Heyworth-Dunne, *Introduction to the history of education in modern Egypt* (London, 1938), p. 166.

45. This is what Nerval wrote to his father on the 25 July 1843. *Oeuvres,* i. 887.

46. In an extract on the merit of the Syrians, Ibn Jābir mentions an amusing story about pilgrims when they reached Damascus in 580. Many women went to meet them and offered them bread: as soon as the pilgrims started eating, the women snatched the bread from them in order to obtain the blessing they had given it by leaving the mark of their teeth on it. See Mohammed Yalaoui, *100 textes français* (Tunis, 1984), p. 46.

47. A. Hourani, *Arabic Thought in the liberal age 1798-1939* (Cambridge, 1983), p. 53.

48. A. Hourani, *A History of the Arab peoples*, pp. 273-74.

49. See Norman Daniel, *Islam, Europe and Empire* (Edinburgh, 1966), p. 14.

50. Jean de Thevenot, *Relation d'un voyage fait au Levant* (Paris, 1664).

51. After wearing the *iḥrām,* for example, the pilgrim proclaims his intention to make the pilgrimage by an act of consecration, the *talbiya*. Burton accurately gives the English version as: 'Here I am! O Allah! Here am I! No partner has Thou, here am I! Verily the praise and the grace are Thine, and the empire', followed by the Arabic text but the Arabic only, in Appendix I. See *Personal Narrative of a pilgrimage to al-Madina and Meccah* (New York, 1893), ii. 139 and ii. 285.

52. Op. cit., i. 2.

53. Ibid., p. xxii. In Appendix 1, ii. 280.

54. At the heart of the *ḥaram,* the sacred area, in Makka, stands the Ka'ba, the rectangular building which Muḥammad had purged of idols and made the centre of Muslim worship, with the Black Stone embedded in one of its walls. Pilgrims would go round the Ka'ba seven times touching or kissing the Black Stone as they pass it.

CHAPTER 6

De Tocqueville's and Gobineau's perspectives on the world of Islam

It is not surprising that De Tocqueville's interest in Islam went beyond his commentaries on the Qur'ān. For De Tocqueville was also interested in the development of world leaders like Muḥammad. In his notes of December 1829 on the lectures on the history of civilization in Europe by the historian and statesman François Guizot (1787-1874), he tries to offer a solution to the problems that Muḥammad, Cromwell and Bonaparte give rise to.[1] He suggests that in the case of these leaders people have been unwilling to take into account the successive development that took place in their moral being. The fact that a man constantly changes in the course of his career has been lost sight of and people fail to isolate factors that prompt the actions of a young leader from factors inspiring those of a mature man. So wishing to avoid the traditional approach that seeks to distinguish between Muḥammad at Makka and Muḥammad at Madina, De Tocqueville seems to prefer a development by age.

There is a shift in focus from individuals to races in the 'Lettres sur l'Algérie' of 1837. In the first of the letters De Tocqueville attempts a classification of the population of Algeria in which he concentrates on the Kabyles living in the Atlas mountains and the Arabs living in the valleys.[2] He accepts a little intermingling between the two races, but stresses the fact that they retain their distinctive characteristics. The criteria he uses to establish a distinction between them are those of language, customs and ethnic origin. These were virtually the same criteria used in the eighteenth century to explain the diversity of peoples encountered by European visitors and to distinguish the native inhabitants of Barbary (the Kabyles or Berbers) from the invaders (the Arabs).[3] The nineteenth-century theorists, however, went further: in their view the Arabs or Bedouin were entirely pastoralists and nomadic plains-dwellers, while the Kabyles were the mountain-dwellers who cultivated the land. This means that the plains were occupied by the invaders only and could therefore be cultivated by French settlers.[4]

De Tocqueville shared in this colonialist mentality of the nineteenth century but he had his own distinct contribution to make in its development. Whereas other thinkers of the century fabricated the image of the wicked Arab and the good Kabyle in the 1840s,[5] he criticized the tendency of Europeans to consider all Arabs as pastoralists. On the other hand, if they are not entirely pastoralists and nomads, they are not quite sedentary and farmers. Rather they alternate between the two positions. De Tocqueville does not see among the Arabs the same complete equality that prevails among the Kabyle people. Yet he finds that the Arabs of the African coast have a vivid and sensual imagination, astute and sagacious minds, the same courage and inconsistency typical of their ancestors. Like them, they belong to that indomitable race which enjoys pleasure, but which sets liberty above all pleasures, which would rather flee to the desert sands than remain idle under a master. Like all 'half savage'[6] races, they respect power and force above everything. Scorning trade and the arts like their ancestors, they particularly like war, pomp and noise: they are more inclined to feel than to think. It is clear that although writing in the late 1830s De Tocqueville does not perceive the Arabs in Algeria as the thriving and lazy descendants of the invaders: rather he subscribes to the current myth of the 'noble Bedouin' on the lines of the 'noble savage' of the eighteenth century.[7]

De Tocqueville, however, is not genuinely interested in Algerian Arabs. For he has his own agenda for the colonization of Algeria. He argues that while the Arabs own all the land they cultivate but a small portion of it; because of their scanty population, they occupy more land than they can cultivate every year. The result of this is that they sell it easily and cheaply and a foreign population can easily settle among them without them suffering. It is easy for the French who are richer and more industrious than the Arabs to occupy much of the land without using force and to settle peacefully and in large numbers amidst the surrounding tribes. De Tocqueville is not satisfied with the French merely settling alongside the Arabs. What he advocates is a permanent link and integration between the two races. He does not perceive the struggle between France and Algeria as a war between Christianity and Islam: the ambition of indigenous leaders more than the religion of the people accounts for the uprising against the French. For religion does not stop the Algerians from becoming the keenest auxiliaries of the French and under the French flag they fight their Muslim co-religionists as fiercely as the latter fight the French. De Tocqueville's firm belief is that if the French can prove that under their domination Islam is not in danger, religious fervour will die down and the French will only have political enemies in Africa. De Tocqueville may have had in mind Arab nationalists like 'Abd al-Qādir who rose against the French in 1839 and was finally defeated by General Bugeaud in 1847.

How should the Kabyles be won over? In the first letter, De Tocqueville points out that the only thing they have in common with the Arabs is religion. Yet he claims that the

Kabyles are lukewarm about Islam and that they are a prosaic race more concerned with this world than the hereafter. It would be easier to defeat them with French 'luxe' and arts than with bullets – an idea he takes up in the second letter where he suggests that they can be won over through their love of material pleasure.[8] In the first letter, he mentions the fierce resistance the Kabyles put up against the Turks who are fleetingly described as a body providing the militia, the civil and military officers. There the Moors too are speedily dismissed: they are simply described as belonging to various races and as Arabs whose sedentary taste and desire to enjoy their wealth in peace made them settle in towns. This witty, gentle, intelligent race is, however, despised by the Arabs of the plains.

Some three years after writing the letters and before his visit to Algeria in 1841, De Tocqueville made notes and reflexions on the situation of French establishments in Algeria.[9] These 'Notes et réflexions' of 1840 are provocative from a sociological and theological point of view.[10] De Tocqueville's comments on the foundation of property betray a profound misunderstanding of property laws in Islam. He begins with the erroneous statement that according to the Qur'ān all property belongs to God and His representative. It is not clear who is the representative of God: he may have the Sulṭān in mind. In any case, if God is master of the world, it cannot reasonably be argued that His representative owns all property. De Tocqueville claims that according to the commentators and usage, God's representative has no right to deprive the Muslim owner of property: the only concession made is that the latter is bound to pay him the tithe or the tenth, the *'ushr* (which he calls *achour*), a tax which is levied on the harvest. According to A. Grohmann the 'ushr' had pre-Islamic origins. T. Sato, however, lays greater emphasis on its levy during Islamic times, quoting *Ḥadīth* and Abū Yūsuf (d. 798).[11] In

North Africa, ''ushr' is sometimes levied on trees and livestock and sometimes on land. De Tocqueville establishes a distinction between the situation in Egypt and in Algeria: in the former country, lands only gradually came out of the hands of the people and the Qur'ānic principle was gradually applied with the result that the Pasha became the owner of the whole of Egypt, whereas in the latter Islam was quickly introduced and all lands remained as individual property, subject only to the 'achour' which every owner had to pay.[12]

In his remarks on the pious foundations of Muslims in Algiers, De Tocqueville contrasts the state of affairs prevailing before and after the French conquest. He mentions the existence in all Muslim countries of a foundation by the name of Makka and Madina. He says this foundation consists of property given in perpetuity and from the usufruct sums are sent annually to these two cities and are spent locally as charity. It is clear that De Tocqueville did not wish to embark on a lengthy explanation of the complex *waqf* system. Avoiding this tricky ground, he concentrates on a factual survey, on the impact of the conquest which, in his view, was responsible for the disappearance of some of the expenses and resources. It reduced the number of buildings to be maintained, since a report of 1837 shows that half of the mosques were no longer used for prayers and that a number of buildings had been demolished or put to public use (*Oeuvres complètes*, iii, 167).

When he tries to account for the absence of a clergy in Islam, De Tocqueville takes up a more controversial position. In all his remarks, he has Sunnī Islam in mind, completely ignoring Shī'ite Islam where a clerical hierarchy exists. He begins with the provocative statement that Muḥammad preached Islam to a backward, nomadic and war-like people. He claims that since Islam had war as its aim, there followed a small number of practices and a simple cult. The form of worship being virtually non-existent, the priest proved hardly necessary. But in his view there was a more powerful reason to explain the almost complete absence of a priesthood among Muslims, which strikes him as odd, since all religions which have made a powerful impact on man's imagination have maintained their influence by means of a priesthood distinct from the rest of the nation. It is that Islam completely merged the two powers (religious and secular) so that the high priest is necessarily the prince and the prince is the high priest and all the acts of civil and political life are more or less based on religious law (iii, 174). What De Tocqueville says about the merging of religious and secular powers may be true of the early Caliphate. For many problems the Caliph 'Umar, for example, instituted precedents as they arose, after consulting with Muslims. De Tocqueville considers the absence of a separate religious body, as in Roman Catholicism, to be a blessing in the midst of all the evil that Islam is supposed to have produced. For he believes that a priestly body is in itself the source of much social unease and one should rejoice when a religion can be powerful without the help of such means. But at the same time he claims that this intermingling of powers due to Muḥammad has been responsible for despotism and particularly for the social stagnation which has nearly always characterized Muslim nations and which makes them succumb to nations which have adopted the opposite system.

De Tocqueville makes no attempt to clarify his remark about the origin of despotism in Islam, while he makes some attempt to account for social immobility. He attributes the root cause for it to the Qur'ān. For he argues that since the Qur'ān is the common source from which stem religious law, civil law and to some extent secular science, the same education is given to those who want to become ministers of religion, doctors of the law, judges and even scholars. The result is that these various professions leave no indelible trait on those who practise them. Forgetting what he had written in the 'Lettres sur l'Algérie', on the sedentariness of some Arabs he now says that the Muslim population is more like the Prophet's Arabs, since it is nomadic and divided into tribes. Even traces of a clerical body are hardly visible among the Arab tribes of Algeria who are compared with the Muslims of Constantinople where a semblance of religious hierarchy apparently exists. He points out that the very word 'clergy' does not exist in Arabic. He concludes this section of the 'Notes' with the remark that temporal power is exercised by the marabouts, a kind of power which is ill defined and similar to that exercised by saints and anchorites at the end of the Roman Empire. The only difference he detects is that among the Arabs this holiness is often hereditary.

Under the section 'Etat civil', De Tocqueville claims that a registry office goes against the habits and religious practices of Muslims. It would appear that they particularly dislike the recording of death, since it compels them to open up their homes so as to give access to the doctor or the civil status officer. Moreover, registration of births, marriages and deaths is unknown to Muslim countries with their enclosed houses. De Tocqueville's view is not borne out by what really happens in such countries. There is no basis for his remark that Muslims hardly ever pronounce the first names of their wives and daughters.

De Tocqueville appears totally confused in his remarks on the Islamic form of worship (iii, 180). Although there is nothing particularly objectionable in his perception of the ceremonies of Islamic worship as simple and consisting of prayers and sermons, unlike Lane, he does not seem to know what a *Khuṭba* really is, as he describes it as a profession of faith and a prayer for the leader of the believers, recited every Friday. The *Khuṭba* or sermon which precedes Friday prayers in congregation is not a profession of faith, although it contains praise of God, blessings on the Prophet and a prayer to God for the welfare of all Muslims. De Tocqueville turns Islamic worship into a primarily urban affair. While there may be fewer mosques away from urban centres, he makes the categorical statement that outside the towns, no mosque or minister of religion exists: Islamic worship is according to him non-existent and the population is abandoned to marabouts. The fact that marabouts may be more in evidence in villages does not of course mean that all Islamic worship is abandoned. On the other hand, his remark on what he calls Muslim sects is accurate. This remark, not based on the *Tableau des établissements français*, refers to the four orthodox schools of thought in Sunnī Islam. As he points out, two of these schools exist in Algeria: the *Ḥanafī* and the *Mālikī*, the former having fourteen mosques in Algiers and the latter ninety-two.

Towards the end of his 'Notes' De Tocqueville has a section on 'Djihad' which he takes in the popular sense of holy war, ignoring the other meaning of 'struggle', 'effort'. He states that holy war is compulsory for all believers, that the state of war is a natural state against the 'infidels' and that one can only have truces. He attributes two motives for this war: fanaticism and greed (III, 187).

In a letter of 22 October 1843 to Gobineau, De Tocqueville says that the latter reminds him of another of his friends whom he met again in Africa and who became a Muslim. (*Oeuvres complètes*, iii, 68). He was not tempted to become a Muslim himself, although he had studied the Qur'ān a lot. He confesses that the study was primarily motivated by consideration of the position the French were taking towards Muslim populations in Algeria and the Middle East. Far from wanting to become a Muslim, he says he became convinced as a result of this study that few religions were as harmful to men as Muḥammad's. In his view Islam was the main cause of the decadence so apparent in the Muslim world. Here De Tocqueville is simply echoing sentiments expressed by Volney in the 1780s. Although less absurd than ancient polytheism, the social and political tendencies of Islam were, he felt, more to be dreaded and, compared with paganism, Islam was more a sign of decadence than progress.

The above letter may be read as an introduction to his substantial comments on the theme of France and Islam in Algeria in his *Rapport sur l'Algérie* of 1847 in which secular matters predominate.[13] The *Rapport* starts with the jingoistic observation that barbarous nations can be studied only with arms in hand and that victory over them had enabled the French to gain an insight into their usage and beliefs and given them the secret to govern these nations. Proudly showing that the French know the history of the different tribes as well as the tribes themselves and that they had the exact biography of all the powerful families, De Tocqueville unashamedly acknowledges that no institution has been more useful in establishing French domination in Africa than the *bureaux arabes*. Indeed, the officials of the twenty-one *bureaux*, the status of which was fixed by ministerial decree on the 1 December 1844, were keen students of various aspects of Arab society and civilization.[14] The author celebrates the 'civilizing' mission of the French with the remark that the better they know the country and the natives, the more obvious become the usefulness and the necessity even of establishing a European population on African soil. There is at first the suggestion that no civilization existed in Algeria before the arrival of the Europeans, as a civilized and Christian society is founded only with the arrival of a European population. But De Tocqueville then modifies his position by admitting that Muslim society in Africa was not uncivilized. Though it had a backward and imperfect civilization, it had a large number of pious foundations which aimed to provide charity and public education. In trying to be fair to Islam in Algeria, he concedes that the French have diverted revenues from areas in which they were formerly used, reduced the number of charitable institutions, let schools fall in ruins and dispersed seminaries. In a footnote, he says that according to general Bedeau there existed in 1837 in Constantine secondary schools where some six to seven hundred pupils studied commentaries on the Qur'ān, the traditions of the Prophet and followed classes in arithmetic, astronomy, rhetoric and philosophy. At the same time there were ninety primary schools frequented by thirteen to fourteen hundred children. Ten years later the number of students in secondary and primary schools and the number of primary schools had been drastically reduced. The recruitment of people of religion and the law had ceased. The disastrous effect of French colonialism is spelt out in unambiguous terms with the frank admission that the French have made Muslim society much more wretched, disorderly, ignorant and barbarous than it was before their arrival.

However, De Tocqueville wanted to look at French colonization in Algeria in contrasting ways. He lists a number of measures taken in favour of Algerians and sometimes at the expense of the French settlers. He points out that respect for the beliefs of the Algerians was carried to such extreme lengths that in certain areas the French built mosques for them without having a church themselves. Every year, the French administration, doing what the outgoing Muslim prince failed to do, transports to Egypt free of charge those pilgrims who want to honour the tomb of the Prophet.[15] In many of the places where the European population mixes with the indigenous population, the legitimate complaint is that the native is better protected and the European finds it hard to obtain justice.[16] These various measures lead him to conclude that the French administration in North Africa is so gentle towards the vanquished that it forgets its position as victor and does for its foreign subjects more than is done for citizens in France. Against this positive discrimination in favour of the natives must be set the other side of the coin. Algerian towns have been invaded and plundered more by French administrators than by French armies. In the vicinity of Algiers, fertile lands have been snatched away from the Arabs and given to the French who, unable or unwilling to cultivate them, have leased them to the same natives who thus became mere farmers on the lands which belonged to their fathers! Using much irony De Tocqueville denounces the theoretical writings that justify such reprehensible practices. Without being specific he says that the doctrine in one of these writings is that the native population having reached the final stage of depravation and vice is incapable of any reform or progress. Far from enlightening it, the French should deprive it of such light as it possesses; far from allowing it to settle, they should drive it away gradually so that they may take its place. Before this happens, they should use force to obtain its submission. In De Tocqueville's opinion, such doctrines deserve not only public condemnation, but also the official censure of the government and the Chamber of Deputies. Like the majority of the commission, he believes that the French government should avoid falling into extremes. Yet the conclusion he reaches is that of a Frenchman who glories in French racial superiority: the Algerians should not be led to believe that the French are bound to treat them like their own compatriots or their equals. For half civilized nations do not understand forbearing and indulgence! (*Oeuvres*, iii, 324). Although he admired American democracy in *La Démocratie en Amérique* (1835), De Tocqueville had no plans to promote democracy in Algeria!

De Tocqueville has a limited programme of reform to propose for Algeria in which a paternalist approach is evident. He argues that Islam is not against individual property, industry and sedentary living. In an understatement reminiscent of Diderot's on Abbasid achievement, at the beginning of the article 'Sarrasins' in the *Encyclopédie*, he adds that Islam is not entirely impervious to light, as it often admitted certain sciences and arts. Therefore why not make these flourish under French domination? The natives should not be forced to attend French schools, but they should be helped to improve their own, to increase the numbers of their teachers and to train men of the law and religion. De Tocqueville refers to the popular French belief that the religious passion inspired by the Qur'ān is hostile to the French and that Algerians should be allowed to wallow in superstition and ignorance through lack of lawyers and priests. He dismisses such a policy, deeming it to be very imprudent. His view is that when religious fervour exists in a nation, it always finds men who incite it and exploit it. The disappearance of regular and natural interpreters of religion does not signify the end of religious fervour which will simply be controlled by fanatics or impostors. As evidence, De Tocqueville refers to the insurrection of Bou Maza in 1844-45, led by fanatical beggars belonging to secret associations which he dubs a type of irregular and ignorant clergy.

The end of the 'Rapport' concentrates on slavery in Algeria. Even the small number of Negro slaves found in Algeria should not be allowed to remain in a country ruled by the French. To support his stand De Tocqueville quotes the example of the Bey of Tunis who had abolished slavery in his empire. So the French could not do less than he. De Tocqueville acknowledges that slavery in Islamic countries is not of the same type as in French colonies and that it has lost some of its rigours in the whole of the Middle East. While conceding that it has become milder, he argues that it has not become less opposed to the natural rights of humanity.

In a letter dated 13 November 1855 to Gobineau who was then serving at the French embassy in Tehran, De Tocqueville asks the latter to what he attributes the rapid and apparently relentless decadence of the Muslim nations whose countries he had crossed.[17] Setting his practical approach against Gobineau's theoretical approach, he hints that this decadence has placed some Muslim nations under the domination of 'our little Europe' which they caused to shudder once but that it will place all of them under the same domination. He wonders what worm is eating into this huge body. He can understand the causes of Turkish decadence, as the Turks are in his view a clumsy people whom nature simply intended to be deceived and defeated by everybody. But he is rather puzzled to explain the cause of the decadence into which Persia has been relentlessly driven for centuries, considering that the Persians, if one is to believe travellers, are intelligent, refined even. A few million men who centuries before lived in forests and swamps, that is, the French and other Europeans, will before a century has passed become the transformers of the globe and hold sway over mankind. De Tocqueville sees clearly in this the designs of Providence. Hence it is evident that the earlier interest he displayed in Islam and the Qur'ān was simply a passing phase, the real interest being colonial in origin. The prophecy about the military and intellectual triumph of Europe over Muslim nations was to prove true and De Tocqueville's intellectual arrogance, though tempered by some measure of fair-mindedness, was shared over a longer period by other Frenchmen when they reacted to different peoples constituting the world of Islam.

It is true that Islamic communities were generally viewed with less discredit by the French Enlightenment than they were later by scholars who embarked on various racial classifications. In *L'homme. Essai zoologigue sur le genre humain* (1827), for example, Bory de Saint-Vincent puts the Arabs in second place after the 'superior' European race.[18] This does not mean that nineteenth-century French writers as a whole had no contribution to make towards our understanding of the world of Islam. For the French contribution did not rest solely on scholars concerned with anthropometry and racial classifications. Chateaubriand, Lamartine and Nerval, for instance, had made an impact on French readers through their observations on Islam in the first half of the century.[19] Moreover, from the end of the eighteenth century the 'Ecole publique des langues orientales vivantes' added considerably to the interest in Islamic Studies through its scholarly output. The paradox here is that one of its most distinguished professors, Sylvestre de Sacy, could have advanced the cause of Arabic and Islamic Studies further with his substantial scholarly publications if he had refrained from serving the political objectives of the French government.[20]

The attitude of the French towards the people of the Middle East and North Africa and towards the main religion of the area – Islam – has sometimes provoked legitimate reactions. But over-reaction and over-sensitivity also have their dangers. Hypersensitivity may lead to what many in the West regard as the hyperbole of Arab rhetoric, a caricatural reading of European thought and an unfair evaluation of writers critical of Islam, yet not blind to its achievements. Such over-reaction may have harmed the standing of Comte Arthur de Gobineau (1816-82), who served France as a diplomat between 1849 and 1877. Apart from noting his controversial observations on race, two points need to be made about him: (1) although he is a diplomat by profession, his interests are not limited to the world of diplomacy and this perhaps ensures the variety of his approach and (2) as his *Oeuvres*, in the Pléiade edition, contain some eighteen hundred pages, many of which are devoted to the world of Islam, they require concentration of attention on selected passages and themes. Now it is by no means easy to pick out relevant themes from such a mass of material. But the reader who is prepared to go through some of these pages patiently and is not easily put off by what may appear like Gobineau's disjointed presentation, especially with regard to his reaction to the Prophet, will find the experience rewarding. The reputation of Gobineau has somewhat suffered because many modern critics identify him exclusively with the ethnological discourse of the period and with authorship of the *Essai sur l'inégalite des races humaines* (1853).[21] A thorough examination of a wider area of his literary output in chronological order may reveal an evolution in his reaction to the world of Islam.

The influence of the *Essai*[22] has been such that it cannot be discarded in any assessment of Gobineau's perspective on Islam. Gobineau leans heavily on the studies of the ethnologists of his day in the *Essai*, where he is more concerned with a variety of peoples, including Arabs, than with the Prophet of Islam. He believes that inequality does not stem from institutions but from race, the white race being superior to any other. Earlier on, he defines what he means by the 'white race'. It includes the Caucasian and Semitic. As the Arabs are Semites, the conclusion to be drawn is that they have recovered some ground since Bory de Saint-Vincent's classification in 1827. The criteria which Gobineau uses to grant superiority are past achievements: cultural, scientific and intellectual. The notion of future progress among the Arabs completely escapes him. In his view, there are only ten great civilizations, all issuing from what he calls 'l'initiative de la race blanche' (I, 346). Indian civilization is at the top of the league. But the ancient Arabs under the old name of Himyarites and the Persians – a branch of the Aryan family – are at least in third place, well ahead of the Germanic races which are seventh. Of course, such a league table could only have limited merit in any evaluation of the Arabs.

In book I, chapter XIV, he concludes his 'demonstration' (i, 301-314) about the intellectual inequality of the human race, with a few words about Arab culture. He has no doubt that French culture and Arab culture are mutually exclusive. He concedes that in the Middle Ages Frenchmen must have admired the wonders of the Islamic State and sent students to the schools at Cordoba. The recognition Gobineau gives to medieval Arab civilization in Spain seems rather vague. He makes no mention of the Neoplatonic philosophy of the Spanish Arabs Ibn Ṭufayl (c. 1105-85) and Ibn Rushd (1126-98) who exerted much influence on Christian Europe. He finds that little remains of Arab civilization in nineteenth-century Europe, where only its wreckage resists transformation. He sees no originality in it: resorting to a stereotyped notion of Islam being established by force, he argues that the Arabs merely assimilated races conquered by their swords. He says nothing about non-Arabs converted to Islam through persuasion. In Gobineau's view, since the Muslim nations were mixed, they produced nothing more than a hybrid civilization, the elements of which can easily be distinguished. One cannot quarrel with him for asserting that the Arabs had always maintained continuous relations with neighbouring nations and for asserting the principle of cross fertilization of cultures, although his vocabulary is not very subtle. He describes Arabs as a bastard nation thriving on a civilization with two origins, one advanced and the other barbarous.[23] There is nothing new in his idea that Islam was tailor-made for the Arabs and was invented by the Prophet to suit his people.

More interesting is Gobineau's idea that Islam, which had already assimilated Greco-Asiatic civilization, spread north and south of the Mediterranean because the populations of these regions shared the same civilization. Gobineau insists that while these various communities all contributed to the common prosperity, it was the small nucleus of Arab tribes from inside the peninsula that provided the impetus: they produced no scholars, but rather fanatics, soldiers and victors. This tendency to polarize, to attribute certain characteristics to entire communities, is also evident in chapter VI. Here Gobineau discusses progress or lack of it among them and argues that such characteristics are independent of geography. He asks rhetorically why the Kabyles of Morocco (that is, the Berbers of Algeria), an ancient race who had all the time for thought and every inducement to imitate others, never found a better way than pure and simple privateering at sea to improve their unhappy lot. In fact, the corsairs of Algiers were of various Mediterranean origins, not Berber. There is, however, some justification in the criticism levelled at North Africa for the attitude of its rulers to piracy in the first half of the nineteenth century. For instance, in 1817, the ruler of Morocco, Mawlay Sulaymān, banned piracy in order to avoid conflict with Europeans. But his successor, Mawlay ʿAbdur Raḥmān, revived it after 1825, thus putting an obstacle in the way of European trade with Morocco.[24]

Gobineau's description of Islamic communities sometimes leads to over-simplification and his reliance on anthropological theories produces a see-saw in the fortunes of the Arabs. But one should still refrain from dismissing the *Essai*. Although the main focus is on races, it does not leave out completely the Prophet and the Qur'ān. For instance, in chapter XI dealing with permanent ethnic differences, Gobineau challenges the anthropologist Prichard who, in the *Natural History of Man* (1843), as we are reminded, seeks to prove the unity of mankind and attempts to show that the time of puberty is the same in both sexes and in all races. In challenging Prichard on the question of the age of marriage among Muslim women, Gobineau pays indirect homage to the Qur'ān and the Prophet. He argues that the Qur'ān does not authorise women to simply marry when they have attained physical maturity. As he says, the Qur'ān requires that they be educated to understand the duties of marriage, which is a serious engagement. He seems to have had the provisions of *Sūra* 60: 12 in mind here:

> 'O Prophet! When believing women come to thee to take the oath of fealty to thee, that they will not associate in worship any other thing whatever with God, that they will not steal, that they will not commit adultery or fornication, that they will not kill their children, that they will not utter slander...'

Gobineau believes that the Prophet took great care to provide for young girls to receive a religious education until the time of marriage. That is why the legislator (that is, Muḥammad) delayed marriage and allowed for women's rational faculties to develop first before rushing to give his authorization.

In book II, chapter V, where Gobineau discusses Egyptians and Ethiopians, the homage to Islam appears mixed. He acknowledges that neither ancient Greece nor ancient Rome had, at the height of their glory, managed to integrate the Abyssinians into their civilization. In his view, the Semites of Muḥammad achieved this conversion not so much on the religious as on the social plane since the blood of the newcomers mixed with that of the ancient inhabitants on a wide scale (I, 448). As Jean Boissel points out (i.1357-58, n.1), it is strange that Gobineau should place dress among the key factors in the assimilation of the Abyssinians by the Arabs when he had promised to search for deep causes. But then Gobineau finds that Islamic civilization did not penetrate deeply and that assimilation was incomplete.

There is, however, no need to concentrate all of our attention on the *Essai*. For an evaluation of Gobineau's assessment of Islam in a different context, should one not consider other writings which are primarily concerned with Muslim communities and which form a coherent thematic whole? Gobineau's five years as a diplomat in Persia enabled him to write knowledgeably about Islam. He was posted to Tehran from 1855 to 1858 and from 1862 to 1863. His posting reflects the continuity in French official relations with Persia, which had grown in importance since the reign of Shāh ʿAbbās I and resulted in many missions to Persia by the French East India Company. The accounts of Persia and Islamic theology in Gobineau's *Mémoire sur l'état social de la Perse actuelle* (1856), *Trois ans en Asie* (1858-59) and *Les Religions et les philosophies dans l'Asie Centrale* (1865) broaden the perspective offered by travellers such as Jean Chardin in his *Voyages en Perse*, first published in 1686 and reprinted many times in the eighteenth century.[25]

Despite its title much of the *Mémoire* is not about Persia in the 1850s, but rather about that country in the centuries following the Islamic conquest. Although Gobineau tries to distinguish between Shīʿa and Sunnī Islam, he sometimes tends to neglect the theological differences between Shiites and Sunnites. He does reduce the five 'pillars' of Islam to four in the case of the Sunnīs. His reading of Islamic history is, however, accurate, as he shows how Shīʿite Islam contested the legitimacy of the Prophet's first three successors and how it became the established religion under the Safavids in Persia towards the end of the sixteenth century. In an attempt to distinguish between Shīʿites and Sunnites, he erroneously claims that the rest of Islam refuses to accept the Shīʿites as Muslims. He rather hopes to set Persians against Arabs who are perceived as barbarous zealots, poor and ignorant, feared but despised, led by a man whom they delighted in describing as the unlettered Prophet. Here Gobineau is obviously thinking of the Qur'ānic description, as in *Sūra* 7: 157, of Muḥammad as a 'nabī-al-ummī'. But he fails to recognize that Islam never forced conversion on the People of the Book and that it was only the Pagans who faced destruction. Instead he simply remarks that in Persia the Arabs proclaimed the annihilation of the old faith.

The reason appears to be that Gobineau wishes to impose one opinion on his readers, namely that the Arabs were bent on burning everything, books, temples and even Persian priests when they could. Persecution is an essential element of this opinion. Gobineau uses what he calls Arab persecution to offset the Persian contribution to Islamic civilization. He argues that the Arabs could destroy the ancient culture of the Persians, but not their taste for intellectual pursuits. The result was that the Arab conquerors became indebted to the Persians for their best grammarians, lexicographers, theologians, doctors and poets. While the point about Arab persecution may by controversial, there is nothing controversial about the debt of Islam to Persia. In theology, for instance, some of the greatest figures were Persian by birth, although they wrote in Arabic: al-Ṭabarī, author *inter alia* of the *Tafsīr* and al-Ghazālī, author of many famous theological works.

The *Mémoire* also acknowledges other qualities of the Persians. Gobineau seems to corroborate the testimony of previous writers like Chardin on Persian tolerance. He states that it is all to the credit of the Persians that they refrained from persecuting the 'infidels' in order to demonstrate their orthodoxy. Apart from the Guebres who, he claims, incurred the particular curse of the Prophet, the followers of all the other religions were not persecuted. The Armenians (Catholics or Schismatics) enjoyed special protection at different periods. No one objected to the high offices held by the latter. What impresses Gobineau is that the Persians are open to foreign, particularly European, ideas. He takes the opportunity to contrast them with the Turks, whose government alone, he thinks, imitates Europe. Whereas the Turks thrive on proud memories of military domination, the Persians have no idea of patriotism: they only claim to be an intelligent, shrewd and witty nation. They are as interested in material well-being like the Europeans whose example they follow with the aim of achieving the same results. The fact that many Persians whom he met spoke French must have made Gobineau feel warm towards them. He adds that even the women in the harems knew some words of French, but he does not say which harems and how he acquired the information.

He thinks that under the cloak of refinement and mysticism Zoroastrian and Hindu notions have crept into Shīʿa Islam. As an illustration, he mentions the belief among some Shīʿites that the invisible Imām is but an illusion. To him, this illusion is none other than the *māyā* of Hindu philosophy.[26] Even if there were some resemblance between Shīʿa ideas and Hinduism, Gobineau could be faulted for drawing a rash conclusion, namely that the Persians had reluctantly become Muslims and had taken delight in becoming the first heretics. He further claims that the Persians practise a unique brand of Islam, a point he takes up in *Trois ans en Asie*. Again, it must be pointed out that Shīʿa Islam which became the state religion in Persia at the beginning of the sixteenth century is also the religion of other Muslims, Arabs and non-Arabs.

Whereas the Arabs tend to fade away towards the end of the *Mémoire*, they come back in *Trois ans en Asie* where Gobineau makes his most disparaging remark about them. As the discussion continues along political and theological lines, he refers to early Islamic history. While acknowledging that the Arabs are a noble race, he denies them the capacity to understand the idea of nationhood. He believes that their greatest achievement was their loyalty to their tribes but to no-one else. Moreover, the Arabs lack everything that binds men to one another; even religious faith among them is simply a matter of sentiment. Such disparaging remarks have led

Jean Gaulmier and Vincent Monteil, who on the whole serve Gobineau well as editors, to the conclusion that he has but a very superficial knowledge of Arab civilization and Islam. However, they do point out that Gobineau was writing at a time when the Arabs had fallen into political decadence. Another valid point made by Gaulmier is that the Arab ideal depended on a linguistic and cultural unity, which could accommodate administrative fragmentation.[27]

In other ways, too, *Trois ans en Asie* may read like anti-Arab propaganda. Its negative impression on the reader may perhaps stem from Gobineau's attempt to elevate the Persians at the expense of the Arabs. Unlike Volney who studied the Arabs in Syria and Palestine rather more closely,[28] Gobineau only met Arabs, whom he dubs 'nomadic' Arabs, during his visit to the Pyramids in Egypt. This does not stop him from pontificating about the nomadic Arabs of Egypt who strike him as being ruffians and looters, who only learnt how to fight and dominate from the Qur'ān. That is why, in his view, the Abbasid caliphs, who deemed them unfit for intellectual work and the subtleties of government, had to call in theologians from Syria and Persia and members of the family of the Barmakids from Northern Afghanistan to act as administrators. Instead of recognizing that the Bedouins are constantly on the move and therefore unable to fulfill their religious duties he finds them lacking in religious feeling.

In *Trois ans en Asie* he takes every opportunity to set Arab against Persian. He sees evidence of nationalism in the esteem shown the Imāms by the Persians. What he conveniently forgets to mention is that other Shī'ites who are not of Persian origin have the same esteem for the Imāms. He claims that every Persian is deeply devoted to the Imāms for reasons that he describes as purely political in origin. He suggests that, although 'Alī was an Arab by birth, he was persecuted by other Arabs. But 'Alī found many supporters in Persia and his eldest son Ḥusain married a Sassanid princess who converted to Islam. The children of Ḥusain and all the survivors of 'Alī's family took shelter in Persia and became Persians. Thus the cause of the Alides became that of vanquished Persia and the Iranians see the woes of their own ancestors in those of this family.

This is obviously an over-simplification of the causes leading to the split between Sunnī and Shīʿa Islam. Gobineau is right to stress the existence of a clergy in Shīʿa Islam and its role in the interpretation of the Qur'ān and to note its absence in Sunnī Islam, but he is mistaken in suggesting that the Persians rely on the authority of countless *aḥādīth* (Traditions) of the Prophet of which no one else has heard. It is true that the Shīʿites use both the *aḥādīth* of the Prophet and those of the Imāms. Gobineau certainly exaggerates the differences between Persian and Arab Muslims. How could one accept the view that the Persians apparently disliked the arid simplicity of their new faith, suitable only for 'coarse' Arabs, so much that one of their first undertakings was to complicate Islam? Moreover, exploiting the sympathy their nation felt for the Alids, which Gobineau sees as a form of disguised protest against the Arabs and against Islam itself, the Persians invented the cult of the Imāms. In his opinion they attached so much importance to it that not only was the Prophet's majesty eclipsed by the brilliance of his grandsons, but God Himself was diminished (*Oeuvres*, ii, 247).[29] This view cannot be taken seriously, for the Persians could hardly have tried to lower Muḥammad and even God.

Although Gobineau makes amends towards Muḥammad in *Les Religions et les philosophies dans l'Asie Centrale*, his reading of Shīʿa Islam borders on travesty here. There is no justification in saying that for the Shīʿa, the Prophet is a lesser figure than 'Alī. Montesquieu had made the same kind of polemical use of his sources in letters I and XVI of the *Lettres persanes*. These letters made no reference to Muḥammad in the *Voyages* of Chardin, who translated the prayers offered by pilgrims at the tomb of Fāṭima, daughter of Imām Mūsā al-Kāẓim, at Qum. Chardin also translated the poem by the Persian poet Ḥassān al-Kātib as *Eloge de Hali*. Only praise of Fāṭima and ʿAlī remained in Montesquieu's letters. In the case of both Montesquieu and Gobineau, therefore, the result is pure caricature.

At other times Gobineau can be very perceptive and he wrote some stimulating pages on the theology, sociology and the philosophy of Islam in *Les Religions et les philosophies dans l'Asie Centrale* where he places increasing emphasis on the Qur'ān and Muḥammad. However, the chapter entitled 'L'Islamisme persan' (ii, 420-432) may be misleading, as much of it does not deal with an Islam which is specifically Persian. For instance, Gobineau proclaims that no religion is more tolerant than Islam because tolerance is an article of faith stemming from the Qur'ān which also teaches that the knowledge of truth does not depend on man's will. In a clear but indirect reference to *Sūra* 24: 35, he states that God guides whom He wills to His light. Many a man who was in complete obscurity has everything revealed to him. Another does not and will not see the truth which blinds him, almost mischievously. Gobineau here paraphrases the Qur'ānic verse (*Sūra* 3: 54) relating to God's *makr* (stratagem, plan) which is superior to man's stratagems. He also says that there is no need to have forced conversions in Islam (or, as he puts it, to bring a neophyte to the path of Providence, if it has not marked him with its seal). As an example, Gobineau, with *Sūras* 2: 256, 22: 78 in mind perhaps, says that in a Muslim state Christians and Jews cannot be forced to change their religion. If they are required to pay a tribute, it is because as non-Muslims they are exempt from military duties and it is therefore right that they should make a contribution to public service. All these examples show that Gobineau was not thinking of Persian, that is, Shīʿa Islam, but of Islam in general.

Likewise, his remark that Islam recommends the principle of a unique God, revealing Himself through His Prophets, which he calls 'the alpha and the omega of its theology' (ii, 422) will find endorsement among Sunnīs, and in fact all Muslims. Gobineau argues that, provided these two articles of faith are recognized, the Muslim is allowed the maximum liberty of conscience: he can differ as much as he likes from other Muslims and still be considered a faithful Muslim as long as he does not commit apostasy openly. Here, however, Gobineau is guilty of the most striking ambivalence, for he regards simplicity of belief as a mixed blessing. Indeed, at various points of the discussion, he criticizes the *shahāda* as vague, inconsistent, lacking in originality and superficial. His grounds for criticism are that the *shahāda* is simply a light veil behind which old beliefs, doctrines and theories maintain themselves. In his own words, Islam never uprooted a single poisonous plant which was blooming before its advent nor did it stop any from germinating afterwards. Heresies sprang up in Islam even before those in Christianity. If one were to believe Gobineau heresies arose in the very lifetime of the Prophet. In fact these took place only after his death when the problem of his succession arose. According to Gobineau Persian Shiism is the best evidence to show the existence of hybrid ideas in Islam. While it is recognised that many sects exist in Islam, as they do in Christianity, their existence has nothing to do with the *shahāda*.

However, Gobineau is at pains to confine his remarks to Persian Shīʿism. Certain qualities that he attributes to it are generally recognized as typical of Islam as a whole. He refutes those who claim that it is hostile to intellectual development.

He shows that the opposite is true. Quoting the *Ḥadīth* to the effect that the ink of scholars is more precious than the blood of martyrs, he argues that Islam could not fairly be deemed hostile to intellectual pursuits, as it teaches that, at the Last Judgement, every man will be seriously questioned about the use he has made of the intelligence given him by God. Besides, from its birth in the seventh century to the end of the sixteenth century, Islam has known material prosperity, sustained and maintained by a scientific and literary culture about which the full story has not been told in the West. In a firm rebuttal to writers such as Volney and De Tocqueville, Gobineau rightly argues that the decline of Central Asia – or much of the Islamic world he might have added – can by no means be attributed to Islam. He finds that there is no foundation for the charge of obscurantism levelled against Islam which he describes as a rather vague philosophy. Perhaps showing more optimism than is warranted, Gobineau is convinced that the critical spirit and spirit of enquiry which the Prophet himself encouraged never died.

He makes an attempt, on the other hand, to minimize the outstanding record of the Prophet. He starts by saying that Islam is nothing more than a corrupt version of Aramaic or Sabean ideas. Gobineau claims that, provided Muḥammad can destroy the idolatry that has crept in, he urges little or no change. Such social changes as are advocated in the Qur'ān are directly attributed to the Prophet. Thus Gobineau says that Muḥammad opposed the burying alive of new-born girls,[30] that he extended the use of financial compensation for murders[31] and that he made it almost impossible for someone to be found guilty of adultery without four eyewitnesses.[32] But he suggests that Muḥammad is merely a reformer and a timid one at that, for the Prophet relied too much on Judaism and

Christianity, the apocryphal gospels and popular Jewish anecdotes. Gobineau declares that the Prophet acquired his knowledge more by oral than written transmission, although he was no stranger to the latter. He does not produce any evidence to support this contention. Nor is there any evidence to substantiate his claim that Muḥammad had direct knowledge of the Gospels. Yet Gobineau is not off the mark when he says that Muḥammad wanted to restore the pure faith of the ancient Arabs, of Abraham in particular. He seems to have a sound knowledge of the Qur'ān when he refers to ideas mentioned in it such as those relating to the Prophetic missions of Abraham, Moses and Jesus and to the status of Muḥammad as a simple mortal who has no gift for miracles and who is the transmitter of God's message through Gabriel.[33]

In the chapter on 'Le soufisme et la philosophie', (ii, 448-483) Gobineau shows an extraordinary grasp of the problem of free-will in Islam, even if his conclusion that free-will is the orthodox teaching in Islam is debatable and needs to be qualified. He was led to this conclusion while trying to exonerate Islam from the reproach that it teaches fatalism which, in his view, is an error and an injustice. As he shrewdly perceives, it is not easy for any religion to reconcile divine prescience with human freedom, though all religions recognize the need for such a reconciliation. He believes that Muḥammad had greater difficulty than any other religious legislator in achieving such a fusion. Muḥammad, he suggests, in wishing to avoid the worst consequences of Aramaic pantheism had exaggerated as much as he could God's omnipotence, omniscience and all the attributes capable of separating the Creator from His creatures. Muḥammad was not unaware of the dangers of this emphasis. Gobineau argues that if one were to set verses of the Qur'ān advocating free-will against those advocating determinism, one could show contradiction, one could prove that the Prophet was a dialectician lacking the skill of the Schoolmen. What is more significant, in his view, is to discern Muḥammad's intention and he finds that there is no doubt here. Muḥammad had clearly tried to save free-will and to give to man, even impose on him, responsibility for his acts. Gobineau perhaps shows a tendency to over-simplification when he suggests that in orthodox Islamic teaching, God, by opening Paradise or Hell for man, simply treats him according to his merit. This clear-cut path to man's final destiny is really Mu'tazilite teaching. To combat it Sunnī Islam used the story of the three brothers or a variant, such as the story of the fourteen-year-old nephew who is killed in Voltaire's *Conte philosophique*, *Zadig*. The main purpose of the story was to show that God was not bound to do the best for an individual, because that would reduce His omnipotence.[34]

In *Trois ans en Asie*, Gobineau claimed that he had tried to cast aside all notions, whether true or false, of superiority over the peoples he was studying. It is doubtful whether any reader of that work or of his other works for that matter could accept such a claim. For it is clear that all his works reveal an author who is often inclined to feel superior to at least some of these peoples and particularly the Arabs. That may be due to his dislike of the Bedouins to whom he denies any possibility of progress, castigating them as looters and as not very Islamic. His feeling of superiority is not too surprising, because in the *Essai* he judges nations by their cultural distinction. According to him, Islam lacks originality. However, his own analysis of the origins of Islam which persuades him that it owes nearly everything to Judaism and Christianity or corrupt versions of these religions is not particularly original. Perhaps he exalts the Persians and belittles the Arabs too much: he clearly seems to have more sympathy for the former than the latter. But how genuine is the sympathy?

At times he gives the impression that the further a nation is or the further it is made to appear from Islam, the better it is. If this reading of his works is correct, then it could be argued that he praises the Persians merely to give credence to his denigration of Islam.[35] Nevertheless, it is difficult to deny his insight. He could certainly teach the reader of Chardin's *Voyages en Perse* a thing or two about Persia omitted from the earlier text. In his observation of Persians making the pilgrimage to Qum, for instance, he easily surpasses other writers, including Chardin. How well he captures the spirit of Persian Muslims wishing to be buried near their Imāms in Persia or Iraq! One may reject the claim he makes about Asia, that is, Persia, being the origin of all thought. But one may legitimately detect some evolution in his approach to the world of Islam in the period of some twelve years that separates the *Essai sur l'inégalité des races humaines* from *Les Religions et les philosophies dans l'Asie Centrale*. It does not necessarily mean that he abandoned all interest in races, but other subjects such as theology and philosophy began to fascinate him. Hence Gobineau's later works offer the reader not the highly emotive debates on racial classification of the *Essai* but a calmer discussion of some theological and philosophical issues in Islam.

One could therefore conclude that in his assessment of Islam Gobineau shows greater depth than De Tocqueville although the latter's perspective on Islam and Algeria was not uninteresting. However, it seems that De Tocqueville studied the Qur'ān over a limited period merely to get to grips with the Algerian situation and that his study of Islam was rather superficial. It is therefore not surprising that the political dimension of his response superseded his fleeting interest in the theology and sociology of Islam.

Notes

1. De Tocqueville, *Oeuvres complètes*, op. cit., Vol. XVI, p. 487.
2. *Oeuvres complètes*, III, p. 131.
3. See Ann Thomson, *Barbary and Enlightenment: European attitudes towards the Maghreb in the eighteenth century* (Leiden, 1987), p. 85.
4. Thomson, p. 88.
5. Ibid., p. 89.
6. *Oeuvres complètes*, iii, p. 135.
7. See Thomson, p. 87.
8. *Oeuvres complètes*, iii, p. 146.
9. Ibid., iii, pp. 163-220.
10. They were mainly inspired by a three-volume study published in 1838, 1839 and 1840 and entitled *Tableau des Etablissements français dans l'Algérie.*
11. See the *Shorter Encyclopaedia of Islam*, eds. H.A.R. Gibb and J.H. Kramers, (Leiden, 1970), art. *'ushr*, pp. 610-611 and *E.I*, (new ed.), vol. x, pp. 917-919.
12. It is not clear what De Tocqueville means by 'Qur'ānic principle'. It may be noted that the term 'ushr' is not found in the Qur'ān, although it is often used in the sense of *zakāt.* This is the case in *Sūra* 6: 141. On this line al-Ṭabarī (VIII, 53-61) says that the *zakāt* is 1/10 or 1/20 of the harvest.
13. *Oeuvres complètes*, iii, pp. 310-330.
14. Every administrative area within the 'military territory' of Algeria was allocated a *bureau arabe*. The army depended on these *bureaux*, which were staffed by specialist officers with some knowledge of Arabic language and culture, for information and advice. See C.A. Julien, *Histoire de l'Algérie contemporaine, 1830-1871* (Paris, 1964), pp. 330-337 and C. Harrison, *France and Islam in West Africa, 1860-1960* (Cambridge, 1988), p. 16.
15. In 1843 at the request of Thomas Bugeaud, commander of the French army in Algeria, the Marine Department put a ship at the disposal of pilgrims to Makka for the first time.
16. Discrimination in favour of the natives was sometimes due to the action of the officers of the *bureaux arabes*, especially Colonel Daumas. The *bureaux* were resented by the early colonists in Algeria who accused them of being arabophile. Julien, p. 337.
17. Correspondance d'Alexis de Tocqueville et d'Arthur de Gobineau, in *Oeuvres complètes*, ix, p. 243.
18. See Ann Thomson, *Barbary*, p. 72.
19. See my article, 'Islam in Nerval's *Voyage en Orient*', *Journal of Islamic Studies*, 2:2 (Oxford, 1991), pp. 195-209.
20. See Henri Dehérain, *Sylvestre de Sacy, ses contemporains et ses disciples* (Paris, 1938), pp. I-XXII.

21. Edward Said discusses the Western perception of Oriental backwardness and degeneracy, and refers to the racial classifications in Gobineau's *Essai sur l'inégalité des races humaines* (1853) which he, however, does not fully discuss. He says nothing about Gobineau's other works. See *Orientalism*, p. 206.

22. All quotations of Gobineau's works are from the Pléïade edition, *Oeuvres*, 2 vols, eds. Jean Gaulmier and Jean Boissel (Paris, 1983).

23. As stated by Jean Boissel (i, 1329, note 1 of p. 311), Gobineau learnt this from Caussin de Perceval, *Histoire des Arabes avant l'islamisme* (Paris, 1847-48), 3 vols.

24. See the section 'Morocco at the cross roads, 1822-1912' in Jamil M. Abun-Nasr, *A history of the Maghrib in the Islamic period* (Cambridge, 1987), pp. 297-298.

25. Chardin's book on Persia made a deep impact on several generations of French readers, the most influential of them being perhaps Montesquieu, who in the *Lettres persanes* (1721) used Chardin as a springboard for his attack on revealed religion. In the *Discours sur l'inégalité* (1755), Rousseau had certainly been hasty in his judgement when he claimed that Chardin left nothing to be said about Persia. As for Flaubert he only noted the countless technical details to be found in Chardin when he wrote to his friends E. Vasse and Maxime du Camp in 1846. He would have found different and thought-provoking ideas in Gobineau if he had read him later on.

26. In *Trois ans en Asie, Oeuvres*, ii, 269, Gobineau distorts Persian Islam by describing it as 'à demi hindou, à demi guèbre'.

27. See *Oeuvres* ii, 1047, notes 1 and 2 of p. 361 and p. 362 and the chapter on 'Arab nationalism' in Albert Hourani, *Arabic thought in the Liberal Age 1798-1939* (Cambridge, 1988), pp. 260-323.

28. Gaulmier and Monteil give more credit to Volney perhaps than he deserves. *Oeuvres* (ii, 980, note 1 of p. 50). It appears that while he was in Cairo Volney did not know enough Arabic to mix freely with Egyptians and that much of what he says comes from European and Syrian merchants. See Albert Hourani, *Europe and the Middle East* (London, 1980), p. 84.

29. In their note 2 of this page (ii, 1022), Gaulmier and Monteil have drawn attention to Gobineau's lack of understanding of the profound nature of Shīʿism which reveals the need for mysticism and the search for a truth which transcends the letter of religious law necessary for the organization of temporal society.

30. Gobineau is referring to *Sūras* 6: 140 and 16: 58-59.

31. See *Sūra* 2: 178.

32. See *Sūras* 24: 4 and 4: 15.

33. This point has been made by Gaulmier and Monteil in *Oeuvres*, ii, 1097, 1098, note 1 of p. 432.

34. See W. Montgomery Watt, *Islamic Philosophy and Theology* (Edinburgh, 1962), p. 67, Fazlur Rahman, *Islam* (Chicago, 1966, 1979), pp. 87-94 and my *Images of Islam*. pp. 142-145.

35. He would then appear to have inherited the tradition of French polemical writing as exemplified by Jurieu, Bayle and Voltaire, who often set one party, one group of people and one set of believers against another. Yet a glance at the private correspondence of Alexis de Tocqueville and Gobineau shows that Gobineau is really well disposed towards the Persians. For example, in a letter (no. 63) dated 7 July 1855 to Tocqueville, he says that the Persians are not as bad as they are made out to be in Europe: while they are neither angels nor perfect gentlemen, they are not perverse monsters either. In another letter to Tocqueville (no. 67) dated 15 January 1856, he says the Persians are only Muslims in name and are not fanatical at all. Some years before, Tocqueville in a letter (no. 6) dated 22 October 1843, to Gobineau, thought that the latter had a weakness for Islam! See *Correspondence d'Alexis de Tocqueville et d'Arthur de Gobineau*, in Tocqueville, *Oeuvres Complètes*, ed. J.P. Mayer, Vol. IX (Paris, 1959).

CHAPTER 7

A French intellectual's response to Islam – Renan

While De Tocqueville travelled to Algeria in the 1840s and Gobineau worked in Persia between 1855 and 1863, Ernest Renan (1823-92) sailed for the Middle East in October 1860 and paid a short visit to Lebanon and the Holy Land in 1861.[1] He took the opportunity to see a region forming the background to the Gospel story, as Chateaubriand had done before writing the *Génie du Christianisme*. Renan hoped this visit would be useful in the composition of his work on the life of Jesus. Before its publication, he had been elected to the Chair of Hebrew at the Collège de France in December 1861. Renan's election followed studies in theology, Biblical exegesis and Hebrew at the seminary of St. Sulpice in 1843 and the publication of his doctoral thesis on Islamic philosophy, *Averroès et l'averroïsme*, in 1852. In the intervening period, he wrote *L'Avenir de la Science* (1848), a few years after the crisis of faith which he experienced as a seminarist training for the priesthood and which made him cease to be an orthodox Roman Catholic. By then no longer believing in the immortality of the soul he rejected the supernatural and the divinity of Christ.

Although Renan was a Hebrew specialist, having won the Volney prize in linguistics in 1847 with a 'Historical and theoretical essay on Semitic languages in general and Hebrew in particular', he had a good Arabic and Islamic cultural background.[2] This enabled him to comment on Islam intermittently over a period of some thirty-five years with some authority. He was sometimes fair but more often unfair, controversial and provocative. Thus in his biographical article on the Orientalist Etienne Quatremère, published in *Journal des débats* in 1857, he showed disgust at what he assumed to be a lowering of standards of morality and intelligence in Muslim countries, especially from the second half of the Middle Ages. This kind of sweeping generalization often recurs in his remarks on Islamic communities. Yet Renan was highly significant in shaping up the European image of Islam in his day.

In *L'Avenir de la Science*, Renan suggests that a true history of philosophy begins with a history of religions, that a philosophical theory of religion has become urgent for human sciences to progress and that such a theory should rest on scholarship. He starts with a defence of Islam because it is made to suffer from its association with the most absurd fables and from a false evaluation in popular books. More significant perhaps is his argument for attaching importance to Islam in a comparative study of religion: unlike other religions, Islam has left authentic documents on its origins and the traces of controversy and unbelief which it went through still exist. He argues that it is an exception among religions as documents from a foreign source rarely cast a light on them in their infancy. Islam, on the other hand, is firmly set in history.[3]

Renan has a novel way of explaining what he calls Muḥammad's 'imposture'. In a footnote (III, p. 1140, n. 120) he makes some extraordinary claims which are not borne out by facts, namely that the great majority of those who followed the daring Qurayshite had no religious faith in him and that after his death serious thought was given to the idea of discarding his religious work and concentrating on his political achievement instead.[4] Using the criterion of original creativity, Renan finds Islam to be the weakest of religions. There is nothing new in his criticism of Islam lacking originality. What is new is his manner of showing this lack of originality. He considers the eclecticism of Islam to be more powerful than Western eclecticism because Muḥammad was lacking in refinement and Muslims knew less than Christians and were less critical: they did not know where the elements they were blending came from. In his view, this led to unscrupulous amalgamation.

In another footnote, Renan quotes the Arabs as saying that the list of prophets is not closed. This leads him to conclude that the success of the Wahhābīs proves that a new Muḥammad is not impossible. What he is proposing goes against the view generally held by Muslims, namely that Muḥammad is the last of the Prophets. Contrary to what he suggests, the Wahhābīs regard the founder of their movement, Muḥammad ʿAbd al-Wahhāb (1703-92) not as a prophet, but as a reformer. They were inspired by the Ḥanbalī leader Ibn Taymiyya (1263-1328) in their attack on the cult of saints and they insisted on a return to the purity of original Islam.[5] Renan also devalues the role played by divine inspiration in securing the foundations of Islam. For he imagines that a clever European with a knowledge of Arabic who claimed to be related to the Prophet's family and preached the doctrine of equality and fraternity could with some eight to ten thousand men conquer the Muslim East and sustain a movement similar to Islam (III, p. 1130, n. 44).

Renan declares war on the supernatural which he associates with Islam and maintains that it is the function of modern criticism to destroy any system of beliefs that shows traces of the supernatural. To the supernatural he opposes the rational method with which he says European science is intimately connected. False prophet, he announces the death of Islam through the influence of European science, seeing the nineteenth century as the period when the basis for this great event would be laid. Muslim youth appears to him as the instrument that will help cause the subversion of Islam. For trained in Western schools, it will learn European science, be influenced by rationalism, the experimental method and find it impossible to believe in religious traditions conceived outside any critical canon (III, 768). Renan may be thinking of some Western-educated Muslims who easily discard their Islamic heritage. He draws attention to the warnings given to migrating youths by traditional Muslim teachers about the apparent dangers to Islam perceived in European books. He believes the 'heretical' thoughts contained in Western science will prove stronger than the Qur'ān. The revolution which he predicts will take place in Islam will be due to Western science, a pure creation of the human mind. Using a medieval perspective, he is convinced that history will repeat itself: as the study of Greek science and philosophy in the Middle Ages produced heterodox Arab thinkers, the study of Western science will produce the same effect in the nineteenth century. Renan seems to make no distinction between Biblical exegetes and Qur'ānic commentators. If Biblical exegesis in the seventeenth and eighteenth centuries led to the undermining of Christian beliefs, it does not follow that Qur'ānic exegesis produced the same result in Islam.

In *L'Avenir de la Science* Islam is not singled out for attack, as Renan's criticism is directed at the Semitic family as a whole, that is, Judaism, Christianity and Islam. He claims that these religions show no attempt at analysis, have produced no indigenous philosophical school and are good only at producing and propagating religion (III, 955). But it is the Arabs he chooses to make his point. In a footnote he admits that the Arabs have offered a philosophical and scientific development, but he insists that they borrowed their science entirely from Greece. He obviously ignores the Arab contribution to astronomy, for example. Moreover, Greco-Arab science flourished not in Arabia proper but in non-Semitic countries subjected to Islam such as Persia, Morocco and Spain which adopted Arabic as a learned language. The Arabs are belittled with the remark that the Arabian peninsula apparently only understood the Qur'ān and the old poetry.

Harsher criticism of the Semitic races, especially the Arabs, was to follow in the *Histoire générale des langues sémitiques*, published between 1855 and 1863 and the text *De la part des peuples sémitiques dans l'histoire de la civilisation* (1862) which formed part of his inaugural lecture on the Hebrew, Chaldean and Syriac languages at the Collège de France. Before these came 'Mahomet et les origines de l'islamisme', an article which first appeared in the *Revue des Deux Mondes* in December 1851 and was subsequently reproduced in *Etudes d'histoire religieuse* (1857). This article seems to have been neglected by most modern commentators and yet its evaluation is essential if a balanced appraisal of Renan's perspective on Islam is to be achieved.[6]

Whereas in *L'Avenir de la Science* Renan hints that Islam is flawed because it is linked to the supernatural and as such is irreconcilable with rational European science, in 'Mahomet et les origines de l'islamisme', he surprises the reader by finding merit in Islam for having, if not virtually abolished the supernatural, at least limited it considerably.[7] He admires the canonical Traditionist Al-Bukhārī whom he calls 'l'infatigable', for he says the latter acknowledges that of the 200,000 *aḥādīth* he had collected only 7,225 seemed to him of sound authenticity (VII, 174). Renan's approach to *ḥadīth* literature appears in harmony with that of modern scholarship which distinguishes between genuine and spurious *ḥadīth*. Although he suggests that European critics could, without appearing too rash, be stricter in the process of eliminating spurious *ḥadīth* he admits that these first narratives show many features of the real physiognomy of the Prophet and are clearly distinct from the pious legends which have been invented by some for the benefit of readers. Moreover, Renan hints that the books and speeches attributed to the founders of other religions are lacking in authenticity: these tell us less about the founders than about the way their disciples conceived the ideal (VII, 176). Not so with Muḥammad: Renan argues that his biography is an ordinary one without miracles and exaggeration. He suggests that Muḥammad had good biographers in men like Ibn Hishām and the ancient historians whom he qualifies as 'écrivains sensés' (ibid.), while the legends surrounding Christian saints – St. Francis of Assissi, for example – have become much more mythical than those surrounding Muḥammad. The aim of Renan's polemic is clear: it is to paint a more favourable picture of Muḥammad than of Christ and Christian saints.

How does one account for the absence in Islam of the fantasy which prevails among Indians, Persians and Greeks with their splendid literary embroidery and divine poems? To Renan absence of fantasy is due to the fact that as a Semitic nation the Arabs' concept of God is clear and simple: God is distinct from the world, He does not beget nor is He begotten and He has no equal. As he brilliantly puts it, the mythology producing pantheism is only possible in the imagination of a people who are happy to let the boundaries that separate God, humanity and the world drift indecisively. While pantheism may characterize the thought of some Arab philosophers such as Ibn 'Arabī, there cannot be disagreement with the view that the Islamic spirit is, on the whole, furthest from it. Renan seems sounder in his evaluation than some modern commentators who would have us believe that Islam is pantheistic.[8]

Renan accepts that Muḥammad's life, like that of other great founders of religion, is surrounded by fables, but these, as he perhaps unfairly suggests, have won the seal of approval only among the Persians over whom the imagination holds sway. He says nothing, for example, about the Persian contribution to the consolidation of Sunnī Islam made by authors such as Ṭabarī and Ghazālī. He claims that under the influence of races foreign to Arabia the story of Muḥammad has been complicated by miraculous circumstances which bring it closer to the great legendary myths of the high Orient. He suggests that despite the imposition of the Arabic language and Islam on her, Persia could claim her rights as an Indo-European nation and create a mythological epic for herself within Islam. As an example of the miraculous, he refers to the popular story of how two angels opened the body of Muḥammad at the age of three, removed his gall and inserted the prophetic light. He finds nothing Arabic in such exaggerations which appear typical of Persian taste, adding that such grotesque stories do not detract from the purity of the original Arab tradition in the same way that the dull exaggeration of the apocryphal gospels does not destroy the incomparable beauty of the canonical gospels (VII, 184). The fables that exist in Islam are in his view not fundamental to it: they have to be taken as accessories, they are tolerated rather than sanctified; they are very much like the mythology of the apocrypha, which the Church neither adopted nor rejected. Renan then offers a sample of Indian mythology dealing with the birth of her heroes in order to stress the sobriety of the miraculous element in Islamic narrative. His explanation of the difference in style between India and Arabia is that the latter had reached too great an intellectual refinement to accommodate a supernatural legend in the Indian mould (VII, 182). The Arabs therefore appear in a better light here than the Persians and Indians because of their limited use of myths.

Renan does not entirely eliminate examples of the miraculous in Islam, but it is only to reduce its significance. He claims that the only time when Muḥammad wanted to imitate the fantasies of other religions was on the occasion of the night journey to Jerusalem, but things went so badly that the Prophet hastened to withdraw his ill-advised suggestion by declaring that the miraculous journey, at first presented as a real journey, had only been a dream. This journey which has a deep spiritual significance in Islam is taken symbolically, not literally, by most Muslims. In any case, it is not accurate to say that the Prophet changed his mind about it. However, Renan insists that the Arab legends associated with Muḥammad and to be found in his biography by Abu'l Fidā' are reduced to a few stories characterized by restraint. Even at the battle of Badr (624), where angels are reported to have fought on the side of the Muslims, Renan expresses surprise that the combatants used their imagination in such sober fashion. The conclusion he wishes the reader to draw is that the legendary elements found in Islam have always remained sporadic traditions lacking in authority.

The article 'Mahomet' seems to have less sympathy with the inaccessible rigour of supernaturalism associated with the Man-God (Jesus) than with the ordinary humanity and its weaknesses which characterize Muḥammad. It uses an ingenious technique which allows Renan to evaluate Muḥammad's achievement and to criticize the Prophet as much as he likes. He argues that in the great supernatural legends everything is settled and absolute, as is proper when God is completely involved, whereas in the life of Muḥammad everything is not clear-cut, everything is approximate in a very human but historical manner. Thus Muḥammad is defeated and makes mistakes. It is perfectly reasonable for Renan to say that Muḥammad makes mistakes: he could have used the incident with 'Abdullāh b. Umm Maktūm as an example (see Chapter

2, above). Although Renan refers to circumstances where he says the Prophet compromised with moral standards for the sake of political expediency, he favours what he considers a legitimate criticism of Muḥammad. So he attacks Voltaire's portrait of Muḥammad in his play *Mahomet*, condemning the ambitious, heartless Machiavellian portrayed there. If he defends Muḥammad from the accusation of having altered Biblical stories it is to say that the latter simply reproduced what he had learnt from rabbinical traditions and the apocryphal gospels, especially that of *L'Evangile de l'enfance* which he says was preserved only in Arabic. This, of course, implies that Muḥammad read the text, but Renan does not say whether he could read.

Having decided, once again, that religious faith did not prevail in early Islam, Renan proceeds to list a number of historical events to fit his thesis: the wars of apostasy after Muḥammad's death, the extermination of the first Muslims, the murder of ʿAlī who, Renan says, had been proclaimed[9] his successor by Muḥammad, and the triumph of the Umayyads. He then concludes that the result of all this was the indecisiveness that prevailed in matters of religious doctrine until the twelfth century and that led to the creation of numerous sects. To a certain extent his conclusion that Islam triumphed over undisciplined elements through the rise of Asharite theology may be appropriate. But the evaluation is fragmented as he completely ignores the existence of Shīʿa Islam. He certainly exaggerates when he claims that from the time of Ashʿarī onwards no doubt or protest arose in the world of Islam. He seems to forget what he had said in *L'Avenir de la Science*, about the appearance, in the eighteenth century, of the Wahhābī religious reform movement in Arabia. Still, the emphasis on the historicity of Islam works to its advantage, although the pro-Arab stance is of short duration.

The tendency to polarize between early and later Islam, to characterize the first six centuries as a period of extreme unbelief and later centuries as a period of certainty, reappears in *Averroès et l'Averroïsme*, but Renan now attempts to account for the polarization. He suggests that as Islam slipped away from the Arabs – a sceptic race – and became the 'property' of races naturally inclined to fanaticism such as the Spanish, the Berbers, the Persians and the Turks, it became austere and exclusive in its dogmatism (III, 43). One is struck not only by the blanket condemnation of various Islamic peoples, but also by the contradiction in Renan's remark on the Persians made in the 'Avertissement', where he described them as a race very attracted to speculation (p. 13). However, his assessment of the theological situation of twelfth-century Islam is generally sound, as he describes the triumph of Ash'arism in the Arab empire, particularly in Egypt under Saladin (1169-93) and in Spain under the Almohads (1130-1269). He rightly sees Ash'arism as a sort of compromise between reason and faith. Yet like many other critics of later times Renan claims that Asharism is still the orthodox doctrine of Sunnī schools of thought. Such a view has been challenged more recently by Fazlur Rahman, for instance, who sees in Ash'arism not so much the doctrine of orthodoxy as the dominant trend in Islam. Rahman even considers it to be an almost total distortion of Islam in that its doctrine of the omnipotence of God is at the expense of all human power and will so that man can be said 'to act' only metaphysically, the only real 'actor' being God.[10]

Renan places greater emphasis on what he sees as the negative influence of the rise of Ash'arism on philosophy – fanaticism and intolerance. He narrates how in Spain the ḥājib Al-Manṣūr pandered to the instinctive antipathy of the imāms and the people to rational studies by having philosophical works burnt in public places in Cordoba. In

Baghdad, in 1160, all works in the library of a *qāḍī* (judge), those of Ibn Sīnā (980-1037) and of the Ikhwān aṣ-Ṣafā (The Brethren of Purity) were burnt by command of the Abbasid Caliph al-Mustanjid. If Renan describes in some detail the persecution to which philosophers and their works were subjected in the main centres of Islam, it is to arrive at a balanced appraisal of Averroes's status in Islam and of his contribution to philosophy. He succeeds in this attempt because he takes care not to exaggerate the importance of Averroes (Ibn Rushd). He gives the persecution of philosophy as the main reason why Averroes for centuries so popular among Christians and Jews, made so little impact on Muslims (III, 47). Apart from Ibn Sīnā, other philosophers such as Avempace (Ibn Bajja, Ibn Rushd's master) and Abubacer (Ibn Ṭufayl) enjoy no popularity in Islam. Renan substantiates his opinion by showing that the bibliographical *Dictionary* of Arabic authors, the *Kashf al-Ẓunūn* of Ḥājī Khalīfa, mentions few philosophical works while the name of Ibn Rushd is mentioned only incidentally in connection with his refutation in *Tahāfut al-Tahāfut* (The Incoherence of the Incoherence) of Ghazālī's work *Tahāfut al-Falāsifa* (Incoherence of the Philosophers) and his commentary on Ibn Sīnā's poem. As he points out, there is no word about Ibn Rushd in Ibn Khallikān's *Lives of illustrious men* and in Ibn al-Qifṭī's *Ta'rīkh al-Ḥukamā'* (History of Philosophy). Renan takes the opportunity to correct d'Herbelot and other writers after him for suggesting that Averroes was the first to have translated Aristotle into Arabic by insisting that such a translation had appeared three centuries before (p. 56). Moreover, suggests Renan, Averroes was not particularly original in his medical and philosophical knowledge. However, he stood out among Muslim critics and in his observations on astronomy he was ahead of his times. In his laconic remark on Arab astronomy, Renan does not say in what way

Averroes was ahead. Of special significance is his remark that Averroes, like many good Muslims, combined secular studies with religious jurisprudence, apparently knowing the *Muwaṭṭa'* of Imām Mālik by heart.[11] This is a recognition that Averroes was a true product of Islamic civilization.

A few pages later, however, in the chapter entitled 'Averroes's doctrine', Renan becomes guilty of the most glaring inconsistency. He starts off by admitting that the Arabs, under the cloak of commentaries on Aristotle, managed to create a philosophy peculiar to themselves and different from what was being taught in the Lyceum. He further acknowledges that the true philosophical movement in Islam is to be found among the theological sects such as the Qadarites, Jabarites, Mu'tazilites and Ash'arites (III, 84). But then he says that the so-called Arab philosophy was really a reaction against Arabism in the remoter parts of the Arab empire (III, 85). Renan's contention is that although written in Arabic, this philosophy has nothing Arabic about it. It is of foreign inspiration and has a low status among Muslims. It is really Persian in origin and it is only when the Persian spirit, represented by the Abbasids, tramples over the Arab spirit that Greek philosophy penetrates into Islam. In Renan's view the true genius of the Arabs is opposed to Greek philosophy. Moreover, they have no notion of science or rationalism. Like Gobineau, Renan sees an irreconcilable opposition between Arabs and Persians; the latter knew how to maintain their rights as Indo-Europeans. If one were to develop his thought to its logical conclusion one could say that the Caliph Al-Ma'mūn almost ceases to be an Arab because he seeks rationalist knowledge outside Islam, from India, Persia and Greece. Why should an Arab cease being an Arab, simply because he seeks knowledge from outside Arabia? Renan unambiguously affirms that Ma'mūn is an eminent representative of Persian reaction against Islam.

Although he may be right in suggesting that the Arab philosophers are often against the teaching of Islam, his tendency to polarize, to set Arab against Persian is dangerous. There is a definite lack of balance in his branding a whole community – the Arabs – with the stigma of irrationality.

Although the term 'Arab philosophy' is a misnomer in Renan's view, he is forced to use it when dealing with Ibn Sīnā (Avicenna). He strikes the right note with the remark that the latter represents the quintessence of Arab philosophy which can be summed up as follows. God is the absolute unity, the necessarily existent from whom everything emanates – a Neoplatonic concept. Beneath Him are the pure intelligences and the spheres and He does not need to intervene directly in individual affairs. Avicenna explains the possibility of prophethood and links it with the highest part of the soul, the intellect.[12] Renan suggests that the highest goal of the rational soul is to become the mirror of the universe and that it succeeds in this through internal purification and moral perfection which prepare the base where divine wisdom is to spread. As he rightly maintains, there are men who need neither study nor asceticism to receive divine wisdom. Such men are the prophets whom he calls the favourites of God. To some extent Renan's view regarding the qualities of prophet and ruler may be compared with that of Montgomery Watt on the subject. The latter suggests that Avicenna avoided Shīʿism, as he was aware of Fatimid propaganda in Bukhara and that in Avicenna there is no attempt to show that the actual ruler receives a more than ordinary portion of divine wisdom (ibid.). By definition, only prophets who are men specially selected by God to receive divine messages receive a greater share of divine wisdom.

Renan admires Ibn Sīnā's sobriety as a philosopher who admits the preservation of human personality after death and who tries to stop short of pantheism by placing the world in the category of the possible. His own view is that this distinction of the possible and necessity is the basis of Avicenna's thought, although he is aware of Averroes's insinuation that Avicenna denied the existence of any substance separate from God and identified God with the world (*waḥdat al-wujūd*).

The chapter entitled 'Averroes's doctrine' is as much about Averroes as about other Islamic philosophers and the reference to Ibn Sīnā there may be viewed as a useful introduction to the main trends in Islamic philosophy which Renan analyses with some subtlety. He is quite perceptive in recognizing the achievement of al-Ghazālī (d. 1111) on whom he provides some interesting insights. His evaluation of him is fairly balanced. To him Ghazālī is undoubtedly the most original thinker in Arab philosophy. Tracing the spiritual and intellectual journey which led Ghazālī to the path of Sufism, Renan shows how in the *Tahāfut al-Falāsifa* he proved the weakness of reason and revealed in this debate a mental perspicacity which was really astonishing. In his judgement, Hume was no improvement on Ghazālī who began his attack on rationalism with a criticism of the principle of causality. But then Renan qualifies his praise of Ghazālī by mentioning rumours circulated by Averroes that Ghazālī attacked philosophy to please theologians and remove hints about his lack of orthodoxy.

Towards the end of the chapter, Renan turns Ghazālī into the philosophers' opponent *par excellence* (III, 141). Listing him among the doctors of orthodoxy in Islam, he points out how every rational science is suspect to them because it denies the importance of revelation. To substantiate his thesis, he quotes three extracts from Ghazālī's *Munqidh min al-ḍalāl* (Deliverance from error) in a translation by Franz August Schmoelders extracted from his *Essai sur les écoles philosophiques chez les Arabes* (Paris, 1842). The first extract portrays the Arab philosophers as believing in the necessity and eternity of the world, denying the resurrection and the last judgement and indulging in their base passions. Here Renan acknowledges that rational science often led Muslim thinkers to a type of materialism. He draws a parallel between them and the seventeenth-century French freethinkers who led a life of revelry. He quotes Avicenna as saying that he drank wine to sharpen his wits. The third extract aims to show how they (the followers of Avicenna and al-Fārābī) observe only the outward ceremonies of Islam, but continue drinking and misbehaving. Renan condemns what he perceives as the gross exaggeration of Ghazālī's fulminations, hinting that Ghazālī was incapable of philosophizing calmly and was led by his wild imagination to slander his former colleagues. Here too, however, Renan suggests that Ghazālī was not completely wrong in attacking the 'heretic' philosophers.

Despite his reservations on Ghazālī, Renan takes care to point out his influence on Arab philosophy, claiming that his attacks on opponents introduced in their reasoning a sharpness that was hitherto unknown. In his wish to pay tribute to Ibn Bajja (Avempace) (d. 1138) who tried to rehabilitate the use of reason, Renan may not have been faithful to Ghazālī's thought, as he implied that Ghazālī favoured the renunciation of rational faculties for the sake of achieving perfection. Rather Ghazālī taught that reason was inadequate without revelation. Renan stresses the thorough analysis of the human mind made by Ibn Bajja in *The Rule of the Solitary*.

Of equal interest to the reader perhaps is Ibn Ṭufayl with whom Avempace shares a lofty rationalism. Famous for his main work, the philosophical tale *Ḥayy ibn Yaqẓān* which was translated by Edward Pococke the Younger into Latin in 1671 as *Philosophus Autodidactus* and by Simon Ockley into

English in 1708 as *The Improvement of Human Reason*, Ṭufayl made quite an impact on European writers. Renan describes the tale as a type of psychological *Robinson Crusoe*, the aim of which is to show how human faculties through their own force arrive at a mystical union with God. He is impressed by the hero Ḥayy who works out a complete philosophical religion for himself by the use of reason on his deserted island. He believes the tale is perhaps unique among Arab philosophical works in offering more than an historical interest. Indeed, *Ḥayy* had a singular fortune in the seventeenth and eighteenth centuries: translated into English, Dutch and German, it was adopted by the Quakers as a book of edification. Robert Barclay saw in it a confirmation of his doctrine of the 'inner light' and included it in his *Apology for the true Christian Divinity*. Renan's comment on its impact is brief but sound. He was right in leaving out the French in his analysis of the influence of *Ḥayy*.[13] Known to Leibniz and Spinoza, it made an unfavourable impression on Voltaire who called it a 'spiritual nauseous romance' in a letter dated February 1727 to Thieriot, written in English. Voltaire thought 'it was a tedious nonsense and consequently very distasteful to the French nation who dislikes madness itself when madness is languishing and flat'.[14] Perhaps Voltaire's reaction explains why *Ḥayy* left the French cold.

Negation of immortality of the soul and resurrection was, according to Renan, the main reproach made against the philosophers by zealous supporters of orthodoxy such as Ghazālī. Renan explains Averroes's opposition to the dogma of resurrection by his antipathy to the too precise description of life after death (III, 130). He points out that objections to such an understanding of the survival of the moral being were not new. Here there is a clear attempt to draw a bridge between Christianity and Islam on the question of resurrection. Renan seems to admire the subtle and original argument of St. Paul in favour of resurrection against the Sadduceans and free thinkers opposed to it. In the first epistle to the Corinthians, St. Paul said with reference to the manner of raising the dead: 'What you saw is not the body that shall be, but a naked grain... and God clothes it with the body of His choice, each seed with its own particular body... So it is with the resurrection of the dead. What is sown in the earth as a perishable thing is raised imperishable... the dead will rise immortal and we shall be changed' (from 15, 37-53). Renan argues that the Qur'ān too is preoccupied with objections to the dogma of resurrection. He invites the reader to concentrate particularly on *Sūra* 51: 57. (He really means *Sūra* 56: 60-64). He claims in a footnote that the Qur'ānic verses are almost a translation of the above quoted passage from St. Paul. There is some exaggeration no doubt, although a broad parallel may be seen between the argument of St. Paul and the Qur'ān, as verses 60-61 of *Sūra* 56 say:

> We have decreed Death to be your common lot, and We are not to be frustrated from changing your forms and creating you (again) in (forms) that ye know not.

The aim of verses 63-64 referring to the seed that is sown in the ground is to stress the creative function of God. Renan suggests that as a defender of freedom of thought against orthodoxy Averroes somehow spared Ghazālī in *Tahāfut al-Tahāfut* by objecting not to Ghazālī's belief in an immortal soul but to his claim that man will assume the same form that has fallen into decay. It should be pointed out that in *Munqidh*, Ghazālī's view is that those who claim that on the Day of Judgement bodies will not be assembled are heretical and that while they are right to insist on the spiritual they are wrong to deny the corporal. Renan relies on Aristotle's work on generation and corruption to support his belief that man will assume not the same, but a similar form. He would have found support in a more orthodox and conservative theologian than Ghazālī – a Fakhr ad-Dīn al-Rāzī, who is closer to Qur'ānic teaching. Rāzī believes that men will come back to life, not necessarily in their earthly form, rather in a form or state that they do not know, physically or psychologically.[15]

Although Renan insists on the idea that the true genius of the Arabs is to be found in the Islamic sects, what he says about the latter is not particularly new. A reader interested in this subject could have found the same information in the 'Preliminary Discourse' to Sale's translation of the Qur'ān in 1734 or in its French version published in 1751 under the title 'Observations critiques sur le mahométisme'. What is new is his explanation of the origin of the dispute on the attributes of God among Islamic sects. He ascribes it to what he calls the extreme rigour of monotheism prevailing in Islam, to the constant efforts to combat the Christian doctrines of the Trinity and the Incarnation (III, 92-93). He actually quotes a verse from the Qur'ān which Muslims often repeat in their prayers, that God has no son, does not beget and is not begotten (*Sūra* 112: 3). This, according to Renan, led to the existence of some groups refusing all attributes to God (the *mu'aṭṭils*) while others such as the *ṣifātīs* and the *tashbīhatīs* who give attributes to God are close to anthopomorphism.

One should also note Renan's attempt to do justice to 'Arab' philosophy in *Averroès et l'averroïsme*. Pointing out how it elucidates with daring and in depth the major problems of Aristotelism, he finds it superior to medieval French philosophy which always tended to narrow down the problems and tackle them through subtle dialectics. He sums up the spirit of Arab philosophy, particularly that of Averroes, by emphasizing two doctrines that are intimately connected and constitute a complete and original interpretation of Aristotelism: the eternity of matter and the theory of divine wisdom. In his view philosophy offered only two hypotheses to explain the system of the universe: on one side, God, free, with attributes and providence; causality of the universe transported in God, human soul substantial and immortal; on the other side, matter eternal, evolution of the germ by its latent force, God indeterminate; laws, nature, necessity and reason. The philosophy of Averroes appears definitely in the second category. On the essence of Arab philosophy there is therefore complete agreement between Renan and Ghazālī. If he had wanted to be thorough in his assessment of Averroes, Renan ought also to have discussed the latter's attempt to reconcile religion and philosophy in *Faṣl al-Maqāl*. However, he is sound in stressing Averroes's faith in the capacity of reason to attain to a knowledge of the inner world.

Less philosophical and more sociological was *De la part des peuples sémitiques dans l'histoire de la civilisation*. One of Renan's aims there is to stress the difference between Semites, especially the Arabs, and Europeans. Renan gives the impression that Arab Muslims and Europeans are almost different species who have nothing in common in their way of thinking and feeling (II, 323). What a gulf separates him from writers of a previous period such as Voltaire and Diderot who showed the affinities, despite the existence of differences, between Muslim and Christian sects on the question of theodicy, for example. He is more reminiscent of Montesquieu who made the Orient, more particularly the Arab Orient, appear synonymous with despotism.[16] He sees Muslim despotism, current in Egypt or Babylon, as a force crushing all individualism and reducing man to perform an abstract and nameless role. But unlike Montesquieu, he mentions not only Europeans, but also Indo-European nations (Indian and Persian?) as the only ones to have known liberty, understood the concept of statehood and the independence of the individual. In his view, the Semitic East never knew the middle ground between the anarchy of the nomadic Arabs and bloody despotism while the concept of common good is totally absent there (p. 324). If he acknowledges that liberty prevailed among the ancient Hebrews and Arabs, it is to insist that it was followed by a leader who beheaded people according to his whims. Renan sets Indo-European nations against Semitic peoples and in a sweeping generalization finds that in politics, as in poetry, religion and philosophy, the aim of the former is to seek nuance and conciliation among contraries, while the latter know nothing of these since their organization has always been of a 'désolante et fatale simplicité' (p. 325). Although Renan sets out to minimize the contribution of the Arabs to civilization in this text, he indirectly pays homage to their achievement. He acknowledges that Arabia, floating between Judaism and Christianity and shocked by the myths which Indo-European races had introduced into Christianity, wanted to return to the religion of Abraham. Indeed, Islam aims to return to the religion of Abraham. As Renan says, Islam brought over to monotheism almost all the pagans whom Christianity had not yet converted.

Since he seems to regret the fact that much of Africa had been converted to Islam, Renan looks forward to a future which promises the triumph of the Indo-European genius. There is nothing genuine in Renan's hope since the Indo element in his thesis soon vanishes. He now sings the triumph of Europe from the sixteenth century onwards purely and simply. He does not conceal his joy at the slow decomposition of the Islamic world while European genius flourishes with incomparable greatness. One is amazed by what he sees as an essential prerequisite for the development of European civilization: the destruction of Islam first. By this he means the destruction of the theocratic power of some Islamic countries, for, according to him, Islam can only exist as the

State religion (II, 333). If it becomes a free and individual religion, that is, if it is not the State religion but co-exists with other religions, it will perish. Renan seems completely unaware that Islam existed and flourished as a minority religion in many parts of the world in his day. Prophet of doom, he predicts an eternal war which will stop only when the last son of Ismā'īl (the Arab) will have died of poverty or been relegated to the depths of the desert. The grounds for his attack on Islam are that it stands for fanaticism, the suppression of civilian society and the narrowing of horizons. Like Gobineau, he traces all such weaknesses back to the simplicity of the Semitic spirit, to the *shahāda* in which he finds an eternal tautology, that 'God is God'. This apparently closes the mind to any subtle notion or feeling and to any rational research! In the *Essai sur les moeurs* (1756) Voltaire had made a sounder judgement on the simplicity of the Muslim creed: he believed it was that very simplicity, as opposed to the mysterious dogma of the Trinity, which had been responsible for the conversion of many nations to Islam in various parts of the world.

The translation of the *Shāh-nāmah* (The Epic of the Kings) of the Persian poet Firdawsī (c. 940-1020) by Jules Mohl in 1856 gave Renan another chance of trying to operate a cleavage between Arab and Persian. He claims that Firdawsī was hardly a Muslim, although the surrounding fanaticism made him pay hypocritical homage to the Prophet and 'Alī. Through the cloak of hypocrisy Firdawsī could develop his pantheistic, fatalistic and materialist ideas and his interest in magic. In fact, Firdawsī was no hypocrite but a devout Muslim who, however, was true to his Persian background. Renan says that Firdawsī's irritation against Islam is hardly concealed as the latter pointed to the fact that his ancestors also had a religion – the worship of fire. It is true that the *Shāh-nāmah* recorded the traditional history of Iran and its rulers in pre-Islamic times, that Iran had a strong, conscious link with its pre-Islamic past, but Iran did not reject its Islamic heritage. Renan's hope is that one day Iran would shake the yoke of Islam and that the *Shāh-nāmah* would become its national poem. His dream of Persia abandoning Islam has not materialized and he sounds ridiculous in saying that Firdawsī is not an Arab, but one of us, that is, a European! (II, 423).

The publication of Reinhart Dozy's *Histoire des musulmans d'Espagne* in 1861 provided Renan with the opportunity to make further negative comments on the Arabs. He thought that despite some remarkable instinct for justice and equality, the Arab race never achieved a series of social improvements. He points out that its intellectual development, for a while superior to that of Christian nations, declined rapidly from the thirteenth century onwards. Renan, of course, ignores the achievement, which took place later, of an Ibn Khaldūn (d. 1406). He attributes the decline to religious reaction within Arab society and to external factors such as the surreptitious introduction of foreign races into it. He insinuates that the Turks in the East and the Berbers in the West (Spain) easily overcame Arab indiscipline. He pontificates about the incurable weakness of the Arab race which appears to him devoid of any political spirit and any sense of organization. He even suggests that it is not simply the Bedouins who are anarchic: it is the whole Arab nation! Invincible in battle, the Arabs become powerless the day they have to form a lasting society. They vie with one another for glory and spend their lives dreaming and exercising their wit.

Such chauvinistic remarks did not prevent Renan from making a more balanced evaluation of Arab civilization when he examined the *Kitāb Murūj al-Dhahab* of Masʿūdī, translated by Barbier de Meynard from 1861. The care with which Masʿūdī varies his fictitious portraits reminds him of the comparable art of La Bruyère. Renan is particularly interested in volume 6 dealing with the history of the Abbasids which, as he rightly says, introduces us to the most brilliant period, followed by decadence, of the caliphate in Baghdad. Appreciating the 'liberal' ideas circulating in Baghdad at the time of al-Ma'mūn, but forgetting to mention the *Miḥna* (Inquisition) against those who refused to subscribe to the doctrine of the created Qur'ān, he says that the Abbasid Caliphs, although of pure Arab blood, in fact showed many traits of Persian character. The last part of the statement has nothing controversial about it. Equally free from controversy is the remark that under the auspices of the Abbasid caliphs translations from Greek and Syriac into Arabic were made of the principal works of science and Greek philosophy. According to Renan, few events in history were more significant than the acquisition by the West, in the twelfth century, of its first fundamental writings in science. As he points out, the original texts in Greek came its way only during the Renaissance. However, he limits the Arabs' contribution to scientific advance by stressing their role as translators.

The abundant coverage given to the travels of Ibn Baṭṭūṭa (1304-77) which were translated into French by C. Defrémery and B.R. Sanguinetti in 1853 allows Renan to offer some interesting perspectives on Islamic religion, society and civilization. The first part of the evaluation contains his most positive comments on Arab achievement in the field of travel. The passion for travel seems to him one of the most striking traits of character by which the Arabs had left a deep impact on the history of civilization. How apposite is his remark that before the great surge in Spanish and Portuguese navigation of the fifteenth and sixteenth centuries few communities had contributed as much as the Arabs towards widening the concept of the universe and giving man an exact notion of our planet. Renan maintains that the absence of distinct nationalities in the world of Islam frees the Muslim from the ties which bind the individual to a particular spot in other societies and that he has no country but Islam. So while travelling from Tangier (his home town) to Malaysia, Ibn Battuta does not really leave his country. Renan was of course referring to an age when the concept of individual nations was rather hazy. Indeed, the travels of Ibn Baṭṭūṭa conveyed the feeling of extension of the world of Islam which contained various societies within it but all linked by a common culture, expressed in Arabic.

Renan explains the wanderings of cultured individuals in a plausible manner: these wanderings are encouraged by Arab hospitality and the extreme diffusion of intellectual refinement with the result that whoever wanted to hear famous doctors of religion, for example, had to travel to Morocco, Cairo, Makka and Samarkand. He is, however, utterly unconvincing when he invokes a belief in fatalism by some Muslims to account for a wandering life: the traveller apparently thinks he is obeying a fixed destiny in 'obeying his mobility'! (II, 533). More reasonable is the explanation that perpetual wandering stems from the way Muslim society is organized. Such an organization ensures that among the Arabs the traveller is no outsider without a role or a family, no stranger who is kept at a distance. More often than not he is a lawyer or doctor who practises his profession while travelling. He stops at each halt on his way, takes root in the country and becomes an important personality until the urge to travel reasserts itself, but he is certain that his services will be sought after everywhere and will be well rewarded. The traveller repays his host with a medical or legal consultation, with a recital of prose or verse narratives, some even indulge in magic. It is rather reminiscent of the kind of situation one encounters in the novel of Tahar Ben

Jelloun who is sensitive to the oral tradition of the Arabs.[17] Renan clinches the point about movement in the world of Islam by suggesting that the peculiar life of Ibn Baṭṭuṭa is also that of countless other men within Muslim society. He is impressed by the incomparable unity achieved by Islam for a few centuries and the incredible dispersion of individuals in various parts of Muslim society.

However, the suggestion that these wanderings were turned into a religious duty to make pilgrimage compulsory is less convincing. Renan seems unwilling to distinguish between wanderings through the secular world of Islam and pilgrimage to the sacred city of Makka. However, he does take into account the views of Muslim apologists regarding the joy pilgrims feel and their desire to renew pilgrimage. He is impressed by the pious foundations which assist poor Muslims in performing their duty and the moving spirit of brotherhood during pilgrimage. The blending of the spiritual with the worldly in pilgrimage is eventually brought out by Renan when he adds that the trading spirit had something to contribute to the charm of pilgrimage. He sees Makka as a vast market and centre for exchange in the whole world. Indeed, the fairs of 'Ukāẓ and Mijanna were very lively commercial centres before Islam while the Qur'ān itself allows legitimate trade in the interests of the honest trader and most pilgrims, provided the profit is sought as a favour from God: 'It is no crime in you if you seek of the bounty of your Lord' (*Sūra* 2: 198).[18]

It is clear that Renan is moved by the description of his visit to Makka by Ibn Baṭṭūṭa who expressed his emotion at God's act in creating in men an instinctive desire to seek the 'sublime sanctuaries' which they leave with grief after their hearts have been taken over completely.[19] Renan imagines that Makka at the time of pilgrimage must be truly one of the greatest religious spectacles in the world (II, 535). He is struck by the description of simple prayers coming from everywhere and addressed to the one God, by the austere sermons of the Imāms, by the extraordinary scene of pilgrims emerging from Mount 'Arafāt, by the endless procession taking place round the Ka'ba night and day and by religious unanimity where the slightest doubt is not entertained. Apart from the exaggeration on unanimity in Islam, Renan manages to capture the spirit of the pilgrimage to some extent. But where Ibn Baṭṭuṭa waxes lyrical about its spiritual significance, he is more impressed by its picturesque element and is mildly critical of Ibn Baṭṭūṭa whom he depicts as a naïve Muslim failing to notice the spectacular in what he describes.

Henceforth Ibn Baṭṭūṭa's account only serves as a pretext for Renan's attack on Islam and the Arabs. He does not agree with Ibn Baṭṭūṭa that the Black Stone of the Ka'ba is beautiful. Far from being beautiful, he finds it a blemish with which Muḥammad could be reproached: this 'great worshipper of God' simply pandered to the beliefs of the old pagan Arabs. Renan is not moved by Ibn Baṭṭūṭa's description of Friday prayers at Makka, which he finds typical of the 'culte triste, sans grâce, sans variété, sévère comme le désert' (p. 536). His comments range from the particular to the general. Without giving any illustration Renan says that Islam was so austere and abstract at the beginning that it rejected as polytheism all dogmas appearing to give God a mother and a father. But it ended up with dubious practices and the small-mindedness of the casuists. To Renan Muslim devotion is a devotion of men, created by men for men: in Islam women have almost remained outside religion. This remark is prompted by the fact that in Islam men and women do not, for practical reasons, pray together. Whereas in Persia there appear permanent revolts against the simplicity of the Islamic faith, Makka is criticized for condoning struggles for revenge and murders; it knows no theological disputes, merely disputes about rank and genealogy and the anarchy that prevails there is like that of pre-Islamic times. The Arabs offer the spectacle of a society that maintains itself in its own way without any kind of government or any ideas of sovereignty. Renan claims that in Africa where they found a soil in harmony with nomadic and patriarchal life, the Arabs spread in a way that one associates with the desert and its undisciplined habits. An even larger claim, not borne out by any evidence, is that Islam is purer in the Sudan than in Syria, Egypt and Constantinople and that superstitious practices have hardly gained access among the nomadic tribes of Africa. On the contrary, the influence of ancestral beliefs on African Islam remains strong.[20] Most objectionable perhaps in that part of *De la part des peuples sémitiques* is Renan's prophecy about and misunderstanding of Islam, namely that it will end up the way it began, by being only the religion of the Arabs, according to the true programme of Muḥammad. The Qur'ān, which describes itself as a guide to mankind in *Sūra* 2: 185 and the Prophet's farewell sermon refute this suggestion emphatically.

However, the fiercest attack on Islam and Islamic communities was made by Renan in his lecture entitled 'L'islamisme et la science', delivered at the Sorbonne in March 1883 (I, 945-65). He claims that any person with a little education would clearly see the inferiority of Muslim countries, the decadence of states governed by Islam and the intellectual nonentity of races deriving their culture and education from it only. Everyone who has been in the Orient or in Africa will have been struck by the kind of iron circle in which the believer's head is enclosed, making him absolutely closed to science, and incapable of learning anything or of opening himself to anything new. As if he had made a special study of Muslim children, Renan declares that the Muslim child of ten or twelve, up to then fairly sharp, suddenly becomes fanatical and foolishly proud of possessing what he thinks is absolute truth. Apparently, this foolish pride is the fundamental weakness of the Muslim. Renan reconstructs the picture of the Muslim as someone who is convinced that God grants fortune and power to whomsoever He wishes without taking into account education and personal merit and therefore has the greatest scorn for education and science (I, 946). Such a view represents a complete distortion of Islamic teaching on guidance and knowledge as proclaimed in the Qur'ān. In addition, the Traditionalist al-Bukhārī, for example, has a whole section entitled 'the book of knowledge' devoted to the importance of knowledge in Islam, which he places immediately after the 'book of belief'.[21]

Not unfairly perhaps, Renan reminds his audience of the habit of certain Muslims of comforting themselves about the future by referring to their past. But this is simply a way of making his oft-repeated point that Abbasid achievement in science and philosophy is of foreign and not Arabic origin. What is new is the manner of making his point. He uses the Christian Arab Abu'l-Faraj to support the view that the genius of the Arabs lay in the science of language only and that God did not teach them anything about philosophy nor did he make them worthy of it (I, 947). That is why, argues Renan, when the pious Arab tries to explain the nature of things he is happy to rely on God as a creator who governs the world directly and reveals Himself to man through successive prophets. That is why as long as Islam was in the hands of the Arabs, that is, of the first four Caliphs and the Umayyads, no intellectual movement of a lay character ever took place. Renan suggests that the Caliph 'Umar did not burn the library at Alexandria, but the principle that he caused to triumph in the world in fact destroyed scientific research and any intellectual pursuits among Muslims.[22] However, towards 750 Persia and its ancient family of the

Barmakids ensured the triumph of the Abbasids who in due course gave way to the Turks. In Renan's view it was the latter's hegemony that was responsible for the absence of philosophical and scientific enquiry in Islam.

In 'L'islamisme et la science', Renan's main thesis is that Islam has always persecuted science and philosophy. But he contradicts himself almost in the same breath by acknowledging that it was tempered by what he calls a form of Protestantism – the Muʿtazila – before the twelfth century when it was less organized and fanatical. However, from the thirteenth to the nineteenth century it fell into the hands of Tartars and Berbers who were 'races lourdes, brutales et sans esprit' (I, 955). Renan gives a simplistic account of religious trends in Islam: a relatively short period of two or three centuries characterized by hardly concealed incredulity is followed by longer periods leading to the triumph of absolute dogma, to coercion and corporal punishment surpassed only by the Spanish Inquisition.[23] It is generally agreed that in Islam, as in other religions, religious controversy is never as clear-cut as Renan makes it appear. As Renan's aim is to paint an increasingly negative picture of Islam towards the end of the lecture, he describes it as a religion that oppresses large portions of the world and is the most opposed to progress, the Islamic state being founded on a 'so called revelation' (p. 956). He admits that Western theology persecutes as much as Islam, but claims it has not managed to crush the modern spirit, as Islam has. Although he acknowledges that he is moved when entering a mosque, he still believes that Islam has destroyed itself by destroying science and that the lasting service one can render a Muslim is to free him from his religion (I, 963).

Jamāl al-Dīn al-Afghānī (1839-97), a Muslim writer and politician who believed in the future progress of Islam, replied to Renan in the *Journal des Débats* of May 1883.[24] His arguments were inspired less by Islamic fervour than political common sense. Often relying on irony, Afghānī argues that if it is true that Islam is a bar to the development of science one could not say that the obstacle would not disappear one day. Moreover, the persecution of philosophy was not unique to Islam. He pokes fun at the idea of comparing a Muslim to an ox tied to the plough. He also ridicules the suggestion that the Muslim patiently follows the dogma to which he is a slave and forever treads the same path that has been carved out for him by interpreters of the law. However ignorant and barbarian the Arabs may have been at the beginning, they revived science and made it flourish as it had never done before. Whatever they took from the Greeks and the Persians, they developed, clarified and perfected with elegant taste and precision. As the French, the Germans and the English were not as far away from Rome and Constantinople as the Arabs, it would have been easier for them to exploit the scientific treasures buried in these cities. But the Europeans welcomed Aristotle only when he migrated and became Arab and they did not think of him when he was Greek and their neighbour! Besides, the Arabs by occupying Spain did not cease being Arab and one cannot say that Ibn Bajja, Ibn Rushd and Ibn Ṭufayl are not as Arab as al-Kindī simply because they were not born in Arabia! (pp. 181-182).

Afghani's stand would have found support in Gustave Lebon who protested against Renan's attempt to show the Arabs as nonentities.[25] Lebon points out that each of his assertions is contradicted by Renan himself on the next page. As an example, he refers to Renan's view that for six hundred years progress in science was due to the Arabs and that intolerance appeared only when they were replaced by Berbers and Turks. But Renan says that Islam has always persecuted science and philosophy! Lebon admits that Renan's prejudices fade away from time to time, although they reappear unconsciously: one such prejudice is that the scholars were not Arabs, but people from Cordoba and Seville. Lebon's reply to this argument is that since these places belonged to the Arabs and Arab blood and education had penetrated there for a long time, one could not challenge the product coming out of their schools because of its origin any more than one could challenge the work of French scholars on the grounds that the latter came from Normandy and Aquitaine!

One may agree with Lebon and others up to a point. Renan indeed contradicted himself on a number of occasions. But then he was not the first Frenchman to have been guilty of contradiction and to have had such an ambivalent attitude towards Islam. One must look beyond the ambivalence and the tendency to polarize if one wishes to understand the crucial role he played in the formation of European ideas on Islam in the nineteenth century. To get the perspective right one must certainly look at a whole range of texts, including the *Histoire générale des langues sémitiques* and the *Vie de Jésus*.[26] While his later reactions do give the impression of prejudice and chauvinism towards the Arabs, one should remember that his earlier reactions expose a similar weakness towards the Persians. Yet the reader who patiently reads his attacks on Persian imagination in the 'Mahomet et les origines de l'islamisme' article can appreciate his efforts in stripping Islam of the supernatural to a large extent. The comparison he makes between the miraculous in Islam and Christianity is often to the advantage of the former. That is because Renan is no modern Crusader championing the cause of the Cross. Like Gobineau, he writes more in the spirit of earlier French polemicists setting one religion against another and one group of nations against another. Above all, Renan's ability to dissociate mainstream Islam from the pantheism found in writers such as Ibn Arabi is impressive. After making due allowance for his controversial remarks, one may conclude that his best insights into Islam are probably to be found in his earlier writings and in sections of his major work, *Averroès et l'averroïsme* where he made a distinct contribution to our understanding of Islamic philosophy. For much of what he says about Islamic philosophers is sound and he never seeks to promote the subject of his doctoral thesis at the expense of other thinkers.

Notes

1. See H.W. Wardman, *Ernest Renan. A critical biography* (London, 1964).

2. In *L'Europe et l'Islam*, pp. 48-58, Hichem Djait makes some valid points on Renan, but gives the impression that Renan had no Islamic background. A glance, for example, at the *Histoire générale des langues sémitiques*, vol. VIII of the *Oeuvres complètes* ed. by Henriette Psichari (Paris, 1947) will disprove this. Quotations come from this edition.

3. This is a view shared by Zakaria Bashier who argues that Muḥammad is the only Prophet to have been born and lived in the full light of history. See *Sunshine at Madina* (Leicester, 1990), p. 14.

4. A point Renan emphasizes in 'Mahomet et les origines de l'islamisme', VII, 198.

5. See Albert Hourani, *Islam in European thought* (Cambridge, 1991), pp. 162-3.

6. In *Orientalism* (London, 1978), pp. 130-148, Edward Said devoted a number of thought-provoking pages to Renan, stressing the philological and anthropological aspects of his work but not a word is said about the article nor about Renan's doctoral thesis on Islamic philosophy.

7. In *Averroès et l'averroïsme*, III, 135, Renan argues that the supernatural hardly appears in the essential teachings of Islam which is close to the most purified form of deism, a European thesis often upheld in the eighteenth century.

8. For example, Mohammed Sharafuddin, in *Islam and Romantic Orientalism* (London, 1994), p. 208.

9. This is rather surprising coming from Renan, as he nowhere shows any sympathy with the Shīʿite stand.

10. Fazlur Rahman, *Islam and Modernity* (Chicago, 1982), pp. 133, 152.

11. The *Kitāb al-Muwaṭṭa'*, perhaps the oldest Islamic legal work, by Mālik ibn Anas (d. 795), the founder of one of the four orthodox schools of thought in Islam, gives a general view of law, justice, rites and practices and establishes a theoretical framework to judge matters not settled by consensus or the practice of the Prophet.

12. cf. W. Montgomery Watt, *Islamic Philosophy and Theology* (Edinburgh, 1962), p. 96.

13. See Shelly Ekhtiar, '*Ḥayy ibn Yaqẓān*: the eighteenth-century reception of an oriental self-taught philosopher', *Studies on Voltaire and the eighteenth century*, ed. H.T. Mason (Oxford, 1992), vol. 302, pp. 217-245.

14. Voltaire, *Correspondence and related documents*, ed. T. Besterman (1968-77), Best. D310.

15. Fakhr ad-dīn al-Rāzī, *At-Tafsīr al-Kabīr* (Cairo, 1950), XXIX, 180. As Si Hamza Boubakeur points out in his commentary on verse 61, *Le Coran*, ii, 1847, this conception of resurrection is not to be confused with metempsychosis in any form or incarnation which are rejected by Islam.

16. In *La Société berbère* first published in the *Revue des Deux Mondes* in 1873, Renan declares that Islam is not republican at all, that all Muslim society quickly turns into the bloodiest absolutism and that the Berber race needed to be resolutely democratic to resist this fatal tendency (II, 558).

17. The first chapter of *La nuit sacrée* (Paris, 1987), describes the storyteller Bouchaib who had entertained kings and princes, trained a generation of troubadours in Marrakesh and spent a year in Makka. But he, like the other storytellers including a woman, lost his audience to the superior storyteller, the heroine Zahra.

18. See Si Hamza Boubakeur's commentary on *Sūra* 2: 198, *Le Coran*, i, 133 and Yūsuf 'Alī's in the *Holy Qur'ān*, i, 79.

19. Ibn Baṭṭūṭa, *Riḥla*, transl. H.A.R. Gibb, *The Travels of Ibn Baṭṭūṭa* (Cambridge, 1958), p. 189.

20. In *France and Islam in West Africa, 1860-1960* (Cambridge, 1988), C. Harrison gives countless examples of fetishism, animism, even human sacrifice, prevailing in West Africa. Pure Islamic beliefs and institutions were rarely noticed in the period surveyed and there was a feeling that indigenous pre-Islamic customs remained strong. See particularly pp. 54, 104, 129.

21. See al-Bukhārī, *Ṣaḥīḥ*, vol. I in the translation (with text) by Muḥammad Muhsin Khan (Madina, 1971).

22. The charge of being hostile to learning and intellectual pursuits is often made against 'Umar who could not have contradicted the teaching of the Qur'ān. *Sūra* 20: 114, for example, reads: 'Lord, increase me in knowledge'. However, the story of the burning of the library at Alexandria is to be found in a late Arabic source, the *Ta'rīkh al-Ḥukamā'* of Ibn al-Qifṭī (1172-1248).

23. As H. Djait argues (op. cit., p. 53), it is not certain that the decline of Islamic culture was due to the strangehold of orthodoxy on the political and social system: it was rather due to varied factors. In any case, the ferment of the tenth and eleventh centuries giving rise to movements such as those of the Khārijites and Qarmatians shows that Islamic culture is rich and not monolithic.

24. Reprinted in A.M. Goichon, *La réfutation des matérialistes* (Paris, 1942), pp. 174-189.

25. *La Civilisation des Arabes* (Paris, 1884), pp. 630-640.

26. For Renan's contribution to Qur'ānic studies in these texts (see Chapter 1, above).

Conclusion

One needs to be true to the spirit of Jacques Berque's lecture referred to in the Introduction. If it is highly desirable for Western scholars to work in partnership with those who know their societies and cultures from within, it follows that Muslim scholars too need to work in partnership with the former. The preceding pages might have revealed some fundamental disagreement on my part with certain Western scholars. This is not simply because they are Orientalists, but because their approach to Islam is too controversial and sensational. Therefore it is legitimate for a Muslim, despite some reservations he may have at times, to prefer the writings of Reland, Ockley, Sylvestre de Sacy, Caussin de Perceval, Gibb, Hourani and Watt to those of some other Western authors. The views of the latter cannot often be reconciled with his deeply-cherished beliefs.

Travel perhaps does not always broaden the mind. If we are to believe W. Kinglake, author of *Eothen* (1844), the 'traveller is a creature not always looking at sights... once having determined to write the shear truth concerning the things which chiefly have interested him, he must and he will sing a sadly long strain about Self' (preface, p. vii). Yet Kinglake piously believes that despite his egotism the traveller must still convey some true ideas of the country through which he has passed. It seems that much of Kinglake's remark will apply to Chateaubriand who is primarily interested in himself and to whom the past is more important than the present. It is this present – nineteenth-century Middle East – that interests Lane, Clot and Schoelcher. Together with Lamartine whose thoughts even include the future of the Middle East and Burckhardt and Burton who travel to a hitherto virtually inaccessible country to report on a central aspect of Islam – the *ḥajj* – they contribute new knowledge about the area and Islam. On the whole, there is no doubt that writers such as Boulainviller, Toderini and Lane achieve a higher standard of fairness and accuracy than many other Europeans in their assessment of the Prophet and Muslim communities.

There have been some outstanding women, including saints, in Islamic history. But in Islam, as in other religions, there are more sinners than saints, more ordinary women than extraordinary women. Myths proliferated about all categories of Muslim women in European literature. One of these myths relating to the soullessness of Muslim women died hard. Opinion remained divided on the subject: the nineteenth century was not fully able to restore their souls to them. Soullessness apart, the depiction of Muslim women is certainly different from that of the previous century. As all myths are meant to be dispelled many of them are in fact being dispelled in the period. The ordinary women of Egypt play their part in this connection by showing that they could take positive action. They were therefore not as passive or helpless as they were made out to be by Byron. One would have liked them not to have to fight for their legitimate rights in the *sharīʿa* courts. But what else could they have done in a male-dominated society? At least the courts were operational.

If refreshing images of women's lives inside or outside the harem sometimes appear now it is in no small measure due to the contribution of some European women writers who offer a salutary corrective to deep-rooted prejudices. They, however, do not touch on a painful evil affecting a small section of Islamic society – prostitution, which cannot be swept under the carpet. It fell to men writers to highlight its prevalence in a wide area of the Islamic world. The Orientalist Venture de Paradis, who had been interpreter in Syria, Egypt, Morocco and Tunisia, also spent two years in Algiers in 1788-89. There he noted soldiers using prostitutes who were apparently tolerated by the government.[1] In later times more respectable women – the great majority of Muslim women – cannot, of course, stop *fatwās* being issued by men in an attempt to debar them from holding public office. But *fatwās* change when times and places change.

In this book Western accounts of the culture of Muslim communities focus on their literary achievement. The extracts of al-Ḥarīrī's *Maqāmāt,* reproduced and edited by Sylvestre de Sacy in the *Chrestomathie arabe,* are, to a certain extent, complemented by Venture de Paradis's translation of some of the sessions in Ḥarīrī's text earlier on. Venture's translation was left in manuscript form[2] until it was published by A. Amer in 1964. Although in the 'Traductions de divers contes et poésies' Venture refers to fifty *séances* being translated, only a few were in fact translated by him. Among these was the one which Sacy later translated as the *Séance d'Alexandrie.* Venture liked the adventures of the old man and his wife and, unlike Sacy, he had no criticism for Arabic literary taste which he thought used delicate, elegant and simple metaphorical expressions embellished by Qur'ānic passages and proverbs. The story varied in details but Venture did not reproduce any Qur'ānic allusions.

Perhaps wishing to avoid the charge of being considered too harsh towards the Persians, Sacy sought to make amends with a manuscript entitled 'Sophisme ou théosophie des Perses. Extraits des manuscrits persans'.[3] His remarks on the origins of sufism are quite provocative. According to him many writers believe that sufi doctrine has Greek or Indian origins. He himself believes that despite Muḥammad's censure of monasticism religious groupings sprang up among zealous Muslims from the days of Abū Bakr and ʿAlī and that these may be regarded as the prototype of the numerous monastic orders that followed. He traces the mystical doctrine of Jalāl ad-dīn Rūmī back to Shaikh Junayd and he is convinced that sufi doctrine is characterized by pantheism. At first he quotes a *ḥadīth* of the Prophet to justify the origins of sufism and the idea of the mystical union of man with God. But then he modifies his position by stressing the fact that this mystical doctrine which he deems so opposed to the Qur'ān was already alive in Persia, reaching it via India before it was conquered by the Arabs. As evidence, he refers to the book *Kalīla wa Dimna*, a collection of moral fables of animal life derived from Sanskrit and put into Arabic prose by Ibn al-Muqaffaʿ, a writer of Iranian origin. In Sacy's view it proves the existence of close relations between India and Persia which suffice to have given rise to the transmission of philosophical and religious doctrines between the two countries. These relations are well established, but do not necessarily lead to the conclusions Sacy wishes the reader to draw. He argues, for example, that if the Indian doctrine of *māyā* (illusion, that is, whatever is is in God and outside God there is nothing) is current among Persians then there is every reason to believe that the same holds good for mysticism, based on the doctrine of emanation and the return of everything to God. There is an evident desire on the part of Sacy to drive a wedge between Arab and Persian and to exaggerate Islam's indebtedness to Indian thought. His position anticipates that of Gobineau in *Mémoire sur l'état de la Perse actuelle* (see Chapter 6, above).

If culture were to be taken in a broader sense it would certainly incorporate historical writing. It seems that Sacy took culture to mean something wider than literature. Hence his inclusion in the *Chrestomathie* of extracts both from Maqrīzī and Ibn Khaldūn. The latter has been mentioned only in passing, since a thorough treatment of him would have been beyond the scope of this work. Yet further reference to him may be worthwhile, if only to show that Frenchmen of the nineteenth century and later times valued his outstanding contribution to historiography in general and his discourse on the history of Arabs, Berbers and other communities, in particular. I do not wish to go into controversial questions such as whether Ibn Khaldūn anticipated modern sociology. Instead I prefer to mention his overall achievement. Celebrating the achievement of the Tunisian historian is celebrating, to a degree, that of Anglo-French scholarship at the same time. It is also to stress once again the paradox that in that age scholarship seems to follow the flag. As in the case of Egypt, discussed in the Introduction and chapter 5, the conquest of Algeria by the French led to the production of state-sponsored scholarly works on North Africa. Among these were the works of the baron MacGucklin de Slane, both British/Irish and French by origins and culture, first interpreter of the French army in Africa. In 1847 and 1851 he published, in Algiers, by order of the French Ministry of War, a two-volume Arabic text of that part of Ibn Khaldūn's *History* concerned with the Maghrib. This was followed in 1852 by its French translation in four volumes. 1863 saw the publication in Paris of his three-volume translation of the *Muqaddima*, which has been deemed to be the best translation that exists to date.[4] The same de Slane translated Ibn Khallikān's *Wafayāt* as *Biographical Dictionary*, between 1842 and 1871. His scholarly output had little to do with French imperialism. That is why the Introduction warned against the dangers of seeing relations between Europe and the Islamic world simply in terms of colonialism. It is clear that there is no basis for the thesis that all Western writings are distorted and biased against Islam.

In the seventeenth and eighteenth centuries Islam was often used by Protestant writers as an instrument of denigration against Roman Catholics. These Catholic-Protestant controversies seem to disappear in the nineteenth century and Islam is no longer caught in between, although it is still used to some extent by Renan in his attack on Christianity. It is not necessarily a sign of progress. For there is now a different strategy in place to divide Islamic communities. In Algeria, the French attempt to separate Arabs from Berbers whom they deem more suitable for assimilation – a policy in line with De Tocqueville's thinking. In their more theoretical writings, Gobineau and Renan derive satisfaction in opposing Arabs to Persians. On the part of Gobineau at least, this leads to a feeling of admiration for the modern Persians, as his private correspondence shows. Perhaps his stay of some five years among them in Persia and his getting to know them fairly well may have been conducive to this feeling. His positive attitude towards Persians of previous centuries also finds some echo in his important published output. Yet one should not stress that residence always widens sympathies and make a general rule from it. For similar residence by Muir and others among the 'natives' in India did not produce the same kindly disposition towards Indian Muslims and Islam. But it could be argued that the former were influenced by the missionary zeal of Anglican proselytizing.

One of the conclusions to be drawn is that in the nineteenth century many European writers are as ambivalent as ever towards Islam. There is, of course, no ambivalence in De Tocqueville, as he has a clearly colonial mentality which is demonstrated by his contribution to the formulation of French policy in Algeria. Gobineau and Renan appear more ambivalent. The latter is even puzzling. Champion of a historical Islam, he yet wants its destruction so that Muslims may progress! What has not perhaps been noticed before by critics is that Renan is an admirer of the Traditionist al-Bukhārī in 'Mahomet et les origines de l'islamisme' for his efforts in checking the growth of spurious *ḥadīth*. Even if he expresses a desire for further pruning of the collection it is gratifying to note that Renan focuses attention on a Traditionist who is held in high esteem by Sunnī Muslims all over the world and who is being given increasing importance by other Europeans.

The great paradox of the age of colonialism and imperialism is that it does not prevent some writers from giving fairly extensive exposure to the Qur'ān, either by direct discussion of it or indirectly through its championing of Islamic literary culture which is replete with Qur'ānic references. Arabic philosophy too is not neglected. Renan himself probably produced the best evaluation of Averroes.[5] Interest in *Ḥadīth* literature develops in the later part of the century with the Germans leading the way. There is some inclination to belittle Muslims and their civilization on the part of Gobineau, but the attempt is not sustained. On the contrary, many efforts are being made by other European writers to translate and edit Arabic, Persian and Turkish texts. Among many of these editions one may note, apart from Sacy's edition of al-Ḥarīrī's *Maqāmāt*, that of Abu'l Fidā''s life of the Prophet by Jakob Reiske. It is certainly sounder than Gagnier's[6] because Reiske refrained from adding material foreign to Abu'l Fidā'.

In the *Journal Asiatique* of July-August 1892 Barbier de Meynard, Vice-President of the 'Société Asiatique', paid homage to its former President. After making due allowance for the kind words normally expected in an obituary, one should still contest Barbier's claim that humanity was in mourning for Renan's death in those parts of the world where scientific research is held in high esteem. Few readers today would share his views on Renan's contribution to the debate on Islam and science. For as this study has shown, Renan's deficiency in knowledge of Islamic science was glaring and that may partly explain some of his preposterous remarks.

That is not saying that his overall assessment of Islam was unbalanced or that his century was deficient. On the contrary, it laid the solid foundation for a future history of science in which justice could be done to the part played by Islamic science. In fact some justice was done to the latter in the late eighteenth century by the abbé Toderini. Justice continued to be done, briefly by Sacy, and in greater depth by specialists such as Delambre, Sédillot and the baron Carra de Vaux. This shows how weak is the thesis that sets out to prove that all Europeans failed to recognize Islamic/Arabic achievement in science and other fields in previous centuries.

Sédillot studied the researches of the tenth-century Persian astronomer Abu'l Wafā' al-Buzjānī on the evection of the moon which he interpreted as the third inequality of the moon, a discovery always attributed to Tycho Brahe. After much controversy Sédillot's views were rejected, but the contribution of Abu'l Wafā' was recognized.[7] Nāṣir al-Dīn al-Ṭūsī (1200-1274), dissatisfied with the Ptolemaic planetary model, proposed a new lunar model identical with that of Copernicus, which was later produced by Ibn al-Shāṭir.[8] In his review of the *Traité du quadrilatère* of Tusi in the *Journal Asiatique* of 1892, Carra de Vaux describes Ṭūsī as one of the greatest representatives of Arab science. He pays homage to Tusi's truly scientific spirit of synthesis of his predecessors' works. Highlighting the considerable progress made by the Arabs in trigonometry, he argues that Ṭūsī's book throws a bright light on that part of the history of science. He shows that Muslim scholars possessed new methods which they had created from the thirteenth century onwards and that they were using techniques similar to those found in the West later. These discoveries reached it only in the Renaissance. The effect of such writings of the nineteenth century is to expose not only Renan's inadequacies on the question of Islamic science but also those of later writers such as H. Butterfield, author of *The Origins of modern science*, a work first published in 1949 and republished many times afterwards. To Butterfield, the Arabs were merely the transmitters of Greek science through translation. Fortunately, these errors have since been put right by a number of contemporary scholars.[9]

Notes

1. See 'Papiers Venture de Paradis', in B.N.F., N.a.f., ms. 9134, fol. 92. The ms. dates from about 1790.

2. See 'Papiers Venture', N.a.f. 9136, fol. 49. The ms. dates from the period 1786-95.

3. See B.N.F., F. fr. 25385, fols. 13-17. The ms. dates from about 1821.

4. See Aziz al-Azmeh, *Ibn Khaldun* (London, 1990), p. 167 and *Ibn Khaldun in modern scholarship* (London, 1981).

5. Oliver Leaman thinks that nothing matches the scope of Renan's doctoral thesis on the question of Averroism in the West. See his book, *Averroes and his Philosophy* (London, 1998), p. 168.

6. To arrive at conclusions different from those of traditional Muslims and other Orientalists on the Qur'ān and the Prophet, John Burton sees no need to shift the centre of Islam away from Makka, to make Muḥammad die after the Muslim conquests and to argue that the Qur'ān was written from the ninth century onwards. In *The Collection of the Qur'ān* (Cambridge, 1977) he attempts to show that Muḥammad himself edited and collected Qur'ān texts and that what we have is not a *muṣḥaf* 'Uthmān but a *muṣḥaf* Muḥammad (p. 239).

7. See S.H. Nasr, *Islamic Science. An illustrated study*, p. 99.

8. Nasr, p. 109.

9. In his book, *A History of Arabic Astronomy*, G. Saliba discusses the contribution of scholars such as E.S. Kennedy, N. Swerdlow and V. Roberts towards rewriting the history of science. Roberts, for instance, has found Ibn al-Shāṭir to be 'a pre-Copernican Copernicus'.

Bibliography

Manuscript Sources

PARIS. ***Bibliothèque Nationale de France. Fonds francais.***

25280 A. Galland. Mélanges sur le mahométisme.

25385 Sylvestre de Sacy. Sophisme ou théosophie des Perses. Extraits des ms persans.

PARIS. ***Bibliothèque Nationale de France. Nouvelles acquisitions françaises.***

8988 Papiers Venture de Paradis. Mémoires pour les affaires étrangères sur les enfants de langue. Projet d'un plan d'éducation pour les enfants de langue.

9134 Papiers Venture de Paradis. Notes sur les états barbaresques.

9136 Papiers Venture de Paradis. Traductions de divers contes et poésies.

20424 Papiers, dessins et estampages d'Emile Prisse d'Avennes. Moeurs et coutumes des Egyptiens au xixè siècle.

PARIS. ***Bibliothèque Mazarine.***

1946 Boulainviller. Histoire de Mahomet et de ses premiers successeurs. Tome 1.

1947 Boulainviller. do. Tome 2.

1948 Boulainviller. do. Autre exemplaire complet.

1949 Boulainviller. Histoire de Mahomet. Autre exemplaire du 1er livre.

LONDON. British Library.
Additional manuscripts.
34080. Lane. Description of Egypt.

OXFORD. Bodleian Library.
Mss. Eng. mis. d. 34. Lane. Account of Egypt.

OXFORD. Sackler Library
Griffith Institute Archives. Mss. 6. 1. Lane. Description of Egypt.

Shaykh Ahmed Zaki Yamani, 'The political competence of women in Islamic law', unpublished lecture, Al-Furqan Foundation, London, 2001.

Printed Sources

Abu'l Fidā', Ismāʿīl. *Mukhtaṣar Ta'rīkh al-Bashar*, extracts ed. by J. Gagnier in Arabic and trans. in Latin as *De vita et rebus gestis mohammedis* (Oxford, 1723).

———, Arabic and Latin version of same extracts from *Mukhtaṣar Ta'rīkh* ed. as *Annales Muslemici* by J.J. Reiske (Leipzig, 1754).

———, 2nd edition, ed. I.G. Adler, 1789-94, 5 vols.

———, Extracts from *Mukhtaṣar Ta'rīkh* trans. by W.M. Murray as *Life of Mohammed* (London, 1833).

———, Extracts from *Mukhtaṣar Ta'rīkh* trans. by Noël Desvergers as *Vie du Prophète Mahomet* (Paris, 1837).

Abun-Nasr, Jamil M. *A history of the Maghrib in the Islamic period* (Cambridge, 1987).

Ahmed, Leila. *Edward W. Lane* (London, 1978).

———, *Women and gender in Islam* (New Haven, 1992).

Andréossy, comte. *Constantinople et le Bosphore de Thrace pendant les années 1812-1814, 1826* (Paris, 1828).

Anquetil-Duperron, A.H., *Législation orientale* (Amsterdam, 1778).

Al-Azmeh, Aziz. *Ibn Khaldun in modern scholarship* (London, 1981).

———, *Ibn Khaldun*. (London, 1990).

Banderier, Giles. 'Trois lettres inédites de Renan', *French Studies Bulletin*, Summer 1999, pp. 11-13.

Bashier, Zakaria. *Sunshine at Madina* (Leicester, 1990).

Al-Bayḍāwī, *Anwār al-Tanzīl*. The original of 1330, published in Egypt. Rep. in 2 vols. in Beirut. No date given.

Bennett, Clinton. *Victorian Images of Islam* (London, 1992).

———, *In Search of Muhammad* (London, 1998).

Berkey, Jonathan P. *The Formation of Islam* (Cambridge, 2003).

Botta, Paul Emile, *Relation d'un voyage dans l'Yemen* (Paris, 1841).

Boudhiba, Abdel Wahab, *La sexualité en Islam* (Paris, 1975).

Boulainviller, Henri de, *Vie de Mahomed* (Paris, 1730), 2 vols.

———, Tr. Venturino, Diego as *Vita di Maometto* (Palermo, 1992).

Brahimi, Denise. *Arabes des Lumières et Bédouins romantiques* (Paris, 1982).

Buaben, Jamal. *Image of the Prophet Muḥammad in the West* (Leicester, 1996).

Al-Bukhārī, (Muhammad Muhsin Khan, ed. and trans.). *Ṣaḥīḥ* (Madina, 1971) 9 vols.

———, ed. Ludolf Krehl as *Le Recueil des Traditions Mahométanes* (Leiden, 1862-68), 3 vols. Vol. 4 ed. Th. W. Juynboll (Leiden, 1908).

Burton, John. *The Collection of the Qur'ān* (Cambridge, 1977).

Burton, Richard. *Personal narrative of a pilgrimage to al-Madina and Mecca* (New York, 1893), 2 vols.

Butterfield, Herbert. *The Origins of Modern Science* (London, 1949, 1962).

Byron, Lord. *The Complete Poetical Works*, ed. J.J. McGann (Oxford, 1980), 4 vols.

Carlyle, Thomas. 'The Hero as Prophet' in *On Heroes, Hero Worship and the Heroic in History* (London, 1841).

Carré, J.M. *Voyageurs et écrivains français en Egypte* (Cairo, 1933), 2 vols.

Castel de Saint-Pierre. *Discours contre le mahométisme* in *Ouvrages de politique* (Paris, 1733).

Caussin de Perceval. *Essai sur l'histoire des Arabes* (Paris, 1847-48), 3 vols.

Chabrol de Volvic, comte. *Essai sur les moeurs des habitants modernes de l'Egypte* (Paris, 1822), vol. 2 of *Description de l'Egypte* (1809-28).

Champollion, J.F. *Lettres écrites d'Egypte et de Nubie* (Paris, 1833).

Chardin, Jean. *Voyages en Perse* (Rouen, 1723), 10 vols.

Chateaubriand, Francois René, de. *Oeuvres romanesques et voyages*, ed. M. Regard (Paris, 1969), vol. 2.

Chaybany, Jeanne. *Les Voyages en Perse et la pensée française au xviiè siècle* (Tehran, 1971).

Cicero. *De Oratore.* Loeb Classical Library translation (London, 1948).

Clot, Antoine. *Aperçu général sur l'Egypte* (Paris, 1840).

Combes, E. and Tamisier, M. *Voyage en Abyssinie ... précédé d'une excursion dans l'Arabie Heureuse...* (Paris, 1838).

Cragg, Kenneth. *The Arab Christian* (London, 1992).

Crone, Patricia and Cook, Michael, *Hagarism* (Cambridge, 1977).

Crone, Patricia. *Meccan trade and the rise of Islam* (Oxford, 1987).

Dacier, Bon Joseph. *Tableau historique de l'érudition française* (Paris, 1810).

Daniel, Norman. *Islam and the West*, revsd. ed. (Oxford, 1993).

———, *Islam, Europe and Empire* (Edinburgh, 1966).

Dehérain, Henri. *Sylvestre de Sacy, ses contemporains et ses disciples* (Paris, 1938).

Delaporte, Henry. *Vie de Mahomet* (Paris, 1874).

Der-Sahagian, G. *Chateaubriand en Orient* (Fribourg, 1914).

Desvergers, Noël. *Arabie* (Paris, 1847).

Djait, Hichem. *L'Europe et l'Islam* (Paris, 1978).

Duff Gordon, Lady. *Letters from Egypt* (1862-69) (London, 1969).

Ekhtiar, Shelly. '*Hayy ibn Yaqzan*: the eighteenth-century reception of an Oriental self-taught philosopher' in *Studies on Voltaire and the eighteenth century*, ed. H. Mason (Oxford, 1992), vol. 302, pp. 217-245.

Encyclopaedia of Islam, 2nd ed. (Leiden, 1960-).

The Shorter Encyclopaedia of Islam, ed., H.A.R.Gibb and J. Kramers (Leiden, 1974).

Fahmy, Khalid. 'Women, Medicine and Power in nineteenth-century Egypt' in *Remaking Women. Feminism and modernity in the Middle East*, ed. Lila Abu-Lughod (Princeton, 1998).

Flaubert, Gustave. *Oeuvres complètes*, ed. R. Dumesnil (Paris, 1954), 2 vols.

———, *Correspondance 1830-1850*, vol. 12 in *Oeuvres complètes* (Paris, 1974).

Fromentin, Eugène. *Une année dans le Sahel* (Paris, 1879).

Gagnier, Jean. *Vie de Mahomet* (Amsterdam, 1732), 2 vols.

Garcin de Tassy, J.S.H.V., *L'Islamisme d'après le Coran* (Paris, 1822, 1874).

Garnett, Lucy. *The Women of Turkey and their Folk-lore* (London, 1890-91), 2 vols.

Gibb, Hamilton. *Modern Trends in Islam* (Chicago, 1947).

Gilsenan, Michael. *Recognizing Islam* (London, 1990).

Gisquet, H. *L'Egypte, les Turcs et les Arabes* (Paris, 1848).

Gobineau, comte Arthur de. *Oeuvres,* ed. J. Gaulmier and J. Boissel (Paris, 1983), 2 vols.

Goethe, J.W. von. *Poems,* selected and edited by H.G. Atkins and L.F. Kastner (London, 1902).

———, *West-Eastern Divan*, trans. E. Dowden (London, 1914).

Goichon, A.M. *La réfutation des matérialistes* (Paris, 1942).

Grossir, Claudine. *L'Islam des Romantiques 1811-1840* (Paris, 1984).

Guer, Antoine J. *Moeurs et usages des Turcs* (Paris, 1747), 3 vols.

Gunny, Ahmad. 'Islam in Nerval's *Voyage en Orient*', *Journal of Islamic Studies,* vol. 2 (1991), pp. 195-209.

———, 'Chateaubriand's encounter with Islam in the Middle East' in Studies in honour of Peter France, ed. John Renwick, *L'Invitation an Voyage*, Voltaire Foundation (Oxford, 2000), pp. 301-308.

———, 'Gobineau's perspective on the world of Islam', *International Journal of Islamic and Arabic Studies* (Bloomington, 1992), vol. 9, pp. 17-30.

———, *Images of Islam in eighteenth-century writings* (London, 1996).

Gutas, Dimitri. 'The Study of Arabic Philosophy in the Twentieth Century', *British Journal of Middle Eastern Studies*, vol. 29 (2002), pp. 5-25.

Haddad, Emily A. *Orientalist poetics. The Islamic Middle East in nineteenth-century English and French poetry* (Aldershot, 2002).

Harrison, Charles. *France and Islam in West Africa, 1860-1960* (Cambridge, 1988).

Hawting, G.R. *The idea of idolatry and the emergence of Islam* (Cambridge, 1999).

Herbelot, Barthélemy D'. *Bibliothèque Orientale* (Paris, 1697).

Heyworth-Dunne, J. *Introduction to the history of education in modern Egypt* (London, 1938).

Hopwood, Derek. *Sexual encounters in the Middle East* (Reading, 1999).

Hossain, Mary. 'Women and Paradise', *Journal of European Studies* (1989), vol. 19, pp. 293-310.

Hourani, Albert. *Arabic thought in the liberal age. 1798-1939* (Oxford, 1962).

Hourani, Albert. *Europe and the Middle East* (London, 1980).

———, *Islam in European thought* (Cambridge, 1991).

———, *A History of the Arab peoples* (London, 1991).

Hugo, Victor. *Les Orientales*, ed. E. Barineau (Paris, 1829), 2 vols.

Husayn b. Muḥammad. *Ta'rīkh Al-Khamīs* (place and date of publication not given).

Ibn Baṭṭuṭa, *Riḥla*, trans. by Gibb as *The Travels of Ibn Baṭṭūṭa* (Cambridge, 1958).

Ibn Isḥāq (A. Guillaume, tr.) *Sīrat Rasūl Allāh* (*The Life of Muḥammad*) (Oxford, 1955).

Ibn Khaldūn. *Ta'rīkh al-Duwal al-Islāmīya bi'l-Maghrib*, ed. Slane, W.M., de (Algiers, 1847), 2 vols.

———, *Histoire des Berbères et des dynasties musulmanes de l'Afrique septentrionale*, trans. Slane, W.M. (Paris, 1852), 4 vols.

———, *Histoire de l'Afrique*, Arabic text and trans by Desvergers, N. (Paris, 1841).

———, *Muqaddima*, trans. Slane, W.M as *Les prolégomènes d'Ibn Khaldun* (Paris, 1863), 3 vols.

Ibn Khallikān. *Wafayāt al-A'yān*, tr. M. De Slane as *Biographical Dictionary* (Paris, 1842-71), 4 vols.

Ibn al-Qifṭī. *Ta'rīkh al-Ḥukamā'*, ed. J. Lippert (Leipzig, 1903).

Jalālayn (Jalāl al-Dīn Maḥallī and Jalāl al-Dīn Suyūṭī). *Tafsīr al-Kabīr* (Istanbul, 1958).

———, Al-Suyūṭī. *Al-Taḥadduth bi-ni'mat Allāh* (text, translation and commentary by Elizabeth Sartain (Cambridge, 1975), 2 vols.

Jaubert, Amédée. *Voyage en Arménie et en Perse* (Paris, 1821).
Journal Asiatique (Paris, 1842, 1843, 1892).
Julien, C.A. *Histoire de l'Algérie contemporaine 1830-1871* (Paris, 1964).
Kabbani, Rana. *Europe's myths of Orient* (London, 1986).
Kahf, Mohja. *Western representations of the Muslim woman* (Austin, 1999).
Kamel, Achira. 'Quelques notes sur l'Orient dans l'oeuvre poétique de Victor Hugo, in *La Fuite en Egypte. Supplément aux voyages européens en Orient*, ed. J.C. Vatin (Cairo, 1989), pp. 149-158.
Khayr al-Dīn. *Aqwām al-masālik fī ma'rifat aḥwāl al-mamālik* (Tunis, 1867), trans. as *Réformes nécessaires aux états musulmans* (Paris, 1868).
Kinglake, W. *Eothen* (London, 1844).
Koelle, S.W. *Mohammed and Mohammedanism* (London, 1889).
Kra, Pauline. *Religion in Montesquieu's Lettres persanes*, vol. 72 in *Studies on Voltaire*, ed. T. Besterman (Geneva, 1970).
La Beaume, Jules. *Le Koran analysé* (Paris, 1878).
Lamartine, Alphonse, de. *Souvenirs, impressions, pensées et paysages pendant un Voyage en Orient* (Paris, 1835), 4 vols.
Lane, Edward. *Manners and Customs of the Modern Egyptians* (London, 1836).
———, *Selections from the Kuran* (London, 1843).
———, *Description of Egypt*, ed. J. Thompson (Cairo, 2000).
Leaman, Oliver. *Averroes and his philosophy* (London, 1988, 1998).
Lebon, Gustave. *La Civilisation des Arabes* (Paris, 1884).
Lewis, Bernard. *Islam and the West* (New York, 1993).
Lings, Martin. *Muḥammad* (London, 1983).
Lopez-Morillas, Consuelo. 'Lost and found? Yça of Segovia and the Qur'ān among the Mudejars and Moriscos', *Journal of Islamic Studies* (1999), vol. 10, pp. 277-292.

Loti, Pierre. *Aziyadé* (Paris, 1879).

Lott, Emmeline. *Harem life in Egypt and Constantinople* (London, 1865), 2 vols.

El-Makīn. *Ta'rīkh,* tr. T. Erpenius as *Historica saracenica* (Leiden, 1625) and P. Vattier as *Histoire mahométane* (Paris, 1657).

Mālik ibn Anas. (Imān Sayad ed. and tr. from French) *Al-Muwaṭṭa'* (Beirut, 1993), 2 vols.

al-Maqrīzī, *Le manuscrit autographe d'al-Mawā'iẓ ... al-Khiṭaṭ,* texte édité et annoté par A.F. Sayyid, Al-Furqan Foundation (London, 1995).

Marais, Matthieu. *Journal et Mémoires sur la Régence et le règne de Louis XV* (Paris, 1863-68), 4 vols.

Marcel, Joseph. 'Exercices de lecture d'arabe littéral' in *Arabic tracts* (Alexandria, 1798).

Michaud, Joseph François. *Histoire des Croisades* (Paris, 1825-29), 10 vols.

———, *Correspondance d'Orient* (Paris, 1833-36), 6 vols.

Montagu, Lady Mary Wortley. *The Complete Letters,* ed. R. Halsband (Oxford, 1965-67), 2 vols.

Montesquieu, Charles de Secondat. *Lettres persanes,* ed. P. Vernière (Paris, 1960).

Morier, James. *A Journey through Persia, Armenia and Asia Minor in the years 1808 and 1809* (London, 1812).

Muir, William. *Life of Mahomet* (London, 1858), 4 vols.

Nasr, Seyyed Hossein. *Islamic Science: An illustrated study* (Westerham, 1976).

Nerval, Gérard de. *Oeuvres,* eds. A. Beguin and J. Richer (Paris, 1956), 2 vols.

Nöldeke, Theodor. *Geschichte des Qorans* (Gottingen, 1860).

Ockley, Simon. *Sentences of Ali* (London, 1717).

Oelsner, C.E. *Des effets de la religion de Mohammed* (Paris, 1810).

Pertuisier, Charles. *Promenades pittoresques dans Constantinople et sur les rives du Bosphore* (Paris, 1815), 3 vols.

Porter, James. *Observations on the religion, law, government and manners of the Turks* (London, 1768).
Quintilian. *Institutio Oratoria.* Loeb Classical Library translation (London, 1921).
Qur'ān (André Du Ryer, tr.) (Paris, 1647).
———, (George Sale, tr.) (London, 1734).
———, (Claude Savary, tr.) (Paris, 1783).
———, (Albin Kazimirsky, tr.) (Paris, 1840).
———, (Text, translation and commentary by Yusuf Ali) (New York, 1946), 2 vols.
———, (Text, translation and commentary by Si Hamza Boubakeur) (Paris, 1978, 1985), 2 vols.
Rahman, Fazlur. *Islam* (Chicago, 1966, 1979).
———, *Islam and Modernity* (Chicago, 1982).
Ramadan, Tariq. *To be a European Muslim* (Leicester, 1999).
Rāzī, Fakhr ad-Dīn. *At-Tafsīr al-Kabīr* (Cairo, 1950), 16 vols.
Reinaud, J.T. 'Notice sur Mahomet', *Biographie générale* (Paris, 1860).
Reland, Adrian. *De religione mohammedica* (Utrecht, 1705).
———, *Of the Mahometan religion* (London, 1712).
———, (David Durand, tr.). *La religion des Mahométans* (The Hague, 1721).
Renan, Ernest. *Oeuvres complètes*, ed. Henriette Psichari (Paris, 1947), 10 vols.
Rodinson, Maxime. *La Fascination de l'Islam* (Paris, 1980).
Ruthven, Malise. *Islam in the world* (Harmondsworth, 2000).
Said, Edward. *Orientalism* (London, 1978).
Saint-Hilaire, J. Barthélemy. *Lettres sur l'Egypte* (Paris, 1856).
———, *Mahomet et le Coran* (Paris, 1865).
Saliba, George. *A History of Arabic Astronomy* (New York, 1994).
Sardar, Ziauddin. 'The postmodern age', *Christian-Muslim relations*, ed. M. Anees (London, 1991).

Savary, Claude. *Lettres sur l'Egypte* (Paris, 1788).

Schacht, Joseph and Bosworth, C.E., eds. *The Legacy of Islam* (Oxford, 1974).

Schoelcher, Victor. *L'Egypte en 1845* (Paris, 1846).

Sédillot, J.A. *Histoire générale des Arabes* (Paris, 1854, 1877).

Sharafuddin, Mohammed. *Islam and Romantic Orientalism* (London, 1994).

Smith, Margaret. *Rābiʿa. The life and work of Rābiʿa and other women mystics in Islam* (Oxford, 1997).

Sprenger, Aloys. *The Life of Mohammad from original sources* (Allahabad, 1851).

Sylvestre de Sacy, Isaac. *Chrestomathie arabe* (Paris, 1806, 1826), 4 vols.

———, *Grammaire arabe* (Paris, 1810).

———, *De l'utilité de l'étude de la poésie arabe* (Paris, 1826).

———, *Mélanges de littérature orientale* (Paris, 1833, 1861).

Aṭ-Ṭabarī. *Tafsīr* (Beirut, 1978), 10 vols.

Taha-Hussein, Moenis. *Présence de l'Islam dans la littérature romantique en France* (Cairo, 1955).

Tancoigne, J.M. *Voyage à Smyrne* (Paris, 1817).

Thomson, Ann. *Barbary and Enlightenment: European attitudes towards the Maghreb in the eighteenth century* (Leiden, 1987).

———, 'L'utilisation de l'islam dans la litterature clandestine' in *La philosophie clandestine à l'Age classique*, ed. A. Mckenna and A. Mothu (Paris, Oxford, 1997), pp. 247-256.

Thompson, James and Scott, David. *The East imagined, experienced, remembered. Orientalist nineteenth-century painting* (Dublin, 1988).

Tocqueville, Alexis de. *Oeuvres complètes*, ed. J.P. Mayer (Paris, 1962), vols. 3, 5, 9, 13 and 16.

Toderini, G.B. *Della letteratura turchesca* (Venice, 1787), trans. abbé de Cournand as *De la littérature des Turcs* (Paris, 1789).

Tott, Francois de. *Mémoires sur les Turcs et les Tartares* (Paris, 1784).

Tucker, Judith E. *Women in nineteenth-century Egypt* (Cambridge, 1985).

Vatin, Jean Claude. ed. *La Fuite en Egypte. Supplément aux voyages européens en Orient* (Cairo, 1989).

Venturino, Diego. 'Un Prophète Philosophe? Une *Vie de Mahomed à l'aube des Lumières, Dix-Huitième Siècle*, no. 24 (1992), pp. 321-331.

———, 'Imposteur ou législateur? Le Mahomet des Lumières' (vers 1750-1789), *Studies on Voltaire and the Eighteenth Century*, vol. 2 (2000), pp. 243-262.

Vertot, abbé de. 'Dissertation sur l'auteur de l'Alcoran' in *Histoire des chevaliers de Malte* (Paris, 1726), 4 vols.

Wadud-Muhsin, Amina. *Qur'ān and woman* (Kuala Lumpur, 1992).

Wansbrough, John. *Qur'ānic Studies* (Oxford, 1977).

———, *The sectarian milieu* (Oxford, 1978).

Al-Wāqidī. *Kitāb al-Maghāzī*, ed. J. Marsden Jones (London, 1955), 3 vols.

Wardman, H.W. *Ernest Renan. A critical biography* (London, 1964).

Watt, William Montgomery. *Muhammad at Mecca* (Oxford, 1953).

———, *Muhammad at Medina* (Oxford, 1956).

———, *Islamic Philosophy and Theology* (Edinburgh, 1962).

———, and Bell, Richard. *Introduction to the Quran* (Edinburgh, 1970).

Az-Zamakhsharī. *Kashshāf* (Beirut, 1979), 4 vols.

Index